Module C

---◇---

CONSCIOUS CONSTRUCTION
of an Inviting School Climate

Module 3 of 6 in *Foundations: A Proactive and Positive Behavior Support System* (3rd ed.)

Randy Sprick
Jessica Sprick
Paula Rich

RANDY SPRICK'S

safe & civil
SCHOOLS

Practical Solutions, Positive Results!

Published in the United States by
Pacific Northwest Publishing
21 West 6th Ave.
Eugene, Oregon 97401
www.pacificnwpublish.com

ISBN: 978-1-59909-071-9

Part of *Foundations: A Proactive and Positive Behavior Support System* (3rd ed.)
ISBN: 978-1-59909-068-9

Cover by Aaron Graham
Book design and layout by Natalie Conaway

TRENDS is a registered trademark of Pacific Northwest Publishing
in the United States.

Pacific
Northwest
Publishing

Eugene, Oregon | www.pacificnwpublish.com

CONTENTS

CONTENTS

ABOUT THE AUTHORS

Randy Sprick, Ph.D.

Randy Sprick, Ph.D., has worked as a paraprofessional, teacher, and teacher trainer at the elementary and secondary levels. Author of a number of widely read books on behavior and classroom management, Dr. Sprick is director of *Safe & Civil Schools,* a consulting company that provides inservice programs throughout the country. He and his trainers work with numerous large and small school districts on longitudinal projects to improve student behavior and motivation. Efficacy of that work is documented in peer-reviewed research, and *Safe & Civil Schools* materials are listed on the National Registry of Evidence-Based Programs and Practices (NREPP). Dr. Sprick was the recipient of the 2007 Council for Exceptional Children (CEC) Wallin Lifetime Achievement Award.

Jessica Sprick, M.S.

Jessica Sprick, M.S., is a consultant and presenter for *Safe & Civil Schools* and writer for Pacific Northwest Publishing. Ms. Sprick has been a special education teacher for students with behavioral needs and Dean of Students. She is a coauthor of *Functional Behavior Assessment of Absenteeism & Truancy, Absenteeism and Truancy: Interventions & Universal Procedures, Functional Behavior Assessment of Bullying,* and *Bullying: Interventions & Universal Procedures* with William Jenson, Randy Sprick, and others. Ms. Sprick's practical experience in schools with positive behavior support techniques drives her passion to help school personnel develop and implement effective management plans.

Paula Rich, B.Mus.Ed., M.Mus.

Paula Rich, B.Mus.Ed., M.Mus., has been a substitute teacher in public schools and was a freelance musician and taught private music lessons for many years in the Boston, Massachusetts, area. Since joining Pacific Northwest Publishing in 2006, she has contributed original stories and poems to the *Read Well* curriculum for second-grade readers and has edited several of Randy Sprick's staff development and behavior management books and papers. She was instrumental in developing TRENDS, Pacific Northwest Publishing's online behavioral data management system, as well as Connections, an online check-and-connect program.

SAFE & CIVIL SCHOOLS

THE SAFE & CIVIL SCHOOLS SERIES is a comprehensive, integrated set of resources designed to help educators improve student behavior and school climate at every level—districtwide, schoolwide, within the classroom, and at the individual intervention level. The findings of decades of research literature have been refined into step-by-step actions that teachers and staff can take to help all students behave responsibly and respectfully.

The hallmark of the *Safe & Civil Schools* model is its emphasis on proactive, positive, and instructional behavior management—addressing behavior before it necessitates correction, collecting data before embarking on interventions, implementing simple corrections before moving to progressively more intensive and time-intrusive ones, and setting a climate of respect for all. As a practical matter, tending to schoolwide and classwide policies, procedures, and interventions is far easier than resorting to more costly, time-intrusive, and individualized approaches.

Foundations and PBIS

Positive Behavioral Interventions and Supports (PBIS) is not a program. According to the U.S. Department of Education, PBIS is simply a framework to help provide "assistance to schools, districts, and states to establish a preventative, positive, multi-tiered continuum of evidence-based behavioral interventions that support the behavioral competence of students" (A. Posny, personal communication, September 7, 2010). That framework perfectly describes *Foundations*. *Foundations* provides instructions for implementing such an approach—with detailed processes and hundreds of examples of specific applications from successful schools. Furthermore, *Foundations* provides step-by-step guidance for involving and unifying an entire district staff to develop behavior support procedures that will prevent misbehavior and increase student connectedness and motivation. *Foundations* moves well beyond a simple matrix into how to guide and inspire staff to take ownership of managing and motivating all students, all the time, every day.

SAFE & CIVIL SCHOOLS

Resources in the series do not take a punitive approach to discipline. Instead, *Safe & Civil Schools* addresses the sources of teachers' greatest power to motivate: through structuring for student success, teaching expectations, observing and monitoring student behavior, and, above all, interacting positively. Because experience directly affects behavior, it makes little sense to pursue only the undesired behavior (by relying on reprimands, for example) and not the conditions (in behavioral theory, the antecedent) that precipitate experience and subsequent behavior.

The *Safe & Civil Schools* Positive Behavioral Interventions and Supports (PBIS) Model is listed in the National Registry of Evidence-based Programs and Practices (NREPP) after review by the Substance Abuse and Mental Health Services Administration (SAMHSA).

Inclusion in NREPP means that independent reviewers found that the philosophy and procedures behind *Foundations, CHAMPS, Discipline in the Secondary Classroom, Interventions,* and other *Safe & Civil Schools* books and DVDs have been thoroughly researched, that the research is of high quality, and that the outcomes achieved include:

- Higher levels of academic achievement
- Reductions in school suspensions
- Fewer classroom disruptions
- Increases in teacher professional self-efficacy
- Improvement in school discipline procedures

For more information, visit www.nrepp.samhsa.gov.

The most recent evidence of the efficacy of the *Safe & Civil Schools* PBIS Model appeared in the October 2013 issue of *School Psychology Review*. "A Randomized Evaluation of the *Safe and Civil Schools* Model for Positive Behavioral Interventions and Supports at Elementary Schools in a Large Urban School District," by Bryce Ward and Russell Gersten, shows how the *Safe & Civil Schools* PBIS Model improves student behavior and school climate. Thirty-two elementary schools in a large urban school district were randomly assigned to an initial training cohort or a wait-list control group. Results show reduced suspension rates, decreases in problem behavior, and evidence of positive academic gains for the schools in the training cohort.

Observed improvements persisted through the second year of trainings, and once the wait-list control schools commenced *Safe & Civil Schools* training, they experienced similar improvements in school policies and student behavior.

Download and read the full article at:
www.nasponline.org/publications/spr/index.aspx?vol=42&issue=3

Safe & Civil Schools acknowledges the real power educators have—not in controlling students but in shaping their behavior through affecting every aspect of their experience while they are in school: the physical layout, the way time is structured, arrivals and departures, teaching expected behavior, meaningful relationships with adults, and more. These changes in what adults do can create dramatic and lifelong changes in the behavior and motivation of students.

ACKNOWLEDGMENTS

As lead author, I owe a huge debt to many people who have guided the development and revision of *Foundations* over the past three decades. Betsy Norton, Mickey Garrison, and Marilyn Sprick were instrumental in the development and implementation of *Foundations* long before the publication of the first edition in 1992. Dr. Jan Reinhardtsen received the very first federal grant on the topic of positive behavior support and, with Mickey, implemented the first edition of *Foundations* as the basis for Project CREST in the early and mid-1990s. Jan also came up with *Safe & Civil Schools,* which became the name of our staff development services. Dr. Laura McCullough implemented a brilliant state-level Model School project in Kentucky, followed by the Kentucky Instructional Discipline System (KIDS) project that taught me so much about the importance of training and coaching to assist schools with implementation of both schoolwide and classroom behavior support.

I want to thank my coauthors of the different modules within this edition. Susan Isaacs, Mike Booher, and Jessica Sprick are outstanding trainers of *Foundations*, and their respective expertise has added depth to the content that makes this edition more practical, rich, and fun than previous editions. Paula Rich has provided both organizational skill and writing expertise to weave together a vast amount of content with many school- and district-level examples to create a highly accessible and user-friendly resource.

Thanks to the awesome staff of Pacific Northwest Publishing: Aaron Graham and Natalie Conaway with design, Sara Ferris and K Daniels with editing, Matt Sprick for directing both video and print development, Sam Gehrke for video editing, Robert Consentino and Jake Clifton for camera and sound, and the rest of the Pacific Northwest Publishing and *Safe & Civil Schools* staff—Jackie Hefner, Karen Schell, Sarah Romero, Kimberly Irving, Brandt Schram, Caroline DeVorss, and Marilyn Sprick—for their great work.

Implementation of *Foundations*, *CHAMPS*, and *Interventions* would not have thrived without the skill and dedication of great staff developers and trainers: Tricia Berg, Mike Booher, Phyllis Gamas, Laura Hamilton, Andrea Hanford, Jane Harris, Susan Isaacs, Debbie Jackson, Kim Marcum, Bob McLaughlin, Donna Meers, Carolyn Novelly, Robbie Rowan, Susan Schilt, Tricia Skyles, Pat Somers, Karl Schleich, Jessica Sprick, and Elizabeth Winford as Director of Professional Development.

ACKNOWLEDGMENTS

Fresno Unified School District and Long Beach Unified School District in California allowed us to visit with the Pacific Northwest Publishing video crew to capture the excitement, professionalism, and commitment of school and district personnel. These districts have taught us so much about the importance of common language and district support in creating a sustainable implementation.

Lastly, I want to the thank the schools and districts that have implemented *Foundations* over the years and graciously shared their lessons, posters, staff development activities, forms, and policies that you will find as examples throughout the print and video presentations. These real-world examples will help your implementation process by illustrating how other schools and districts have successfully implemented and sustained *Foundations*.

—R.S.

HOW TO USE FOUNDATIONS

This third edition of *Foundations* is constructed as six modules to accommodate schools that are just beginning their implementation of multi-tiered systems of behavior support (MTSS) as well as schools that already have some, but not all, pieces of behavior support firmly in place. For example, a school may have done great work on improving behavior in the common areas of the school but very little work on intentionally constructing a positive, inviting climate or addressing conflict and bullying in a comprehensive way. This school could go directly to Module C: *Conscious Construction of an Inviting Climate*, and after implementing those strategies, move to Module E: *Improving Safety, Managing Conflict, and Preventing Bullying*.

Each module incorporates multiple resources to assist you: video presentations on DVD, the book you are reading now, and a CD with forms and samples. The videos can guide a building-based leadership team through implementing *Foundations*. The same content is available in print format; we provide eight copies of this book for each module, one for each member of the leadership team. Teams can decide which content delivery form works best for them—video or print.

Each book comes with a CD that contains reproducible forms, examples of policies and procedures from real schools that have implemented *Foundations*, and other implementation resources. The CD also includes PowerPoint presentations that correspond directly to the video and print content. Your leadership team can use these presentations to deliver the most relevant *Foundations* information to the entire staff.

Beginning Behavior Support

For schools and districts that are just beginning with behavior support or are unsure where to begin, we suggest starting with Module A: *Foundations of Behavior Support—A Continuous Improvement Process*. This module is the foundation of *Foundations*. It describes the importance of a well-designed leadership team, a formalized continuous improvement cycle, how to use multiple data sources to drive that cycle, and how to involve and unify the staff in implementation. Without laying this groundwork, any specific work on procedures, such as improving the cafeteria, is unlikely to be effective or sustainable.

Once your team is collecting and analyzing data, you will probably move through Modules B–F (described below) in order. You'll work on the common areas of the school, then positive climate, and so on. Once a module has been implemented, you are not done with that module. For example, after implementing the procedures in Module B for a couple of common areas and a couple of schoolwide policies, such as dress code, you may move on to Module C to work on improving school climate. However, you will concurrently continue to implement Module B procedures for additional common areas and schoolwide policies. Working through all six modules will take about two to five years of development and implementation.

MTSS in Progress

Schools and districts that have been effectively implementing other approaches to PBIS should follow these guidelines when implementing *Foundations*.

You may be able to use the modules in a nonlinear fashion if your school has a highly functional team, uses multiple data sources to involve the entire staff in continuous improvement of behavior support, and has worked to improve several common areas or schoolwide policies. To self-assess where to begin, a resource for each module called the Foundations Implementation Rubric and Summary is included in Appendix A of the book and on the CD. The rubric can help your leadership team assess which modules have information useful to your school at this time and help you make judgments about where to begin. Print the rubric, work through it as a team, and summarize your findings, and you will see patterns emerge. (Instructions are included with the rubric.)

For example, if all the conditions described at the beginning of this paragraph are in place, you will probably find that you are already implementing many of the procedures delineated in Modules A and B. One school may have an urgent need to go directly to Module E because the school has no programs or policies to address conflict and bullying, whereas another school may go directly to Module D because staff are very inconsistent about when and how to use disciplinary referral to the office. Another school may go directly to Module F because their schoolwide structures are relatively well established, but they have yet to address classroom management or the integration of universal, targeted, and intensive interventions.

HOW TO USE FOUNDATIONS

Appendix B of each module presents an Implementation Checklist for that module. The Implementation Checklist details the summarized items on the rubric. You will use this tool as you near completion on any module to ensure that you have fully implemented it, and it's also useful for reviewing the implementation every three years or so. The checklist can identify strengths to celebrate and catch gaps in your implementation that you may be able to fill before a major problem emerges.

OVERVIEW OF MODULES

The modules in *Foundations* are designed to be used sequentially by a school or district that is just getting started with behavior support. However, if a school or district is already implementing a team-based, data-driven approach to continuous improvement of climate, safety, discipline, and motivation, the modules can be used in any order.

This module—**Module C:** *Conscious Construction of an Inviting School Climate*— guides the entire staff in creating and sustaining a school environment that makes all students feel welcomed and valued. This process includes developing Guidelines for Success, a set of behaviors and traits that provides a common language and common values among staff, students, and parents. This module explains how and why to maintain at least 3:1 ratios of positive interactions and covers the importance of regular attendance and strategies for improving attendance. Strategies for meeting the basic human needs of all students are also discussed. Finally, the module outlines how to welcome and orient staff, students, and families who are new to the school in a way that connects them to the school community.

- Presentation 1: Constructing and Maintaining a Positive Climate
- Presentation 2: Guidelines for Success
- Presentation 3: Ratios of Positive Interactions
- Presentation 4: Improving Attendance
- Presentation 5: School Connectedness—Meeting Basic Human Needs
- Presentation 6: Programs and Strategies for Meeting Needs
- Presentation 7: Making a Good First Impression—Welcoming New Staff, Students, and Families
- Appendix A: Foundations Implementation Rubric and Summary
- Appendix B: Module C Implementation Checklist
- Appendix C: Guide to Module C Reproducible Forms and Samples

Other modules in *Foundations: A Proactive and Positive Behavior Support System* are:

Module A: *Foundations of Behavior Support—A Continuous Improvement Process* covers the essential processes for involving the entire staff in developing, implementing, and sustaining positive behavior support. It includes detailed information about establishing a building-based leadership team (Foundations Team) to represent the entire staff. This module advises the team on how to collect and analyze data, identify and rank a manageable number of priorities for improvement, and guide the staff in revising, adopting, and implementing new policies and procedures for each priority. This process creates a cycle of continuous improvement that empowers and unifies the entire staff.

- Presentation 1: Foundations: A Multi-Tiered System of Behavior Support
- Presentation 2: Team Processes
- Presentation 3: The Improvement Cycle
- Presentation 4: Data-Driven Processes
- Presentation 5: Developing Staff Engagement and Unity
- Appendix A: Foundations Implementation Rubric and Summary
- Appendix B: Module A Implementation Checklist
- Appendix C: Guide to Module A Reproducible Forms and Samples

Module B: *Managing Behavior in Common Areas and With Schoolwide Policies* delineates processes for ensuring that common areas (arrival, cafeteria, hallways, and so on) and schoolwide policies (dress code, electronics use, public displays of affection, and so on) are structured for success and that expectations for behavior are directly taught with clarity and repetition to students. In addition, this module includes detailed information for all staff about how to provide positive and systematic supervision and how to correct misbehavior calmly, consistently, and respectfully.

- Presentation 1: Laying the Groundwork for Consistency in All School Settings
- Presentation 2: Structuring Common Areas and Schoolwide Policies for Success
- Presentation 3: Teaching Expectations to Students
- Presentation 4: Effective Supervision, Part 1—Protect, Expect, and Connect
- Presentation 5: Effective Supervision, Part 2—Correct and Reflect
- Presentation 6: Supervising Common Areas and Schoolwide Policies—for All Staff
- Presentation 7: Adopting, Implementing, and Monitoring Improvements to Common Areas and Schoolwide Policies
- Appendix A: Foundations Implementation Rubric and Summary
- Appendix B: Module B Implementation Checklist
- Appendix C: Guide to Module B Reproducible Forms and Samples

Module D: *Responding to Misbehavior—An Instructional Approach* focuses on the vital importance of an instructional approach to correction in reducing future occurrences of the misbehavior. It provides information on training and inspiring all staff to correct all misbehavior by giving students information about how to behave successfully and by using the mildest consequences that reasonably fit the infractions. Module D describes how to get consensus among staff about when (and when not) to use office discipline referral. It provides menus of corrective techniques for mild and moderate misbehavior, from gentle verbal correction to time owed after class to restorative justice. All staff learn strategies for de-escalating emotional situations, and administrators are introduced to a comprehensive game plan for dealing with office referrals and implementing alternatives to out-of-school suspension. This module includes sample lessons for students on how to interact with people in authority.

- Presentation 1: The Relationship Between Proactive Procedures, Corrective Procedures, and Individual Student Behavior Improvement Plans
- Presentation 2: Developing Three Levels of Misbehavior
- Presentation 3: Staff Responsibilities for Responding to Misbehavior
- Presentation 4: Administrator Responsibilities for Responding to Misbehavior
- Presentation 5: Preventing the Misbehavior That Leads to Referrals and Suspensions
- Appendix A: Foundations Implementation Rubric and Summary
- Appendix B: Module D Implementation Checklist
- Appendix C: Guide to Module D Reproducible Forms and Samples

Module E: *Improving Safety, Managing Conflict, and Reducing Bullying* guides the Foundations Team in assessing school strengths and weaknesses related to safety, conflict, and bullying. The module begins by examining the attributes of safe and unsafe schools and offers suggestions for moving your school toward the evidence-based attributes that contribute to safety. One potential risk to safety is poor conflict management, so this module includes a simple conflict resolution strategy that students can use to manage conflict in peaceful and mutually beneficial ways. Bullying is another serious risk to safety. Module E provides a step-by-step process for analyzing strengths and gaps in your school's bullying policies and procedures as well as suggestions and examples for turning gaps into strengths. This module includes lessons for students on safety, conflict, and bullying prevention and intervention.

- Presentation 1: Ensuring a Safe Environment
- Presentation 2: Attributes of Safe and Unsafe Schools
- Presentation 3: Teaching Conflict Resolution
- Presentation 4: Analyzing Bullying Behavior, Policies, and School Needs
- Presentation 5: Schoolwide Bullying Prevention and Intervention
- Appendix A: Foundations Implementation Rubric and Summary
- Appendix B: Module E Implementation Checklist
- Appendix C: Guide to Module E Reproducible Forms and Samples

Module F: *Establishing and Sustaining a Continuum of Behavior Support* outlines how the Foundations Team can analyze and guide an integration of universal prevention, targeted support, and intensive support for students. This process includes adopting and supporting a schoolwide or district approach to classroom management that creates a common language and ensures that teachers, administrators, and support staff are on the same page about classroom organization and management. For students who need individual support, this module provides staff training in early-stage interventions and a variety of problem-solving structures that match the intensity of student need to the intensity of school- and district-based resources. Finally, Module F provides guidance in sustaining *Foundations* at the building and district level so that effective procedures are maintained and improvement continues, even when school administration changes.

- Presentation 1: The Vision of a Continuum of Behavior Support
- Presentation 2: Supporting Classroom Behavior—The Three-Legged Stool
- Presentation 3: Articulating Staff Beliefs and Solidifying Universal Procedures
- Presentation 4: Early-Stage Interventions for General Education Classrooms
- Presentation 5: Matching the Intensity of Your Resources to the Intensity of Your Needs
- Presentation 6: Problem-Solving Processes and Intervention Design
- Presentation 7: Sustainability and District Support
- Appendix A: Foundations Implementation Rubric and Summary
- Appendix B: Module F Implementation Checklist
- Appendix C: Guide to Module F Reproducible Forms and Samples

Constructing and Maintaining a Positive Climate

PRESENTATION

ONE

CONTENTS

Introduction to Module C

For all staff

DOCUMENTS*

- Anytown High School Grateful Dads program flyer (C-13)

* This document is available on the CD.

5

INTRODUCTION TO MODULE C

What is climate? Climate is the atmosphere on the school campus. It can be positive and inviting or negative and uninviting (or somewhere in between). Do students and staff want to be there? Are students able to learn? A positive climate encompasses many factors, including staff dedicated to student learning, high expectations for academic performance and behavior, meaningful relationships, a sense of order and discipline, involved parents and families, and respectful interactions among students, staff, and families.

This entire module is about the conscious construction of an inviting school climate. We believe that staff behavior creates the climate of the school, and a positive, welcoming, and inviting climate can and should be intentionally created and continuously maintained. The presentations in this module are all designed to help you evaluate the strengths of your current climate and guide you in developing ideas for *designing* (that's the conscious part) and then *creating and implementing* (that's the construction part) a climate that is so inviting that students, families, and staff are all grateful to be part of your amazing school.

Creating a positive school climate rests on the base of the work you've done in previous modules to implement continuous improvement processes and clear expectations for behavior in common areas and with schoolwide policies, as illustrated in Figure 1a, the Foundations continuum graphic. Creating an Inviting Climate is at the same level as Responding to Misbehavior (Module D) and Addressing Safety, Conflict, and Bullying (Module E). These three aspects of a safe and civil school go hand in hand. When implemented well, they create the layer in your continuum of behavior support on which your positive classroom management and individual student intervention efforts will be built.

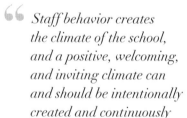

Staff behavior creates the climate of the school, and a positive, welcoming, and inviting climate can and should be intentionally created and continuously maintained."

Why is it important for students to feel connected to school?

School climate is sometimes considered synonymous with other terms—*school connectedness, school bonding, teacher support, student engagement*—and many researchers have looked at this issue using those various names. Klem and Connell (2004) found that by high school, 40% to 60% of all students—urban, suburban, and rural—are chronically disengaged from their schools. Although the percentages are not quite as high at the elementary and middle-school levels, the number of children

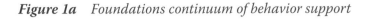

Figure 1a *Foundations continuum of behavior support*

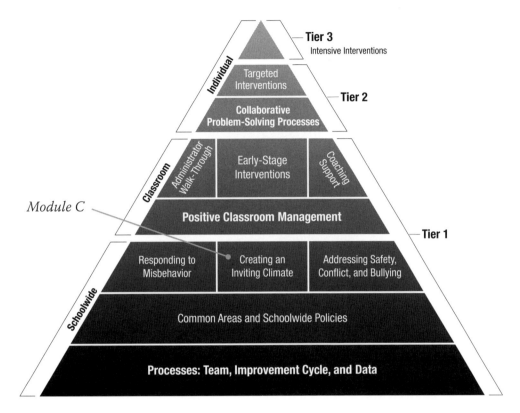

who are emotionally detached from their schools is troubling at those grade levels, too. Why are these statistics alarming? The Centers for Disease Control and Prevention (CDC, 2009) states:

School connectedness is an important factor in both health and learning. Students who feel connected to school are

- *More likely to attend school regularly, stay in school longer, and have higher grades and test scores.*
- *Less likely to smoke cigarettes, drink alcohol, or have sexual intercourse.*
- *Less likely to carry weapons, become involved in violence, or be injured from dangerous activities such as drinking and driving or not wearing seat belts.*
- *Less likely to have emotional problems, suffer from eating disorders, or experience suicidal thoughts or attempts.*

Four factors can help strengthen school connectedness for students: adult support, belonging to a positive peer group, commitment to education, and a positive school environment. School staff members are important adults in students' lives; the time, interest, attention, and emotional support they give students can engage them in school and learning.

This module discusses three of the four factors noted by the CDC: adult support, commitment to education, and a positive school environment. The fourth, belonging to a positive peer group, is addressed in Module E, Presentation 2, Task 3: "Teach Lessons to Increase Connectedness and Safety."

Why is an inviting climate important?

William Purkey published the first edition of his book *Inviting School Success: A Self-Concept Approach to Teaching, Learning, and Democratic Practice in a Connected World* in 1984. Purkey was a forerunner in pointing out that some well-intentioned words and actions can be uninviting to students.

For example, imagine a high school math teacher who tries to motivate students to be proactive in their study habits by telling the class that one third of her students failed the previous year. That is a little like a maître d' welcoming you to his restaurant by saying, "Good evening! We are delighted to have you here. We poisoned one third of our customers last night, but we hope you have a great meal tonight. Follow me." You would probably not find that restaurant very inviting. In fact, you would probably want to leave that restaurant as quickly as possible and never go back.

Many researchers from many different disciplines have determined that climate influences connectedness, which in turn influences academic achievement, dropout rates, healthy choices, and much more.

What is most important in creating the school climate?

Based on decades of experience working in schools, we maintain that the daily behavior of the staff is the most important factor in constructing a positive climate. Climate is slightly influenced by the building architecture, building maintenance, and the amount of natural light. But those factors pale in importance next to the daily collective behavior of your staff.

Imagine you're a student. From the moment you walk onto campus, the adults you see in the arrival area, in the hallways, and in your classroom are silent and frowning, with their arms folded across their chests. Then imagine walking onto a campus where the adults smile and say, "Good morning, Malik, how are you today?" "Justine, welcome. Hope you have a good day at school today." Your teacher is at the classroom door and greets you by saying, "Hey, nice to see you today. Get going on that challenge problem. We're going to have a great day." In which school would you feel more welcome? Which school would you rather attend each day?

Every adult, in his or her own style, needs to make an overt effort to make all students feel valued and welcomed in the school. And, believe it or not, students value and need the adults in the school. They want adult guidance and role models. School staff don't always capitalize on that need, but you can use it to your and your students' advantage.

How do students view teachers?

In 2006, Michael Hock of the University of Kansas Center on Research and Learning researched teenagers' perceptions of themselves—their self-images. As part of his research, he conducted surveys. One of the survey questions was, "How much influence does each of the following have on your life?" The results are displayed in Figure 1b below.

Figure 1b *Sources of influence as reported by teens (from* Survey on Teen Perceptions of Self *conducted by M. Hock, University of Kansas Center on Research and Learning, personal communication, 2006)*

Q: How much influence does each of the following have on your life?		
	A Lot or Some	**None**
Parents	96%	4%
Teachers	**80%**	**20%**
Other kids	78%	22%
Religion	70%	30%
Girlfriend/Boyfriend	63%	37%
Celebrities	63%	37%
TV shows	44%	56%
Advertising	36%	64%

Parents top the list—96% of students said that their parents influence them a lot or some, and only 4% said their parents have no influence. Next were teachers; 80% (four out of five students) said that teachers have a lot or some influence in their lives. Only 20% said teachers have no influence. The six other categories of potential influences rank below teachers. Advertising—marketing specifically designed to influence people—ranks last, way below teachers. In other words, teachers have far more influence on students' lives than marketing specifically designed for that purpose. Keep this in mind—students say that teachers significantly affect their lives.

Hock also asked students, "Who understands you the most?" The results are displayed in Figure 1c on the next page.

Friends top this list, at 42%. Teachers rank second to last, at 1%. So students say that teachers have a significant influence on their lives but also that teachers don't understand them. Or at least students perceive that teachers don't understand them.

Figure 1c *Teens' perceptions of who understands them (from* Survey on Teen Perceptions of Self *by M. Hock, University of Kansas Center on Research and Learning, personal communication, 2006)*

Q: Who understands you the most?	
Friend	42%
Parent	28%
Girlfriend/Boyfriend	10%
No one	8%
Sibling	5%
Religious leader	1%
Teacher	**1%**
Other	5%

How do teachers view students?

After hearing about the research discussed above, a middle-school administrator told us about a survey he had conducted at his school. He randomly selected 50 of his middle-school students and asked them, "What three things would you like your teachers to know about you?" He anticipated answers such as "I'm good at soccer," "I like hip-hop music," and "I really hate math." He was shocked that almost all students shared very personal things about their lives—both their struggles and their joys. He was surprised by the seriousness of the issues and by how forthcoming students were about their parents' divorces and separations, moves to new cities, medical concerns, and other significant worries that we adults have, too.

Then the administrator set up a matching exercise for staff. He displayed pictures of the participating students with their names, and he distributed to each staff member a typed list of the 50 responses, without student names. He asked the staff to write a student's name next to each response. The students who participated had all attended the school for at least several months, so they were known to staff. But most staff members matched only one to three students out of the 50 to the correct response. One person got four out of 50 students correct. And one staff member, the in-school suspension aide, identified *47 of the 50* students correctly.

Remember, the students were chosen at random. Many had never been assigned in-school suspension. The aide did not know these students so well because she dealt with them in the ISS program. She knew them because, in her words, "I spend time in the halls talking to students." She made an overt effort to be consciously inviting with all students, not just those she knew from ISS. As she talked with students, they shared things they wanted adults in the school to know. She knew 47 students, when no other staff member knew more than four. Remarkable.

Connect with students.

This module is all about making an overt effort to connect with students. An example of a simple yet powerful program to provide more positive attention to students comes from Lewisville High School in Lewisville, Texas. School staff saw a need for positive male role models for their students, so they developed a program called Grateful Dads. It's very simple: Each Friday, volunteer dads, other male relatives of students, and male community members greet students at the front doors of the school for half an hour during the arrival period. The mission of the Grateful Dads program is simply to provide active, visible, and positive male role models for the students. For dads who aren't involved in other high school activities or booster clubs, the program provides a way to participate in school activities. The students have so much fun that they sometimes circle back through the door to be greeted again! From all reports, the volunteers love it, too, as they enthusiastically greet, encourage, and cheer on the students.

Figure 1d on the next page shows an informational flyer we adapted from the Lewisville High School program. Note that all participants are required to submit a completed volunteer application and undergo a background check.

Grateful Dads is just one example of a program that can contribute to a positive climate. You'll read about many other programs and procedures as you progress through Module C, *Conscious Construction of an Inviting School Climate*. This module contains six additional presentations:

- Presentation 2 covers a concept we call *Guidelines for Success*. The guidelines are three to five brief statements or phrases that describe skills, traits, and attitudes that students need to possess to be successful in school and in life. They become the spiritual core of your school culture. We explain why Guidelines for Success are important, how to develop them, and how to use them well.

- Presentation 3 is about ratios of positive interactions. All adults should pay at least three times more attention to students when the students are meeting behavioral expectation than when they are misbehaving. We discuss why maintaining a high ratio of positive to corrective interactions is important and suggest ways to keep the ratio high.

- Presentation 4 examines attendance, tardiness, and the vital importance of creating and sustaining a climate that motivates students to *want* to come to school. Attendance is also a measure of a positive, inviting climate. When you have worked on school climate and attendance data show improvement, you can safely say that you are making school a more comfortable place where students want to be.

Figure 1d   Anytown High School Grateful Dads program flyer (C-13)

- Presentations 5 and 6 explain basic human needs and suggest ways to meet those needs in your students. Does your school climate allow every student to feel acknowledged and recognized? Do students feel like they belong to the school community and have a sense of purpose? Do some students need more attention and nurturing? Students whose basic needs are not being met are more likely to behave inappropriately and lack motivation. These presentations help you assess whether all students' needs are being met and design programs to meet those needs.

- Presentation 7 is about welcoming and orienting students, families, and staff who are new to the school. First impressions can be lasting impressions, so staff need to be consciously inviting, welcoming, and helpful to newcomers. You want them to begin connecting to the school immediately.

Guidelines for Success

CONTENTS

Introduction

Task 1: Understand Guidelines for Success

For the Foundations Team or Guidelines for Success task force

Task 2: Develop Guidelines for Success

For the Foundations Team or Guidelines for Success task force

Task 3: Implement Guidelines for Success

For the Foundations Team or Guidelines for Success task force

DOCUMENTS*

- Examples of Guidelines for Success (C-23, C-25, C-26, C-28, C-29, C-31, C-30)
- Sample elementary and secondary classroom behavior rubrics based on schoolwide Guidelines for Success (C-14, C-15)
- Sample Staff Handbook entry for Guidelines for Success (C-16)
- Sample lessons on Guidelines for Success

* All documents listed are available on the CD. Other documents that are not shown in this presentation are also available on the CD (see Appendix C for a complete list).

INTRODUCTION

Guidelines for Success are three to five brief statements or phrases that describe skills, traits, and attitudes that students need to be successful in school and in life.

As an educator, what legacy do you want to leave your students? Thirty years from now, when students reflect on their years in your school, what will they remember? Will they think, "I was so lucky to attend Ben Franklin Middle School because those teachers really taught me the importance of . . . "? Your school's Guidelines for Success should embody the lifelong traits that you want your students to remember.

This presentation provides information on developing three to five traits that the entire staff will work to instill in students. The staff will be preaching these traits over and over to the students. We use the word *preach* intentionally here. The effective preacher doesn't state the Ten Commandments once and expect the congregation to follow them perfectly. The preacher continually communicates the lessons of the Ten Commandments with hymns, parables, and scripture readings, and models the traits for his or her followers. The core message is so important that it can't be left to chance.

Task 1: Understand Guidelines for Success describes the features of and rationale for Guidelines for Success.

Task 2: Develop Guidelines for Success explains how to gather constructive input from staff, students, and others and reach consensus about the Guidelines for Success. We encourage you to take your time on this task.

Task 3: Implement Guidelines for Success gives ideas for launching and maintaining the Guidelines for Success so they become the hub of behavior management procedures and the traits that students will remember for the rest of their lives.

If you already have Guidelines for Success or something similar, we suggest you read Task 1 to review the rationale behind them and think about whether you are using your guidelines as effectively as possible. If you determine that your current guidelines are working well, skip to Task 3 to read about ways to implement and revitalize them. If you do not have anything like Guidelines for Success, or you have them but don't use them every day—they have become lifeless words on a wall—we suggest you work through all three tasks in this presentation.

TASK 1

Understand Guidelines for Success

The first task describes the features of Guidelines for Success and explains the rationale for promoting them in your school.

What are Guidelines for Success?

Guidelines for Success represent a set of skills, traits, and attitudes that everyone in the school always strives to demonstrate. The guidelines are *not* rules—they are more like goals, lifelong learning strategies, or codes of conduct. Here's a sample set of guidelines:

- Always try.
- Do your best.
- Cooperate with others.
- Treat everyone with respect.

You should, of course, develop guidelines that reflect the values you want to emphasize in your school. Just remember that they should not be rules. Driving a car is a good analogy to explain the difference between rules and Guidelines for Success. Many rules apply to driving: Come to a complete stop at stop signs, do not exceed 65 mph on the highway, turn left only when oncoming traffic is clear. Other aspects of driving—drive safely, be courteous to other drivers, drive defensively—are values that good drivers follow and that make the roads safer and more pleasant for everyone. Guidelines for Success are not the rules of the road. They are the big-picture values, characteristics, and attitudes that good drivers and responsible citizens follow.

Guidelines for Success should encompass ideals that the staff can be passionate about. They are the hub, or basis, of all staff efforts to create a safe, civil, and productive school. Guidelines for Success can serve as:

- The framework for behavioral expectations in all settings. All expectations are framed in terms of the key attitudes, beliefs, and behaviors set forth in the guidelines.

- The foundation for lessons that teach students how to be successful.

- A reference for staff members as they encourage responsible student behavior and correct irresponsible student behavior. The guidelines are not just words—they are *used* by staff to clarify what students should and should not do.

- A guide for staff members and students to evaluate their own behavior.

Figure 2a shows some examples of Guidelines for Success from *Foundations* schools. Additional examples are available on the Module C CD.

Figure 2a   *Examples of Guidelines for Success (C-23, C-28)*

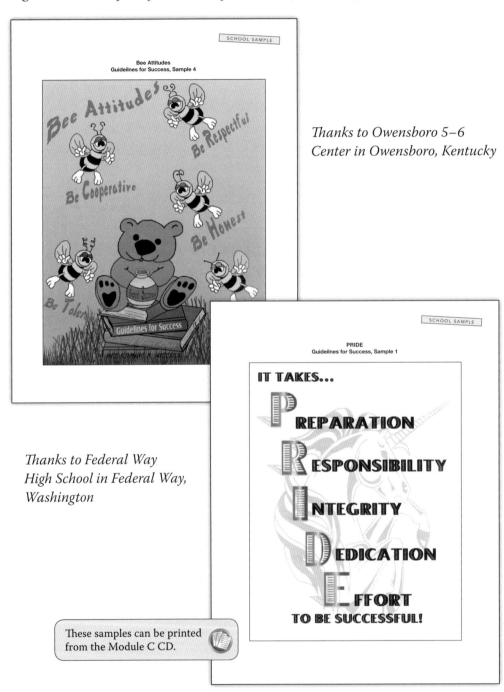

Thanks to Owensboro 5–6 Center in Owensboro, Kentucky

Thanks to Federal Way High School in Federal Way, Washington

These samples can be printed from the Module C CD.

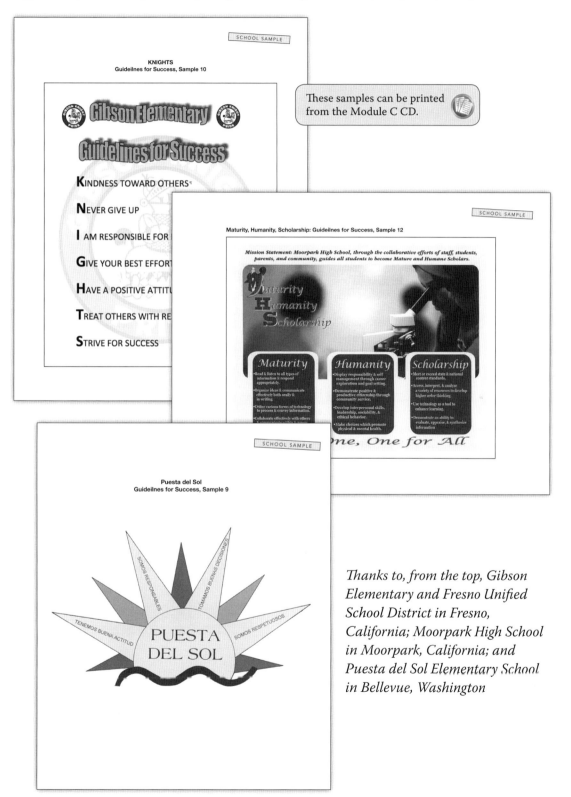

Thanks to, from the top, Gibson Elementary and Fresno Unified School District in Fresno, California; Moorpark High School in Moorpark, California; and Puesta del Sol Elementary School in Bellevue, Washington

These samples can be printed from the Module C CD.

Thanks to Easterby Elementary and Fresno Unified School District in Fresno, California

Thanks to Foothills Elementary School and White River School District in Washington

When every staff member is passionate about teaching the school's Guidelines for Success and incorporates the values into lessons, the resulting repetition and variety ingrains those values into students. For example, let's say that *integrity* is one of the guidelines, and a high school student has seven periods during each school day when a teacher might emphasize integrity. If each teacher mentions integrity just once a week, the student still hears about it seven times during every week of the school year. That number multiplies to a few hundred lessons about integrity every year of the student's 4 years of high school.

A science teacher might include integrity as part of instruction about the scientific method. Imagine a scientist who adjusts his test data to give the results he wants to see, and a new medicine for children is approved based on that erroneous data. Children take the medicine and get sick, and the scientist is prosecuted for his actions. The lesson for students is that integrity is important; lack of integrity can hurt you and others. In English class the next day, students might learn about copyright laws and their relation to personal and professional integrity.

The power of Guidelines for Success is that if an entire staff is passionate about teaching them, the necessary repetition and variety will inherently occur.

What is the rationale for Guidelines for Success?

Not all students come to school knowing what is required for success. Some students have had little or no training in or role models for qualities such as respect, integrity, cooperation, responsibility, and self-motivation. When the skills, attitudes, and traits required for success are incorporated and deeply embedded in the school culture, students do not have to *guess* what they are.

Lessons about the Guidelines for Success can make a real difference in the lives of students. Teaching students the skills for being successful in life is equally important as teaching them academic skills.

Guidelines for Success set the tone for a school's climate and provide a common focus for all members of the school community.

Task 1 Action Steps & Evidence of Implementation

Action Steps	Evidence of Implementation
1. Identify whether your school has something comparable to Guidelines for Success (e.g., Character Traits, Schoolwide Goals, a pledge). If so, determine whether the comparable guidelines serve as a hub for all your behavior management practices. Are they: • Taught to students? • Incorporated into school culture and activities? • Used by staff to provide positive and corrective feedback? • Known by students and families? 2. If you have something similar to Guidelines for Success and they serve as a hub for school practices, you may wish to skip Task 2 about developing guidelines and proceed to Task 3 to learn about ways to implement and revitalize them. If you do not have anything like Guidelines for Success, or you have them but don't use them every day—they are just lifeless words on a wall—work through Tasks 2 and 3.	Foundations Process: Guidelines for Success

TASK 2

Develop Guidelines for Success

Task 2 explains how to gather constructive recommendations and opinions from staff, students, and others and reach consensus about the Guidelines for Success you will implement in your school.

Decide on a name or title for your guidelines.

Think about using *Guidelines for Success* as your title. It clearly indicates the purpose of your set of behaviors and attitudes, and parents and community members are unlikely to object to it. Parents might object to names such as Character Traits because they think (understandably) that parents, not schools, are supposed to teach their children character. No one is likely to object to teaching students how to achieve success at school.

Other name possibilities include Goals and Keys to Success. A great example of a creative name is Ben's Keys to Success for Ben Franklin Middle School:

> **K**now: Seek knowledge and be active in your own learning
> **E**xcel: Do your best. Try your hardest and strive for excellence in all you do.
> **Y**earn: Desire to be successful. Set goals and work hard to accomplish them.
> **S**erve: Work with others. Give of yourself, your time, and your talents.

A student in an administrative training class developed the KEYS acronym. Whether it's Guidelines for Success, KEYS, Goals, or something else, you'll use the name frequently as you remind and motivate students to follow them.

Decide who should be involved in the development process.

The Foundations Team or a dedicated task force guides the development, but ensure that the entire staff is included in the brainstorming and decision-making process. You might also involve students, parents and families, and community members. The example we give below illustrates one way to include all these groups.

Design and implement a plan for developing your guidelines.

Decide on the steps and timeline for developing Guidelines for Success. "Sample Process for Developing Guidelines for Success" on the following page is the process adopted by Federal Way High School in Federal Way, Washington.

Through this process, Federal Way High School adopted PRIDE as their Guidelines for Success: It takes Preparation, Responsibility, Integrity, Dedication, and Effort to be Successful!

Sample Process for Developing Guidelines for Success

1. Each homeroom or advisory group brainstorms suggestions for guidelines with students. To begin the brainstorming process, teachers should:

   - Pose this question to students: What traits, qualities, behaviors, or attitudes are required to be successful in school or a job?

   - Remind students that effective guidelines should:

     ◦ Be simply stated.
     ◦ Include verbs ("be prepared" is more effective than "responsible preparation"). The verb could be a starter statement—for example, "At Interlake High School, we all demonstrate Integrity, Humanity, and Scholarship."
     ◦ Be free of slang or jargon that could go out of style ("peeps," "chill out," "just sayin'," for example). The guidelines should be timeless and not seem outdated when a student reflects back on them 20 years later.
     ◦ Pass the *stranger test*. The guidelines should be clear enough that someone unfamiliar with the school will immediately understand them.

2. Each homeroom or advisory group submits a list of suggested guidelines to the Foundations Team or task force.

3. Student leaders consolidate the brainstorming lists and eliminate any redundant guideline ideas. (At Federal Way High School, they reduced the number to about 40 at this step.)

4. Parents review the consolidated list and vote for the five guidelines they want emphasized. Reduce the list to the 20 guideline ideas that receive the most parent votes.

5. A group of student leaders seeks community input by going to a local mall and asking area residents their opinions about the list of guidelines. Reduce the list to the top 10.

6. Hold a schoolwide election. Each student and staff member can vote for five guidelines. Identify the five guidelines that get the most votes as the school's Guidelines for Success.

Task 2 Action Steps & Evidence of Implementation

Action Steps	Evidence of Implementation
1. Determine a name for your Guidelines for Success.	Foundations Process: Guidelines for Success
2. Identify who should be involved in the development of your Guidelines for Success. Staff need to be involved, and also consider including students, parents, and community members.	
3. Design and implement a plan for developing your Guidelines for Success.	

TASK 3

Implement Guidelines for Success

In Task 3, we provide ideas for how to launch and maintain the Guidelines for Success so they become the hub of your school's behavior management procedures and the traits that students will remember for the rest of their lives.

Effectively launch your Guidelines for Success.

Once you develop your Guidelines for Success, consider these suggestions for introducing them with a splash and embedding them into your school culture.

Celebrate the completed guidelines with an assembly or a schoolwide party. Announce the winning guidelines with fanfare. Communicate pride in the cooperative process, and reinforce the idea that the guidelines are more than just words—they represent how students and staff members can take charge of their own success.

Make the Guidelines for Success highly visible. Enlist student groups or the art department to make large posters of the guidelines. Post them in all common areas, and ensure that they are posted in every classroom. The next page shows examples of how two schools display their guidelines to great effect. Figure 2b shows how Aynesworth Elementary School's Guidelines for Success are displayed on banners in the hallways (right side of hallway). Aynesworth also displays their antibullying policy on banners (left side of hallway). Figure 2c shows a bulletin board poster made by a first-grade classroom from Miller Heights Elementary School. Each student signed the poster as a pledge to follow the guidelines.

Figure 2b *Guidelines for Success displayed on banners in the school hallway; thanks to Ermelinda Sanchez of Aynesworth Elementary and Fresno Unified School District in Fresno, California*

Figure 2c *Guidelines for Success poster created by first-grade students; thanks to April Robinson of Miller Heights Elementary School in Belton, Texas*

Develop behavior rubrics. Consider encouraging teachers to use the guidelines to create behavior rubrics for their classrooms. Rubrics can help clarify the expectations and guide constructive feedback to the class, both positive ("Everybody was exemplary about being respectful") and corrective ("This behavior is only satisfactory. Tomorrow you'll need to do _____ to move to exemplary.") Figure 2d below shows examples of elementary and secondary behavior rubrics created by teachers for classroom use, with the schoolwide Guidelines for Success as a framework.

Figure 2d   Sample elementary (top) and secondary (bottom) classroom behavior rubrics based on schoolwide Guidelines for Success (C-14, C-15); thanks to Stef Neyhart of Sunnyside Elementary in Roseburg, Oregon, and Matt Connolly of Aiken High School in Austin, Texas

SCHOOL SAMPLE

Behavior Rubric Using Guidelines for Success (Elementary Level)

GUIDELINES FOR SUCCESS	EXEMPLARY	RECOGNIZED	SATISFACTORY	UNSATISFACTORY
Always try.	Seek out challenging projects and activities. When stuck, use different resources. Help others. Attitude: I like challenges.	Try different ways to solve problems. Seek help in positive ways. Attitude: I can try harder.	Try first before asking for help. No whining. Attitude: I can.	Give up and/or refuse help. Refuse to try. Attitude: I can't, or won't.
Be responsible.	Recognize that their behavior determines their success. Consistently take the initiative to make sure that they are successful. Role models for other students.	Recognize that their behavior determines their success. Occasionally take the initiative to make sure that they are successful.	Recognize that their behavior determines their success in the classroom, but they need to be redirected and show more initiative to be fully successful.	Allow outside influences to determine their success in the classroom. Make excuses instead of taking initiative.
Cooperate.	Consistently make the best possible use of class time. Help others to be more productive Produce work of the highest quality.	Make good use of time and produce good-quality work. Follow all rules and correct behavior when reminded once.	Make good use of time and produce good-quality work. Follow all rules and correct behavior when reprimanded once. Work well in groups.	Make unproductive use of time. Work lacks quality. Occasionally prompt others to be unproductive. Difficulty working in groups.
Do your best.	Always have supplies ready. Always have assignments completed. Apply extra effort with or without credit. Go above and beyond what is required.	Usually have all supplies and all assignments completed. Immediately correct any shortcomings on their own. Will take extra time to ask for help or improve quality.	Usually have all supplies and all assignments completed. Immediately correct any shortcomings when reminded by teacher. Sometimes ask for help to improve quality of work. Work at rate and level.	Occasionally not prepared for class and do nothing to improve. Do not participate in some class activities. Work is frequently late, and the quality is poor.
Everyone deserves respect.	Exhibit total respect for themselves, others, the classwork, and the physical classroom at all times.	Exhibit acceptable levels of respect for themselves, others, the classwork, and the physical classroom at all times. Language, dress, and actions are mostly appropriate. Self-correct and/or apologize without prompting.	Exhibit repeated minor instances of lack of respect for themselves, others, the classwork, and the physical classroom, or are occasionally dangerous or disruptive. Language, dress, and actions are usually appropriate. Correct actions when reminded, and actions do no pose significant danger or disruption.	Exhibit repeated minor instances of lack of respect for themselves, others, the classwork, and the physical classroom, or are occasionally dangerous or disruptive. Language, dress, and actions are often inappropriate. Need adult intervention to change actions.

SCHOOL SAMPLE

Behavior Rubric Using Guidelines for Success (Secondary Level)

GUIDELINES FOR SUCCESS	EXEMPLARY	RECOGNIZED	SATISFACTORY	UNSATISFACTORY
Respect	These students exhibit total respect for themselves, others, the classwork, and the physical classroom at all times.	These students exhibit acceptable levels of respect for themselves, others, the class work, and the physical classroom at all times.	These students exhibit acceptable levels of respect for themselves, others, the classwork, and the physical classroom most of the time. The few lapses that they have do not pose significant danger or disruption.	These students exhibit repeated minor instances of lack of respect for themselves, others, the classwork, and the physical classroom, or are occasionally dangerous or disruptive.
Preparedness	These students always have all supplies and have done all of the assignments necessary for them to be successful in class.	These students usually have all supplies and have done all of the assignments necessary for them to be successful in class. These students immediately correct any shortcomings on their own.	These students usually have all supplies and have done all of the assignments necessary for them to be successful in class. These students immediately correct shortcomings when reminded by the teacher.	These students occasionally are not prepared for class and do nothing to correct this. As a result, they can not fully participate in some of the class activities.
Productivity	These students consistently make the best possible use of time, both in and out of class, and help others to do the same. As a result, they always produce work of the highest quality.	These students consistently make good use of time, both in and out of class, and help others to do the same. As a result, they always produce work of high quality.	These students consistently make good use of time, both in and out of class. As a result, they usually produce work of high quality. They only occasionally help others to be more productive.	These students occasionally make unproductive use of time, both in and out of class. As a result, their work lacks the quality it would have with more time devoted to it. They occasionally prompt others to be unproductive.
Responsibility	These students recognize that their behaviors determine their success in the classroom, so they consistently take the initiative to make sure that they are fully successful.	These students recognize that their behaviors determine their success in the classroom, so they occasionally take the initiative to make sure that they are fully successful.	These students recognize that their behaviors determine their success in the classroom, but they need to show more initiative to make sure that they are fully successful.	These students allow outside influences to determine their success in the classroom. They make excuses instead of taking initiative, so they are therefore not fully successful.

These samples can be printed from the Module C CD.

Incorporate the guidelines as part of the Student and Parent Handbook, school calendar, school planner, meeting agendas, and so on. You might include them on disciplinary referral forms—the referring or receiving adult can check off the guideline the student violated and ensure that the student knows how to do better the next time. Consistent, frequent use of the guidelines creates a common language between teachers and administrators, and students receive a consistent message about how they are expected to behave.

Interlake High School of Bellevue, Washington, did a great job of incorporating its guidelines—Integrity, Humanity, Scholarship—into all aspects of school life. Figure 2e below shows one example: The Guidelines for Success graphic is displayed five times during the back-to-school staff inservice presentation, and the guidelines are integrated into both academic and behavior management information for staff.

Figure 2e   Sample PowerPoint slides from staff inservice; thanks to Interlake High School and Bellevue School District in Bellevue, Washington

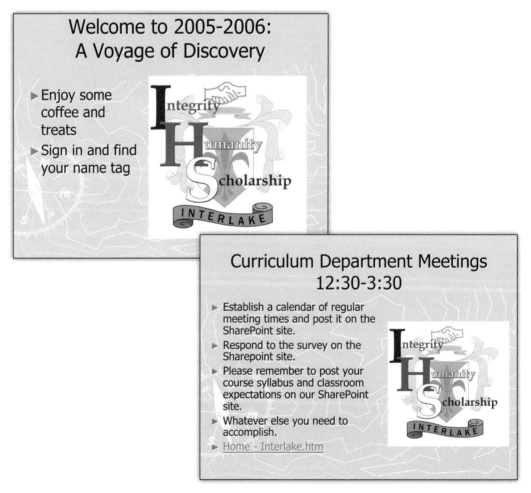

Frame new improvement priorities within the Guidelines for Success. For example, tie improvements in the homework completion policy to the guideline "Be responsible."

Document the Guidelines for Success. Include the guidelines in the Foundations Archive, Staff Handbook, and Student and Parent Handbook. For staff, provide specific examples of how to use the guidelines to acknowledge responsible student behavior and correct irresponsible behavior. Also describe major school programs for implementing the guidelines, such as monthly themes. Figure 2f below shows a sample of how the Guidelines for Success can be included in the Staff Handbook.

Figure 2f *Guidelines for Success information provided in staff handbook (C-16)*

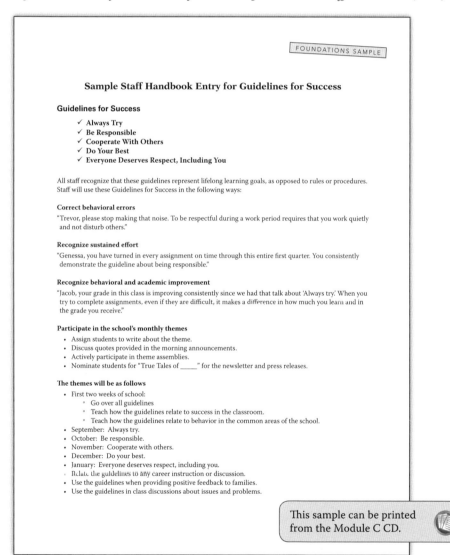

FOUNDATIONS SAMPLE

Sample Staff Handbook Entry for Guidelines for Success

Guidelines for Success

✓ **Always Try**
✓ **Be Responsible**
✓ **Cooperate With Others**
✓ **Do Your Best**
✓ **Everyone Deserves Respect, Including You**

All staff recognize that these guidelines represent lifelong learning goals, as opposed to rules or procedures. Staff will use these Guidelines for Success in the following ways:

Correct behavioral errors
"Trevor, please stop making that noise. To be respectful during a work period requires that you work quietly and not disturb others."

Recognize sustained effort
"Genessa, you have turned in every assignment on time through this entire first quarter. You consistently demonstrate the guideline about being responsible."

Recognize behavioral and academic improvement
"Jacob, your grade in this class is improving consistently since we had that talk about 'Always try.' When you try to complete assignments, even if they are difficult, it makes a difference in how much you learn and in the grade you receive."

Participate in the school's monthly themes
- Assign students to write about the theme.
- Discuss quotes provided in the morning announcements.
- Actively participate in theme assemblies.
- Nominate students for "True Tales of _____" for the newsletter and press releases.

The themes will be as follows
- First two weeks of school:
  ◦ Go over all guidelines
  ◦ Teach how the guidelines relate to success in the classroom.
  ◦ Teach how the guidelines relate to behavior in the common areas of the school.
- September: Always try.
- October: Be responsible.
- November: Cooperate with others.
- December: Do your best.
- January: Everyone deserves respect, including you.
- Relate the guidelines to any career instruction or discussion.
- Use the guidelines when providing positive feedback to families.
- Use the guidelines in class discussions about issues and problems.

This sample can be printed from the Module C CD.

Design and teach lessons to introduce and re-teach (when necessary) Guidelines for Success to students. Lessons should be age appropriate. They should explain the rationale for the guidelines and how they can help students. Include examples of what it looks and sounds like when a student is and is not following the guidelines. You might prepare a schoolwide lesson for the launch of the guidelines and teach all students during an assembly, then follow up by providing lesson plans to teachers and having them teach the guidelines to their classes. A good project to reinforce the guidelines is to have older students prepare lessons for younger students, perhaps on video. See the sample lessons for KEYS (Know, Excel, Yearn, Serve) for Success at the end of this task. These sample lessons show how you might teach Know and Excel.

Ensure the continued innovative and effective use of Guidelines for Success.

Incorporate the guidelines into a creative variety of school activities throughout each school year. Here are some suggestions:

- Include a celebration of the guidelines during the annual kickoff to the school year.

- Establish monthly themes (October is Cooperation month, November is Respect month, and so on) that are the basis for common area posters and decorations, classroom discussion and assignments, and special awards for students.

- Award Student of the Month honors based on the Guidelines for Success.

- Have teachers assign students to write about the guidelines.

- Provide the guidelines to outside guest speakers and ask them to incorporate the values into their presentations, if possible.

- Give tangible rewards, such as lottery tickets, to students for following the guidelines. (More information about reward programs appears in Module C, Presentation 6.)

- Ask students to nominate (in writing) other students for exemplary behavior according to the Guidelines for Success. Forward the nominations to the corresponding nominated students so they know that others recognize their positive behavior.

Create an annual Guidelines for Success implementation calendar to ensure that the guidelines are fully used by the entire staff. Include specific tasks, people responsible, and timelines, and be sure to include on your long-term planning calendar the tasks of teaching and celebrating the guidelines every year. Figure 2g on the next page shows a sample calendar. Thanks to Federal Way High School in Federal Way, Washington—this example was adapted from a document its staff developed.

Set up a reminder system to ensure that a new implementation calendar will be created each year.

Figure 2g *Guidelines for Success Sample Implementation Calendar*

Guidelines for Success • Sample Implementation Calendar

Guidelines for Success (GFS) Task Force: John Wilkins, Abigail Cho, Evan Odom, Cathy Cortez, Harry Smith

Date	Task	People Responsible
September 1–15 School begins.	Each class brainstorms suggestions, and five guidelines are selected.	Mr. Wilkins will instruct teachers how to lead brainstorming sessions; GFS Task Force and principal will make final decision.
September 15	Hold a schoolwide assembly to reveal the final guidelines.	Principal organizes.
September 15– October 15	Student artists create posters of the guidelines, and student leaders help with installing them in all common areas.	Ms. Cho and Mrs. Lewis, the art teacher, lead this effort.
	Staff volunteers create lesson plans to teach the guidelines.	Mr. Odom will facilitate.
	Document the guidelines and how to use them in the staff handbook.	GFS Task Force
	All staff begin using the guidelines when they correct misbehavior. "Tom, it's not respectful to call others names. Remember the Guideline for Success: Treat everyone with respect."	Mrs. Cortez ensures that all staff know how to use the guidelines when correcting misbehavior.
October 15–31	Staff teach the lessons on the guidelines to their classes.	Mr. Odom will distribute lesson plans and provide support.
November	Teachers are encouraged to develop rubrics to clarify the expectations and guide constructive feedback to their classes.	Principal communicates this idea.
	Begin using monthly themes (December: Be responsible; January: Cooperate with others; February: Do your best; March: Everyone deserves respect, including you).	GFS Task Force establishes schedule and guides staff in how to use the theme with students.
December	Hold a school assembly to discuss how the guidelines have improved the school so far, celebrate their success, and reveal the reward systems that will begin in January.	Principal organizes assembly. Mr. Smith develops reward system and presents it at assembly.
January	Implement reward system: Staff give RESPECT tickets to students who are following the guidelines. Students can enter their tickets in weekly drawings for small prizes.	Mr. Smith facilitates this implementation.
February	Review how the guidelines are working in the school, brainstorm ways to make them even more visible, and invite opinions and recommendations from staff.	GFS Task Force
March	Special event: As part of the annual Community Partners week, local employers come to school and talk about their businesses and what they look for in an employee. Inform the guest speakers ahead of time about the Guidelines for Success and ask them to include those qualities in their talks.	Mr. Wilkins and principal are primarily responsible for this program.
April May	Prepare and implement an end-of-year celebration that includes awards for students and staff who exemplify the guidelines.	GFS Task Force and principal will organize.
June	Review current year's implementation activities and determine calendar for next school year.	GFS Task Force and principal

Conclusion

Remember that the Foundations Team's job is to establish the Guidelines for Success as the hub for all behavior management procedures and to keep the staff excited about using the guidelines. The staff's job is to keep students excited about the guidelines and to teach the guidelines as life lessons that students will never forget. Guidelines for Success are not just words—they define the climate and culture of the school, and everyone should strive to live them every day.

Task 3 Action Steps & Evidence of Implementation

Action Steps	Evidence of Implementation
1. Develop and implement a plan for celebrating the completion of your Guidelines for Success. 2. Develop and implement a plan for making your Guidelines for Success highly visible in the school. 3. Identify ideas for creatively incorporating your Guidelines for Success into school activities.	Foundations Process: Guidelines for Success Foundations Archive: Guidelines for Success (final guidelines)
4. Design lessons for teaching the guidelines to all students. Sample lessons follow these Action Steps and are also available on the Module C CD. Develop a plan and timeline for teaching the lessons.	Foundations Archive: Lesson Plans for Teaching Guidelines for Success
5. Prepare a Guidelines for Success section for your Staff Handbook. • Include specific suggestions for how staff can and should use your Guidelines for Success. • Include descriptions of any major school programs for implementing your Guidelines for Success.	Staff Handbook: Guidelines for Success
6. Create a Guidelines for Success implementation calendar for the current year. 7. Set up a reminder system to ensure that a new implementation calendar will be created each year. Teach and celebrate the guidelines every year, using creative ways to reward behavior that exemplifies the guidelines.	Foundations Process: Planning Calendar

Figure 2h *Guidelines for Success, Lesson 1 Scripted Lesson and Worksheet*

Guidelines for Success
Lesson 1 • KEYS for Success: Know

KEYS for Success: Know

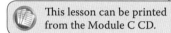 This lesson can be printed
from the Module C CD.

OBJECTIVES

Students will explain the guideline **Know** and the attitudes, behaviors, and attributes
needed to exhibit the guideline.

MATERIALS

- Document camera, interactive whiteboard, or PowerPoint
- Student copies of the Student Worksheet for Lesson 1—Keys for Success: Know

Introduction

1. Introduce the Guidelines for Success.

   At Ben Franklin Middle School, we have KEYS for success. If you remember and
   always strive to do your best with each of the four KEYS, you will be successful
   at Ben Franklin. These things will also help you be successful in other areas of
   your life—for example, in a job, with your family, and in relationships.

   Point to each guideline as you read it. You may have students read them
   chorally with you or do cloze reading by having students complete the
   last half of the sentence. Have them fill in the blanks on their worksheet.

   (**Know**): Seek (knowledge) and be active in your own learning.

   strive for excellence in all you do.

Guidelines for Success
Lesson 1 • KEYS for Success: Know

Name _____ Class/Teacher _____ Period ____

KEYS for Success: Know

Ben Franklin Middle School KEYS for Success:

_____: Seek _____ and be _____
in your own learning.
Excel: Do your _____. Try your hardest and strive for excellence in all
you do.
Yearn: Desire to be successful. Set _____ and _____
to accomplish them.
Serve: Work with _____. Give of yourself, your time, and your talents.

1. To *seek* something, I would:
   - _____
   - _____
   - _____
   - _____
   - _____

Guidelines for Success
Lesson 1 • KEYS for Success: Know

2. The qualities, behaviors, and attitudes someone needs to be active in something include:
   - _____
   - _____
   - _____
   - _____

3. One example of how the guideline **Know** will help me be successful in school is:
   _____
   _____

   Another example is: _____

Lesson Body

1. Analyze what *seek knowledge* means. Use the analogy of hidden treasure to explain the word "seek" and the efforts someone would put in to seek something.

   Seek means to try to find something. Let's think about what you do when you seek something, especially something that is worth a lot, like knowledge. If you were seeking a hidden treasure with two million dollars' worth of diamonds and rubies and gold in it, what would you do to try to find it?

   Show me a thumbs-up or thumbs-down for each question:

   • Would you try to find the treasure? Would you seek it? **Cue thumbs up or down.**

   • Would you try hard, putting in your best effort? **Cue thumbs up or down.**

   • Let's say there was a map to the treasure, and it had words on it that you didn't understand. You knew the guide could help translate the words for you. Would you ask for help or give up? Thumbs up if you would ask for help. Thumbs down if you would give up.

   • What if you got to a difficult spot on the journey to find the treasure? Let's say it was going to take longer than you expected, or you made a wrong turn and had to start over again. Would you keep trying or give up and go home? Thumbs up for keep trying. Thumbs down for give up and go home.

   So, if you were seeking a treasure, you would do everything you could to try and find it. You would do your best. You would ask for help if you needed it. You wouldn't give up, even if it was difficult.

   For Item 1 on their worksheets, have students write a list of things someone might do to seek something.

   Let's list those things that you would do to seek a treasure. I'm going to write these on the board, and I want you to write them on your worksheets.

   To seek something, I would:

   • Try hard
   • Put in my best effort
   • Ask for help if needed
   • Keep trying, even when it is difficult

Figure 2h (continued)

Have students brainstorm additional actions, attitudes, and attributes needed when someone seeks something. To prompt their thinking, ask them to consider things such as:

- What would you need if you were seeking the next level in a video game? How would you get the answer or abilities to defeat a challenge in the game?

- What things would help you if you were seeking a promotion in a job? What attitudes and efforts would make you more likely to get a promotion?

- If you were seeking to buy a cell phone and calling plan, what things would you need to do to figure out the best information? What qualities and attitudes would help you get the best information.

Circulate and write student responses along with their names. Share the ideas and add them to the list on the board. If needed, rephrase so that they apply to broad situations and to seeking knowledge. Some possibilities include:

- Read instructions or other material.
- Talk to friends for suggestions.
- If it's not working one way, try another.
- Be polite to those in charge.
- Go above and beyond what is expected.
- Listen to and follow directions and rules.
- Compare different items.
- Do research to find the best option

Use the list to refer back to what students can do to seek knowledge. Use the treasure-seeking analogy to discuss how seeking knowledge is like unlocking a treasure chest—it helps them financially, helps them succeed in the world, helps them form healthy relationships, etc.

At Ben Franklin, our guidelines tell us to *seek knowledge.* If you always do your best to seek knowledge, it will help you be successful at Ben Franklin and in your life. If we look at our list, all of these things will be helpful as we seek knowledge.

And seeking knowledge is almost like looking for and finding that hidden treasure. If you actively seek knowledge and are successful in school, you can graduate from high school and have more options for the jobs you want or college you want to go to. On average, during the course of their working lives, high school graduates make a quarter of a million dollars more than people who drop out. College graduates earn a million dollars more than

Foundations: A Proactive and Positive Behavior Support System   © 2014 Pacific Northwest Publishing

Module C, Presentation 2

Scripted Lesson

Page 4 of 5

Guidelines for Success
Lesson 1 • KEYS for Success: Know

those who graduate from high school. And people with an advanced degree earn another million on top of that! So seeking knowledge really is like seeking treasure.

Just as with treasure, to seek knowledge you need to try to put in your best effort. Give me a thumbs-up if you are ready to put in your best effort this year. **Cue thumbs up or down.**

As with a treasure map, at times you won't be sure what to do next and could use some help. That's what we, your teachers, are here for—to help you learn and give help when needed. If you never needed help and already knew everything, you wouldn't need to be in school! Give me a thumbs-up if you are ready to ask for help when needed. **Cue thumbs up or down.**

Seeking knowledge can be difficult sometimes. It can be uncomfortable when you don't know something or are struggling to learn something. But the only way to grow is to push through and keep trying, just like you would if you were seeking that treasure. When you seek knowledge at Ben Franklin, give me a thumbs-up if you are going to push through and keep trying even when things are tough. **Cue thumbs up or down.**

You are all going to be successful if you do these things and the other things on our list to seek knowledge.

2. Analyze what *be active in your own learning* means.

Point to the next part of Know. The guideline says that you should seek knowledge and . . . (*be active in your own learning*).

Use an analogous situation—a marathon runner, for example—to explain the concept of *be active.*

I think of people who run marathons when I think of someone active. They get up and train every day. They don't sit around and do nothing and then expect to do well without having practiced. So let's think of the qualities, behaviors, and attitudes that marathon runners have that help them stay active and engaged in their running.

Demonstrate writing a list of qualities, behaviors, and attitudes someone would need to *be active* in something. Think aloud as you list items.

Marathon runners need to have a lot of motivation and determination— they can't be lazy. I'll write that down—"motivation," "determination," "not be lazy!" I know a lot of marathon runners have a training partner to stay motivated, so I'll write down "help" and "partners to stay on track." Let's think of other things . . .

Figure 2h (continued)

Guide students as they add to the list, using other examples that you and students come up with for being active in something and the traits, behaviors, and attitudes that are needed.

Use the list you and the students generate to explain what students can do to *be active* in their own learning. Have students complete Item 2 on their worksheets.

How does this apply to school? Well, let's think about what you can do to be active in your own learning. We listed motivation and determination. Are those traits true for school? Will you be more successful if you stay motivated and determined, even if you are having a bad day or struggling with something?

What about *don't be lazy*? That means coming to school every day you aren't seriously ill, putting in your best effort, and actively looking for opportunities to improve in school . . .

Conclusion

- Summarize and review what students should do to seek knowledge and be active in their own learning.

- Explain and give some examples of how **Know** will help them be successful outside of school.

  • If you actively seek knowledge in whatever job you have, you will continue growing and learning, which is one of the best ways to get a promotion, continue improving in your field, and set yourself apart from the rest of the pack.

  • If you have a hobby and you actively seek knowledge about it, you will become better at it and you may enjoy it more.

  • If you actively seek knowledge in a relationship, working to learn about the other person, you will be more likely to develop a real and lasting connection.

- **Exit Ticket:** Have students complete Item 3 on their worksheets, in which they explain with at least two examples how the guideline **Know** will help them be successful in school.

Module C, Presentation 2

Scripted Lesson

Page 1 of 4

Guidelines for Success
Lesson 2 • KEYS for Success: Excel

KEYS for Success: Excel

This lesson can be printed from the Module C CD.

OBJECTIVES

- Students will explain how to excel in a subject or activity.
- Students will describe how to apply these qualities and decisions to school.

MATERIALS

- Document camera, interactive whiteboard, or PowerPoint
- Student copies of the Student Worksheet for Lesson 2—Keys for Success: Excel

Introduction

1. Review the Guidelines for Success and key points from Lesson 1. Have students fill in the missing words.

   (Know): Seek (knowledge) and be <u>active</u> in your own learning.

   Excel: Do your <u>best</u>. Try your hardest and strive for excellence in all you do.

   Yearn: Desire to be successful. Set <u>goals</u> and <u>work hard</u> to accomplish them.

   Serve: Work with <u>others</u>. Give of yourself, your time, and your talents.

   Point to each guideline as you read it. You may have students read them chorally with you or do cloze reading by having students complete the last half of the sentence. Have them fill in the blanks on their worksheet.

Module C, Presentation 2

Student Worksheet

Page 1 of 2

Guidelines for Success
Lesson 2 • KEYS for Success: Excel

Name _____ Class/Teacher _____ Period ____

KEYS for Success: Excel

Ben Franklin Middle School KEYS for Success:

_____; Seek _____ and be _____

in your own learning.

Excel: _____

_____

Yearn: Desire to be successful. Set goals and work hard to accomplish them.
Serve: Work with others. Give of yourself, your time, and your talents.

1. How to Excel Chart

Things they did/Effort	Attitude/Mindset
Relationship skills	Things avoided

Module C, Presentation 2

Student Worksheet

Page 2 of 2

Guidelines for Success
Lesson 2 • KEYS for Success: Excel

2. One area in which I would like to excel is: _____

_____

3. Things I can do to excel in this area include: _____

_____

Figure 2i (continued)

to the top of their field. Examining what these experts do and think will help you learn what you need to do to excel in school and any other field or area in which you desire to do well!

Lesson Body

1. Demonstrate filling out the How to Excel chart on the student worksheet for a specific field (musician, athlete, engineer, writer, etc.) Talk aloud and explain your thinking as you fill out the chart. Have students write responses on their worksheet.

   Let's look at what an expert in the field of music might need to do in order to excel. I'm going to think about a classical musician, but we could also break this down for a pop star, rock musician, or some other expert in the music industry.

   What does a musician do, or what effort does a musician put in to become the best in the field and excel? Well, I know that professional musicians have to practice, practice, practice. When they are younger, they take lessons. All musicians that I know set goals for practice and performance, such as practicing 6 hours a day or continuing to practice one passage until it is perfect. Then they stick to those goals. I'm going to write these things down in the "Things they did/Effort" box.

   Now, what kinds of attitudes or mindsets do musicians need so that they excel? They . . .

   How to Excel: Musicians

Things they did/Effort	Attitude/Mindset
Practice, practice, practice Take lessons Set goals and stick to them	Don't give up—strong Confident Positive
Relationship skills	**Things avoided**
Respectful Willing to work with others Show humility Help others and accept help	Distractions—certain people, certain activities Naysayers

   Ask additional examples in each box. Have students share one idea with a partner first, then randomly call on students to share their partner's response.

Module C, Presentation 2

Scripted Lesson

Page 3 of 4

Guidelines for Success
Lesson 2 • KEYS for Success: Excel

2. With students, develop a list of topics or fields in which someone may excel. For example:

   - Sports (have students select specific sports)
   - Science
   - Art
   - Business
   - Technology
   - Chess
   - Medicine

3. Divide students into partners or groups, then have each partnership or group select a topic from the list generated in Step 2. Direct students to think of things that leaders in the field they selected had to do in order to excel and get to the top. Students will brainstorm and write their answers on the How to Excel Chart on their worksheets.

4. When students finish brainstorming, randomly call on groups to share something from each box. Add their ideas to your original How to Excel Chart.

5. Have a class discussion about how each of the listed efforts, attitudes, skills, and things avoided will help them be successful at Ben Franklin Middle School. Also discuss the following points:

   The second part of the guideline Excel says, "Do your best. Try your hardest and strive for excellence in all you do." What things listed on your How to Excel chart are similar or have the same meaning? Do you think that experts in the field you chose follow this guideline—doing their best, trying their hardest, and striving for excellence?

   The point is not to be the best at everything but to do your own best in whatever you do. This is about *personal best*. Strive for excellence and excel, not in comparison with other people, but to be the best you can be. Many musicians, athletes, public speakers, writers, etc., are not trying to beat anyone else. Their goal is to create their personal best and excel.

   Notice that most of what is on the How to Excel Chart doesn't have to do with talent, IQ, or something you are born with. It has to do with how hard you try, how well you work with others, and the choices you make.

Foundations: A Proactive and Positive Behavior Support System   © 2014 Pacific Northwest Publishing

Figure 2i (continued)

Conclusion

- Summarize and review what students should do to excel at Ben Franklin Middle School.

- Explain that students can apply these same efforts, attitudes, relationship skills, and positive decisions to become successful in any endeavor—classes, a job, relationships—so that they excel in life.

- **Exit Ticket:** Have students complete Items 2 and 3 on their worksheets—identify an area in which they would like to excel and list at least five things they can do to excel.

Ratios of Positive Interactions

DOCUMENTS*

- Ratios of Positive Interactions Monitoring Forms, three versions (C-03a, b, and c)
- Strategies for Increasing Positive Interactions (C-04)
- The Power of Three: Increasing Positive Behaviors (C-17)
- Caught You Caring! instructions and nomination form (C-18)

* All documents listed are available on the CD. Other documents that are not shown in this presentation are also available on the CD (see Appendix C for a complete list).

INTRODUCTION

As we said in Presentation 1, school climate is defined mainly by staff behavior. Therefore, staff behavior needs to be consciously inviting and positive. There's another very compelling reason why all staff should work on being positive: When adults pay more attention to positive behavior than to misbehavior, students' motivation to behave responsibly can increase.

Understand the Criticism Trap.

The term *Criticism Trap* was coined by Dr. Wesley C. Becker, a pioneer in the study of behavior. In the 1960s, Dr. Becker was working in elementary schools and noticed that some teachers repeatedly nagged students about minor misbehavior, such as being out of seat or talking inappropriately. He wondered if the misbehaviors would decrease if the teachers gave more attention to the *desired* behavior than to the misbehavior. He had baseline data on out-of-seat behavior for several classrooms, and he tried to convince those teachers that students would be more likely to stay in their seats if the teachers paid more attention to students when they were following expectations. However, the teachers were reluctant to curtail their reminders. They said, "Are you crazy? If we quit nagging these students about sitting down, our rooms will be chaotic!" They were convinced that their reprimands were the force that kept their classes in control.

So Dr. Becker got creative. He decided to encourage the teachers to reprimand and remind students about out-of-seat behavior even more immediately and consistently. The data collectors stationed in the classrooms helped by prompting the teachers to correct students when the teachers didn't notice the misbehavior. The result was that every out-of-seat behavior was reprimanded.

The teachers assumed this would decrease the behavior, but the number of students getting out of their seats at the wrong times actually increased. Dr. Becker called this phenomenon the Criticism Trap. Although the teachers thought they were doing something effective, the students, some of whom were starved for attention, were getting out of their seats at least in part to get their teachers to look at them and talk to them.

Dr. Becker then had the teachers ignore most out-of-seat behavior and instead praise students who were in their seats and students who were following the rules. In every classroom, student behavior improved and misbehavior decreased. So what does Dr. Becker's experiment suggest? The only real way out of the Criticism Trap is to have more interactions with students when they are behaving responsibly than when they are misbehaving.

Understand Ratios of Positive to Corrective Interactions.

Dr. Becker's work (Becker was one of Randy's professors at the University of Oregon) led to the *Safe & Civil Schools* recommendation that instructors and supervisors always pay at least three times more frequent attention to every student when the student is meeting expectations than when the student is behaving inappropriately. The concept of ratios of positive interactions (RPI) is about the strategic use of your attention as a tool in the classroom.

Over the years, many researchers have studied the efficacy of this approach. Sheets and Gay (1996) wrote that "the causes of many classroom behaviors labeled and punished as rule infractions are, in fact, problems of students and teachers relating to each other interpersonally." Way back in 1977, O'Leary and O'Leary wrote that "teacher attention is perhaps the most basic of all influences on student behaviors, and the systematic use of attention should characterize every teacher's classroom repertoire."

These and other researchers have observed in many different classrooms and repeatedly found that when teachers do not overtly strive to be positive, they are very likely to fall into patterns of paying 3 to 15 times more attention to misbehavior than to positive behavior. We emphasize RPI in *Foundations* because it's so easy to forget, even when you know it works.

Avoid the Criticism Trap.

People don't fall into the Criticism Trap because they don't care or because they are inherently negative. When students are behaving well, you don't think about behavior management. You think about the pace of your lessons, the clarity of your questions, the quality of your instruction, the degree to which you're following the curriculum. You tend to think about behavior only when a student misbehaves:

- "Get back to your seat. You're disturbing people in the lab area."
- "Please quiet down. It's too loud in here."
- "You two, stop talking and get to work."

You think about behavior as soon as behavior goes wrong. When behavior is going well, you are thinking about instruction.

Another reason that you might fall into negativity is that most of the time when you reprimand, most students do what you ask. When you say, "Sit down," most students sit down, and you are reinforced for reprimanding them. A student who is starved for attention, however, learns that when she behaves, you ignore her. When she misbehaves, she gets immediate attention. The misbehavior is probably not even a conscious choice. So a vicious cycle begins in which everybody gets immediate gratification but nobody gets what he or she wants in the long term.

Correctives are not bad or wrong. In fact, for consistency they're vital—most misbehavior needs to be corrected, and your first response to misbehavior should be corrective. (Planned ignoring is a specialized procedure that should be used only with chronic attention-seeking behavior and only when corrective techniques haven't worked.) But given that correctives are necessary, and given that most students improve their behavior when we correct them, the reinforcement you receive for correcting might lead you to become increasingly negative. You'll have to work hard to provide much more attention to positive behavior than to correctives. That's the theme throughout this presentation.

*E*xample From the Field

The concept of RPI has surprising power, but it is easy to forget. A few years ago, I was presenting *Foundations* to a large urban district. During a lunch break, I was conversing with a veteran teacher, Kathy, from one of the high schools. Kathy described her current third- and fourth-period classes as her "classes from hell"—among the toughest classes she had ever taught in her decades-long career teaching inner-city youth. She felt as though these classes were always on the verge of being out of control, and she related incidents when she had to call in security officers to pull students out of class. She asked if I had any suggestions, so I talked with her about re-teaching expectations and setting up some classwide incentives. I didn't even think about mentioning RPI to Kathy, although later that day I presented some information about classroom management techniques, including RPI, to the group.

The next day, I received an email from Kathy. Here's what she said: "Randy, I could cry. As they entered the classroom, I greeted the students in my 'classes from hell' with big smiles for each *individual*. The kids smiled back and said that I seemed to be in a good mood. (Wow, if they see a difference that quickly, I *have* been grouchy.) I started them on the first assignment with enthusiasm and told them how this particular assignment would benefit them relative to the subject I'm teaching. While students worked, I walked around the room with a pad of sticky notes. When I found a student working or asking questions or cooperating with other students to understand the process, I wrote a personal, specific note thanking him or her for that behavior.

"I am amazed. My students are working and happy. I am happy for the first time in a long time in these classes. Thank you. Thank you. Thank you!"

I emailed Kathy and asked whether I could share her words with other schools in her district that I was working with. She wrote back: "Absolutely. I felt so hopeless. I know it won't always be this good every day, with every class, and with every kid, and I will have to constantly come up with new ways to show the positive, but I'm so encouraged that I can do this. When you explained the positive-to-corrective ratio yesterday afternoon, I could hear my own voice saying, 'Stop that.' 'Don't do that.' 'Sit down.' I had to think long and hard to find any positive things that I say to my class.

"This concept really touched my heart, and if I can hold on to it, I know that I can truly say at the end of the day that I did the right thing. RPI is a remarkably powerful strategy. If my words help spread this message to others, please feel free to use them."

I kept in touch with Kathy, and we remind each other about how we—everyone—needs to be constantly vigilant about keeping those positive interactions at a high level. I've known this concept for decades, yet I still need to remind myself.   —R.S.

RPI is an objective technique that you can quantify with data. You can identify positives and correctives and count the ratio. You control the ratio in the same way a pilot controls an airplane. When something goes wrong, a pilot has the training to know how to fix it. He or she adjusts the variables—altitude, speed, and so on. When behavior management is going badly, you can use your training to adjust the variables, and RPI is one of your most powerful tools.

Note: In previous publications, we've referred to this technique as the ratios of interactions or ratios of positive to negative interactions. To emphasize the positive, we've adjusted our language just a bit. We now use the phrases *ratios of positive interactions* (RPI) and *ratios of positive to corrective interactions.*

The tasks in this presentation are designed to help you understand why and how to keep adult attention to positive student behavior at least three times more frequent than adult attention to correcting misbehavior.

Task 1: Understand Positive and Corrective Interactions defines positive and corrective interactions so the entire staff knows how to deliver them and can objectively and consistently identify and count them.

Task 2: Increase Your Positive Interactions describes ways to increase your interactions with students when they are behaving appropriately, and this strategy is the main approach to improving your RPI.

Task 3: Fine-Tune Your Positive and Corrective Interactions suggests how to fine-tune both positives and correctives and ensure that you are getting as much out of the RPI strategy as possible.

Task 4: Work on Ratios of Positive Interactions Continuously explains how the Foundations Team can work on RPI regularly with the entire staff and keep the concept of RPI alive in your school long term.

TASK 1

Understand positive and corrective interactions

Susan Isaacs, a fabulous trainer for *Safe & Civil Schools* and one of the codevelopers of this third edition of *Foundations*, says this about ratios of positive interactions (RPI):

> *It's easy to believe that a classroom full of positive interactions springs from having responsible students who are exceedingly well behaved and responsible, yet in reality this belief is exactly backwards. In truth, positive interactions are more like the fuel that drives good behavior and personal responsibility. Unfortunately, some students with chronic misbehavior have learned that it is easier and more reliable to get attention by doing things wrong than by following the rules.*

This powerful concept of RPI is measurable—that's why it can be expressed as a ratio—and it's concrete enough to be analyzed and modified to be even more powerful. In this task, we define positive and corrective interactions so that your entire staff can objectively and consistently identify and count them. Briefly, both interactions involve the student getting adult attention, and both are defined by the student's behavior at the time of the adult attention, rather than by what the adult did.

The ability to identify an interaction as either positive or corrective is important so that the entire staff shares a common language and a common understanding of how an interaction is categorized as either positive or corrective. RPI is such a powerful concept, both productively and destructively, that we encourage all staff members to periodically self-monitor their ratios of interactions. We recommend that you address RPI as a whole-staff project and that you collect and analyze data. Data on RPI are very useful for coaches and mentors who are helping teachers, both novice and experienced, hone their skills.

ℰ FOUNDATIONS RECOMMENDATION ℭ

RPI is such a powerful concept, both productively and destructively, that we encourage all staff members to periodically self-monitor their ratios of interactions. We recommend that you address RPI as a whole-staff project and that you collect and analyze data.

What is a positive interaction?

When a student is engaged in positive behavior and you pay attention to the student, you've interacted positively. When a student is on task and you verbally praise the student, give a thumbs-up, ask "Do you have any questions?" or make eye contact, you've interacted positively with the student—not because *you* were positive, but because *the student* was engaged in positive behavior. When a student is walking down the hallway and you ask, "How was the basketball game?" or you greet the student, you've interacted positively. The student was following expectations and behaving responsibly and you gave him attention. The attention does not have to be praise—noncontingent attention can be a positive interaction, too. So any time the student is not misbehaving and you give attention, the interaction is positive.

What is a corrective interaction?

Note: In previous editions of *Foundations*, we used the term *negative* interaction, but we now use *corrective* interaction. The word *negative* implies bad or wrong, but there is nothing wrong about correcting student behavior! The term *corrective* gives a more accurate description of the interaction.

When a student is not following behavioral expectations and you pay attention to the student, you've engaged in a corrective interaction. Corrections include reminders, assigning consequences, stating that the behavior is unacceptable, and gestures or looks that indicate disapproval of the student's behavior. For the purpose of documenting RPI, interactions with the student to correct *academic* errors are *not* corrective. When the student is behaving appropriately, an interaction to correct an academic error is positive and can be recorded as attention to positive behavior.

Corrections are not wrong—they are necessary. Gentle reminders during the beginning of the school year, following through on consequences for rule violations, and giving the "teacher eye" as a quick correction for off-task behavior are all fine ways to correct misbehavior. They are important tools in your repertoire as a teacher. Your goal is not to reduce correctives to zero, but to ensure that you always place more emphasis on noticing students when they are behaving positively than noticing students when they are behaving negatively.

Identify corrective interactions correctly.

Some corrective interactions can seem like positives, but in the schema we're creating here they are considered correctives. For example, a student is off task and you say, "Reiko, you did such a nice job on the first part of this assignment and there's only 10 minutes left, so keep working."

Or you walk past a cooperative group and hear a student saying rude comments to another student, so you say, "Rashid, you are such a responsible young man—please apologize to Armando." (Notice that these statements express disagreement with what the students said, not with the students.)

In both examples, your words sound positive. For determining RPI, however, both examples would be counted as corrective because you gave the student attention as the student was engaged in an undesirable behavior. What you say doesn't matter—the student's behavior at the time of the interaction defines it as either positive or corrective. Both of the above examples are perfectly fine ways to correct misbehavior, but when you are counting positives and correctives, both would be considered correctives.

Read the following example and judge whether the interaction is positive or corrective:

> *The teacher is supervising an independent work period. She is circulating around the room and visually scanning. She walks up to a seated student and says, "Caitlyn, do you have any questions? Let me know if you need anything."*

Did the teacher praise the student? Did she correct the student? No, she gave noncontingent attention. If you were counting RPIs, how would you count this interaction?

 Interactions are identified as positive or corrective based on what the student is doing at the time you provide attention, not on what you do or say to provide the attention."

If you are having trouble answering the question, it's because an essential piece of information is missing from the scenario. (That's right, it's a trick question!) You don't know *what the student was doing* when the teacher paid attention to her. If the student was on task, the interaction would be marked positive. If the student was off task, the interaction would be marked corrective—the teacher was using her attention to re-engage the student.

We've observed teachers whose styles are very stern and brusque, yet they are very positive. They praise and give attention to students who are meeting expectations much more than they pay attention to misbehavior. Style doesn't matter. The timing of the attention is what matters.

A teacher who misunderstands the concept of positives might say to an off-task student, "Dani, you worked so hard yesterday. Why don't you get going on this assignment?" This teacher's words sound positive, but what he's saying doesn't matter. He's talking to the student while she is not meeting expectations, so the interaction is corrective. He is saying these ostensibly positive words in the hope that the student will get on task, but what he is really doing is paying attention to misbehavior. When determining whether an interaction is positive or corrective, *what* you say matters less than *when* you say it.

What about planned ignoring?

Planned ignoring can help reduce attention-seeking behavior. For example, you tell the class clown in advance that you will no longer pay attention to his misbehavior—you are going to maintain the flow of instruction and ignore his inappropriate behavior. If you are truly ignoring the misbehavior, you will have no positive or corrective interactions to record.

But ensure that you really pay no attention to the student when he is misbehaving! We have seen teachers tell students (as they misbehaved), "I'm ignoring you now." Clearly, according to the definitions we've established, that is a corrective interaction.

What if you ignore the student but praise other students? "You're doing a fine job of staying on task." "Keep up the good work." "You're behaving very responsibly." If you are truly giving deserved attention to the other students while ignoring the target student, you are providing positive interactions to those other students. If you praise a student ("You're doing a fine job of staying on task"), then look meaningfully at the target student (indicating the student needs to get to work), you have provided a positive interaction to the other student *and* a corrective interaction to the target student.

Collect data on your positive and corrective interactions.

To self-monitor, print Form C-03a, one of the Ratios of Positive Interactions Monitoring Forms provided on the Module C CD. See Figures 3a–3c on pp. 50–52 for examples of completed forms. Think about a 30-minute period of the day when you tend to have the most trouble being positive with students. Arrange one day to video record those 30 minutes. Later, watch the video and tally the number of positive and corrective interactions. Do not count instructions to the group ("Class, open you books to page 14"). However, do count instructions to individual students ("Alana, please turn out the lights") as positive if the student was behaving responsibly at the time and corrective if the student was misbehaving. You might also have a colleague or a coach observe and tally your interactions.

Calculate your ratio by reducing the positive to corrective fraction. For example, 20 positives to 10 correctives is a 2:1 ratio. Five positives to 23 correctives is a ratio of 1:4.6. Remember, your goal is 3:1 or higher.

For more detailed data, use codes for categories such as gender, type of instructional activity, and type of attention instead of simple tally marks. Then calculate separate ratios for each category. The sample text in Figures 3a, 3b, and 3c shows how you might use codes.

Ratios of Positive Interactions Monitoring Form
During a Particular Time of Day

Teacher: __Ms. Ng__   Date: __10/12__   Time of Day: _8:45-9:30_

Coding system used (if any):

M = Male   C = Class (as a whole)
F = Female   N = Nick

Positive Interactions (Praise or noncontingent attention while student is behaving appropriately)	**Corrective Interactions** (All attention while student is misbehaving)
M, M, M, F, M, F F, C, F, N, F, M C, M, M, N, F, M	N, N, M, M, F, F, N N, C, M, M, N

Analysis and plan of action:

My overall ratio is 3:2, so I need to double positive interactions to reach a 3:1 ratio. If Nick's data are pulled out, I am almost at 3:1!

My interactions with Nick are 2:5 (2 positive interactions for every 5 corrections), so I should work on improving this ratio and monitor my interactions with Nick a week from now.

I think my feedback was fine in terms of clarity and style.

 This form can be printed from the Module C CD.

Figure 3b *Sample Ratios of Positive Interactions Monitoring Form, With a Particular Student (C-03b)*

Ratios of Positive Interactions Monitoring Form
With a Particular Student

Teacher: __Mr. Fleming__   Date: _____10/15_____

Student: __Rasheef__

Coding system used (to indicate specific activities or transitions):

BC = Before class	L = Lining up	TI = Teacher-directed instruction
RG = Reading group	P = Partners	ED = End of day

Positive Interactions (Praise or noncontingent attention while student is behaving appropriately)	**Corrective Interactions** (All attention while student is misbehaving)
BC, TI, L, L, RG, ED	TI, RG, RG, RG, P, P, P, P

Analysis and plan of action:

My ratio with Rasheed is 3:4 positives to correctives, so I definitely need to increase positives (and decrease correctives if possible). I will look for more opportunities to praise during reading group and partner work, where he tends to lose focus and make too much noise. I will also look for opportunities to praise Rasheed when he is on task during lessons.

 This form can be printed from the Module C CD.

Figure 3c   *Sample Ratios of Positive Interactions Monitoring Form, for a Particular Behavior (C-03c)*

Ratios of Positive Interactions Monitoring Form
For a Particular Behavior

Teacher: __Mrs. Hazarbedian__   Date: ___10/17___

Behavior: ___Respecting others___

Coding system used (to indicate gender, activity):

M = Male   TI = Teacher-directed lesson   T = Transition
F = Female   I = Independent work

Label the positive and negative behaviors that will be monitored (e.g., attention to respect and attention to disrespect)

Positive Interactions (Praise or noncontingent attention while student is behaving appropriately)	**Corrective Interactions** (All attention while student is misbehaving)
Respect for others (Behavior Label)	Disrespect (Behavior Label)
M-TI, F-TI, F-TI, F-I, M-I	M-I, M-TI, F-TI, M-I, F-I

Note: Decide if you will use a public posting monitoring system or if you wish to keep a less observable record (e.g., marks made on a clipboard).

Analysis and plan of action:

My ratio is 1:1, so I need to find more opportunities to pay attention to respectful behavior, especially during class time.

 This form can be printed from the Module C CD.

Analyze your data.

- Think about why you nag so much during this time—probably because so much misbehavior occurs. But why is there so much misbehavior? At least in part, it's because you're nagging so much.

- Evaluate whether your ratio of positives to correctives varies by category (for example, it's lower with females than males).

- Evaluate the overall style of your interactions (corrections too harsh, praise sounds insincere or is too friendly) and whether you are comfortable with it.

- Evaluate the contingency of the positive feedback you give to individual students.

- Evaluate whether one or two students receive most of the negative interactions. If so, plan to monitor your interactions with those individual students (Form C-03b).

- Evaluate whether you had to correct a particular category of behavior (for example, off-task talking) more frequently than other problems. If so, plan to re-teach your expectations for on-task behavior for a few days and then monitor your RPI specifically related to feedback for on-task behavior (Form C-03c).

Conclusion

RPI is a powerful tool for motivating students and setting a positive school and classroom climate, so periodically monitor your ratio of positive to corrective interactions and continually work to keep the positives at a high level. Remember that the goal is for every student over time to receive at least three times as much attention when he or she is engaged in positive behavior as when he or she is engaged in misbehavior.

In subsequent tasks, we suggest ways to increase the number and effectiveness of your positive interactions and ways to ensure that your correctives in no way reward misbehavior. On the DVD for this presentation are some brief video clips (titled Exercises) that you can use to practice counting positives and correctives. Each of the exercises is followed by an explanation of how we would have counted the interactions, so you can compare your count to our suggested count.

Note: Use the Counting RPI Exercises video clips on the Module C DVD to practice counting positives and correctives.

Task 1 Action Steps & Evidence of Implementation

Action Steps	Evidence of Implementation
1. Have the staff view or read this task so that every staff member understands the concept of RPI (ratios of positive interactions), knows how to deliver positive interactions, and can objectively and consistently identify and count them. You might conduct a training and show the video presentation of the task, then have staff view the exercises and practice identifying and counting positive and corrective interactions.	Foundations Process: Presentations/ Communications With Staff
2. Encourage every staff member to periodically monitor their RPI by video or audio recording themselves for 30 minutes or having a coach or mentor count their interactions.	
3. Create opportunities for staff to get together and discuss their RPI data, what they learned, and their plans for action.	

TASK 2

Increase your positive interactions

In this task, we suggest ways to improve your ratios of positive interactions (RPI) by increasing the number of positives, which include both noncontingent attention and feedback for responsible behavior. These strategies will work in both the classroom and the common areas of the school. Throughout this task, we discuss the items on the document "Strategies for Increasing Positive Interactions" (Form C-04 shown in Figure 3d); you can print copies from the Module C CD. You can use this document as a checklist as you develop a plan for increasing your positive interactions with students. Note the strategies on the list that you might add to your repertoire for increasing positives.

Remember that correctives are not bad or wrong. To increase RPI (initially, at least), you need to increase the frequency of your positives. More positive interactions with students will improve their behavior, making it even easier to be positive. Your interactions with students create a cycle that either spins upward toward the positive or, if you're not careful, downward toward misbehavior and correctives.

We learned many of these strategies from teachers and supervisors we've had the privilege of working with while implementing *Foundations*, and we thank them for sharing their creativity with us.

a. Provide frequent noncontingent attention.

Think about times when you can easily increase your contact with students in noncontingent yet positive ways. Many teachers find opportunities to interact with students while the students are engaged in positive behavior in these contexts:

> The lettered items within this task correspond to items on Reproducible Form C-04 (shown in Figure 3d on the next page).

- Before the bell rings or right at the beginning of class
- During class transitions, free time, or earned time
- At dismissal
- During the first few minutes of an independent work task, before too many students have questions and need assistance

Elementary teachers might ask one student each day to help with cleaning and packing up at the end of the day. During those few minutes, converse with the student about his or her family, interests, weekend plans, and so on. Secondary teachers might ask a student to come to the desk for 30 to 45 seconds during the beginning of an independent work period for a brief conversation about the student's interests or weekend plans.

Figure 3d   *Strategies for Increasing Positive Interactions Checklist (C-04)*

Strategies for Increasing Positive Interactions Checklist

☐   a.   Provide frequent noncontingent attention:
       ____ As students enter common area
       ____ When you are circulating through the halls, cafeteria, or playground
       ____ Before the bell rings or at the beginning of class
       ____ During class transitions, free time, or dismissal
       ____ At the beginning of an independent work task
       ____ Other: _____

☐   b.   Use nonverbal gestures.
☐   c.   Use brief physical contact.
☐   d.   Use first names.
☐   e.   Use positive nicknames.
☐   f.   Give positive farewells.
☐   g.   Express interest in classwork (for your and other classes).
☐   h.   Learn foreign-language greetings and farewells (for ELL students).
☐   i.   Offer help frequently.
☐   j.   Ask about activities outside of school.
☐   k.   Every third or fourth student, make eye contact and smile (in common areas).
☐   l.   After a corrective interaction, remind yourself to deliver at least three positive interactions.
☐   m.   Use visual reminders to deliver more noncontingent attention.
☐   n.   Use reminders to provide noncontingent attention to specific students who are struggling.
☐   o.   Use the 10–10–10 approach (10 comments to 10 students by 10:00 a.m.).
☐   p.   Use the 10 by 2 approach (for 10 days, spend 2 minutes talking with an individual student).
☐   q.   Recognize student birthdays.
☐   r.   Program your phone or computer to remind you to deliver positive feedback for appropriate behavior.
☐   s.   Deliver a Crazy Handshake.
☐   t.   Pick a student to be famous for the day or period.
☐   u.   Increase opportunities to respond.
☐   v.   Post an on-task list on the board (or a list about any other specific, positive behavior or trait).
☐   w.   Conduct individual conferences.
☐   x.   Use a common occurrence as a reminder to interact positively.
☐   y.   Scan for reinforceable behaviors.
☐   z.   Write brief positive notes.
☐   aa.   Publicly post examples of positive work.
☐   bb.   Praise one student, then another for similar behavior.
☐   cc.   Tell the student, "You remind me of . . . ."
☐   dd.   Make two positive phone calls to parents each week.
☐   ee.   Precorrect.

> This form can be printed from the Module C CD.

If you begin a program like this one, ensure that every student in your class gets attention at least once before you restart the class list because students you've missed will notice and feel slighted. You might focus on your average students—give them longer periods of attention or more frequent attention—because they are often overlooked by other adults in the school.

If you are supervising a common area, greet students as they enter. When all the adults are greeting students, the positive interactions really add up. When you are circulating through the hallways, cafeteria, or playground, interact as often as possible with students who are not engaged in misbehavior; you're adding to the positive bank for those students.

b. Use nonverbal gestures.

Remember that the noncontingent attention we just discussed can be as simple as a smile. Positive nonverbal gestures include making eye contact, smiling, nodding, winking (if that fits your style), giving a thumbs-up, and waving.

c. Use brief physical contact.

By brief physical contact, we mean shaking the student's hand, bumping fists, or patting the student's shoulder, for example. Ensure that other adults are present.

One third-grade teacher we worked with established a morning ritual for her students. As she greeted them at the classroom door, each student either gave her a hug or shook her hand. The students chose the greeting they preferred, but each got a dose of positive physical contact from this nurturing teacher every morning.

d. Use first names.

Use students' first names in both the classroom and common areas. Try to learn the names of unfamiliar students, not just the students you know from class. When you see a student in the hall three or four times, say, "Hi! What's your name? Great, I'll try to remember that." This contact takes very little time but can be very powerful. The student knows that adults notice her and that she is important enough that they want to know her name. (And if she misbehaves, adults know her name!) Make a point to greet that student by name over the next 3 to 5 days.

e. Use positive nicknames.

Make sure the student likes the nickname and is comfortable with your using it.

f. Give positive farewells.

A positive farewell at the end of the day or class period can be simply, "I look forward to seeing you tomorrow." This strategy is particularly powerful when you've had to correct a student for misbehaving several times that day. You are sending the message that you don't hold a grudge and the student will get a fresh start the next day.

g. Express interest in classwork (yours and other classes).

Ask the student to tell you about a project or report he is working on, or ask him how he is doing in other classes.

h. Learn foreign language greetings and farewells (for ELL students).

Ask an English language learner how to say the traditional greeting and farewell in her native language, then try to use those phrases as you see her during the next 5 days. You are also communicating to the student that you value learning about her language and that you are a learner, too. "Did I pronounce that correctly? OK, tell me again. I'll try to do better tomorrow."

i. **Offer help frequently.**

Repeated offers of help convey that you are aware of the student, you care about his success in school, and you want to be a resource for learning. "Let me know if you need anything." "Do you need any assistance?"

j. **Ask about activities outside of school.**

Don't be invasive or ask overly personal questions, but as you're walking down the hall with students, ask what sports they like, what kind of music they listen to, or what their plans are for the weekend. Then try to ask about their interests or activities later. "Hey, how was the soccer game? I know it was an important one for you." Because you remembered what the student said, she will feel valued.

k. **Every third or fourth student, make eye contact and smile (in common areas).**

When you're supervising any common area—arrival, hallways, cafeteria, playground, dismissal—establish eye contact with every third or fourth student and smile, nod your head, give a quick greeting, or give a thumbs-up. This strategy keeps you actively engaged with the students and with your job, and over time, every student will get several of your positive interactions. You can vary the number every couple of days or so.

l. **After a corrective interaction, remind yourself to deliver at least three positive interactions.**

Each time you have to correct a student, tell yourself that you need to deliver three positive interactions to that student as soon as you can reasonably do so. The follow-up positives break the ice and communicate that you are not angry and don't hold a grudge. They also convey to the student that you notice him when he is behaving responsibly, not just when he's misbehaving.

Remember, you are a professional and cannot dislike students on company time. You owe it to the student to interact positively as soon as he begins behaving positively.

m. **Use visual reminders to deliver more noncontingent attention.**

In the classroom, post visual reminders in your planner, on the wall, on your desk, or on your computer (with sticky notes). A simple smiley face or thumbs-up icon can remind you to deliver more noncontingent attention to make students feel noticed and valued. When supervising a common area, put a sticky note on your telephone or your clipboard, or wear a neon rubber band around your wrist to remind you to deliver noncontingent attention.

n. Use reminders to provide noncontingent attention to specific students.

You might also want to remind yourself to deliver more noncontingent attention to specific students. After students have left for the day, think of two or three students who struggled academically or behaviorally that day and who could benefit from some extra attention the next day. Write the names of those students on a sticky note and put the note on the next day's page in your planner.

o. Use the 10–10–10 approach.

At the beginning of the school day, tell yourself to deliver 10 positive comments to 10 students by 10 a.m. Just remember 10–10–10!

p. Use the 10 by 2 approach.

For 10 days, find 2 minutes each day to interact with a target student in noncontingent ways: Walk with the student down the hallway or speak to her before or after class, for example, and find out about her hobbies, interests, family life, weekend activities, and so on.

Target a student who is usually difficult to interact with positively. Perhaps her behaviors are so persistent and negative that it's difficult to find positive things to reward with contingent attention. Or maybe she is withdrawn or shy, and gets little attention from others.

After 10 days, the student's behavior probably will have improved. At the least, your relationship with the student will have changed enough that when you reprimand or correct, there is less likelihood of conflict.

q. Recognize student birthdays.

Keep track of each student's birthday in your planner and recognize each birthday with a card or a sincere "happy birthday" and a brief conversation.

r. Program your phone or computer to remind you to deliver positive feedback for appropriate behavior.

Program your smartphone, tablet, or computer to make a sound every 15 minutes or so. When you hear the prompt, give contingent positive feedback or noncontingent attention to a few students.

s. Deliver a Crazy Handshake.

Have students brainstorm creative ways to shake hands. Then use the handshakes as part of your contingent attention. "Hey, you did a great job straightening up the bookshelf. What handshake would you like?"

t. Pick a student to be famous for the day or period.

Write the names of all your students on slips of paper and put the slips into a basket. Draw one name to identify the student who will be famous for that day or that period. Give the selected student lots of positive attention—nonverbal interactions, noncontingent verbal comments, and contingent praise. Ask him to assist with meaningful jobs, such as delivering messages to the office. You might establish a regular schedule for this program—every Friday or every third period, for example. Don't put the drawn name back into the basket. You want to make sure that every student is selected before you start over.

u. Increase opportunities to respond.

Give students more opportunities to respond within academic tasks by encouraging discussion and asking questions. Ensure that many students have opportunities to participate in lessons. Remember that even when a student answers incorrectly, your academic correction counts as a positive interaction if she is behaving appropriately when she participates.

v. Post an on-task list on the board (or a list about any other specific, positive behavior or trait).

Instead of writing names on the board for misbehavior, create a space on the board that says something like On Task. Then periodically write students' names when you see them exhibiting that positive behavior. This simple strategy can also remind you to focus especially on your middle- and low-performing students. Over time, vary the positive behavior you write on the board. You might use a different behavior each day—examples include perseverance, cooperation, kindness, team player, and encouraging others.

w. Conduct individual conferences.

Conduct individual conferences with students to praise their academic efforts and review their behavioral progress. Just a few minutes of one-to-one formal discussion is a very positive way to build your relationships with students and increase your positive interactions.

x. Use a common occurrence as a reminder to interact positively.

Use a fairly common occurrence in the classroom or common area, such as a student using the pencil sharpener or getting up to hand in work, as a prompt to interact positively with some students. Whenever you see the action you're using as a reminder, scan the room, identify two or three students who are behaving well, and give some positive feedback or noncontingent attention.

y. Scan for reinforceable behaviors.

Periodically scan your classroom or common area and search specifically for important reinforceable behaviors. For example, a student who throws away trash or helps another student with an assignment is exhibiting responsibility. By actively scanning for good behavior, you are reminding yourself to be cognizant of all the positive things that go on in your classroom (or common area) and to pay attention when those things happen.

z. Write brief positive notes.

As you are walking around the room supervising independent seatwork or cooperative group activities, carry a pad of sticky notes and a pen. Write brief notes and stick them on students' desks. "Brandon, you're doing a fine job of understanding subjects and predicates." "Tina, you're being so responsible in remembering to turn in your homework." Noncontingent attention is fine, too: "Looking forward to seeing you tomorrow." Try to write notes to one or two students each day, and ensure that every student gets them over time.

aa. Publicly post examples of positive work.

A powerful way to provide positive feedback is to post examples of student's positive work on the bulletin board.

bb. Praise one student, then another for similar behavior.

After praising one student for positive behavior, find and praise another student. This strategy is a way to double your ratios—tell yourself you always give positive feedback in twos.

cc. Tell the student, "You remind me of . . . ."

Tell a student that a certain positive behavior or mannerism reminds you of someone you know or admire, such as a family member or a famous actor or athlete.

dd. Make two positive phone calls to parents each week.

Set a goal for yourself to make two phone calls to parents each week to provide only positive feedback about their child's school work, efforts, and behavior. Because your goal is to make as many positive parent calls as possible, don't repeat a call to a parent until all of the other parents have been called. If the parents don't have a phone, mail a positive letter or note to the home.

ee. Precorrect.

A precorrection is a reminder of how to behave appropriately when you anticipate that students might have problems. A precorrection can also be a positive when you give the reminder when the student is behaving appropriately. For example, just as students are leaving for recess, precorrect a student who has had problems recently during recess: "Hey, Jacob, I know you're going to have a great recess and be really responsible about remembering to keep your hands to yourself." That precorrection is a positive because you interacted with Jacob before he had a chance to exhibit the misbehavior.

Task 2 Action Steps (for each staff member)

Using the document "Strategies for Increasing Positive Interactions," identify at least three strategies that you will use in the next few weeks to increase the frequency of your interactions with students when they are engaged in positive behavior.

Plan to add more strategies to your repertoire in the future. Put reminders in your planner throughout the year to try new strategies.

TASK 3

Fine-tune your positive and corrective interactions

When you understand the concept of RPI and have mastered the basics of emphasizing positives over correctives, you will want to maximize the effectiveness of your positives and your correctives. The phrase "Catch them being good" describes a good starting point, but it's a touch too simple for long-term maintenance of your RPI. In this task, we explore ways to be more strategic with delivering positive feedback and corrections.

Because you're making a conscious effort to be more positive, you might be concerned that students will perceive your positives as phony. There is perhaps a slight risk of that initially, but you'll become more comfortable as you practice, and you'll find that students will adjust to your style over time. To increase your comfort level with delivering positives to all students, think about how you interact positively with one of your favorite students—a student who is easy to interact with—and then try to duplicate that ratio and style with the student who is more difficult to interact with. Remind yourself of this: You are very important to each and every student, and your effort to deliver positives will probably benefit students and not do any harm.

Remember, positives include noncontingent attention ("Good morning, it's nice to see you") as well as contingent positive feedback. Here are a couple of tips for non-contingent attention: Don't try to be a friend to the student, and don't embarrass the student. You're always going to be an adult who is in authority at the school, so your conversations and actions should not be at the student's level as if you are a peer. You are just expressing interest, which communicates value.

William James (1890), often called the father of American psychology, wrote, "No more fiendish punishment can be desired, were such a thing physically possible, than that one should be turned loose in society and remain absolutely unnoticed by all the members thereof."

Be strategic with your positive feedback.

The following suggestions will help you refine your delivery and ensure the effectiveness of your positive feedback.

Give specific and descriptive positive feedback. Avoid falling victim to the *Good Job* syndrome. In your positive feedback and praise, tell the student what she did well and describe why and how it was good. Many of you can probably remember a time when you received specific, descriptive praise from a teacher. It may have been years ago, but you remember reading the red-pencil note on a paper or being pulled aside and given praise for an achievement. "Your summary of the causes of the Civil War shows real understanding of the issues of the time. You address each major issue, and you chose excellent references. Your writing is very clear and concise, too." If the teacher wrote or said only "good job," you wouldn't remember it. When someone you respect and admire takes the time to give specific positive feedback, it's extremely valuable.

Give useful and meaningful positive feedback. Consider the context and timing of your praise. If you're not careful, you can provide specific, descriptive feedback that is in reality insulting. For example, imagine another adult complimenting you about your driving. "Wow, great right turn into the parking lot. You didn't even hit anything." You would probably not be pleased to receive this praise. In fact, you would probably think this person is being obnoxious and sarcastic rather than complimentary. Why? Because a great right turn, for an experienced driver, is no big deal. The context and timing of the feedback is wrong, even though it is specific and descriptive.

Context and timing come into play in three situations: new skills, difficult tasks, and complex tasks.

New skills. When students are practicing a recently learned skill, whether it's an academic, behavioral, or social-emotional skill, they need frequent feedback. In the early stages of learning and using a new skill, students might not know what they are doing right and what they are doing wrong. Frequent specific feedback at this stage is not insulting—it's very helpful and encouraging.

Difficult skills or tasks. When a student is struggling with a skill or task, positive feedback will be meaningful. For example, let's say a student who has been working on anger management has a difficult interaction with another student. In the past, interactions like this have triggered the student to display anger, but in this instance the student makes a conscious effort to stay calm. Later, you praise the student for working through a difficult concept. Positive feedback in these types of situations will not be the least bit insulting—it's not the "great right turn" kind of meaningless feedback. Provide praise for difficult tasks frequently.

Complex skills or tasks. Positive feedback is meaningful when given for complex tasks, such as writing an excellent essay, showing respect for others, and displaying positive leadership. Praise for these kinds of complex achievements and behavior is not insulting. Think of a particular skill that you have—knitting, for example. When someone compliments you on a beautiful sweater you made, you are not insulted, because knitting is a complex set of skills. Provide praise for complex tasks and accomplishments occasionally.

Avoid attribution statements. An example of an attribution statement is, "You are so smart." This concept comes largely from the work of Carol Dweck and her book *Mindset.* She has examined a great deal of research and suggests that when people who are praised for being smart have difficulty with a task, they may shut down and not continue with the task because (they think) they might lose their appearance of intelligence or have to confront their lack of intelligence.

Praise students for effort, perseverance, and staying focused. Praise them for the behaviors and the processes that are under their control. People can't choose to be smart; they differ in their natural abilities, but it is their continued effort that can make abilities blossom.

Avoid "I" statements. Don't place yourself at the center of the positive feedback. It's easy to fall into patterns of saying, "I like the way you're doing this" or "I'm pleased with the way that you are doing that." Instead, try to attribute the accomplishment to the student: "You should be very proud of how you did this." It's not about you—it's about the student and the behavior he or she was exhibiting.

Distribute your feedback appropriately. At the prekindergarten and kindergarten levels, all students need lots of attention for everything they do, so this concept applies only to older students. In high school, for example, you will probably provide attention of varying types and at varying rates of frequency to different types of students. For example, imagine approaching an on-task student and quietly saying, "Jamie, for the last 10 minutes you've been on task. Great job of staying focused." A highly secure, academically capable, and motivated student will probably give you a puzzled look while thinking, "The last 10 minutes? I've been on task for the last 9 years. What's the big deal about 10 minutes?" On the other hand, that praise would be meaningful for a student with whom you've been having planned discussions about keeping his attention focused during class.

Who should get the most frequent feedback? Your students with the highest needs. Who gets it in some high schools? The most talented students. They get positive grades, notes on papers, invitations to join teams and clubs, and so on. These high achievers need relatively infrequent feedback in the form of (for example): "You are such a self-disciplined, highly responsible learner. You should be very proud of how successful you are in this school." Hearing something like that a couple of times a quarter is probably enough for those students.

High-needs students, on the other hand, may need you to catch them doing well as often as a couple of times per class period, with verbal or nonverbal acknowledgment of what they've done. Average students need positive feedback at a moderate level, somewhere between the high achievers and the high-needs students.

Kindergarten students need lots of feedback all of the time, and high school students have different needs, depending on whether they are independent and motivated learners, high-needs students, or somewhere in between. Upper elementary and middle school students will be moving away from the lots-of-feedback-for-everyone model toward the differential model of high school.

Earlier, we discussed why providing contingent positive feedback for new skills, difficult skills, and complex skills is important. The students with the highest social, emotional, behavioral, and academic needs will fill the first two categories. They will have the most new behaviors, and they'll be working on skills that are difficult for them—anger management, staying focused, staying on task, being respectful, being cooperative. For success with complex skills, you can praise all students and not worry too much about the distribution part of positive feedback.

Deal with students who do not respond well to positive feedback. Even when you are praising appropriately, some students may not respond. In fact, their behavior might even worsen after positive feedback. Following are possible reasons for this common phenomenon and some suggestions for handling such situations.

Consider whether the student is embarrassed by the praise. If so, modify the style of your feedback. Make it more private or more businesslike, or move away sooner after giving the feedback—when you linger, the student might think you expect a response.

The student might have a reputation or an image of himself as being tough and feel peer pressure to maintain that image. In the student's mind, success in school doesn't conform with being tough. For this student, it is often more effective to deliver positive feedback in private by writing a short note or seeing the student after class so that peers are not a factor. You and the student might establish a subtle nonverbal signal—for example, you touch your ear—that tells the student she is doing well. A signal isn't as specific as verbal praise, but it might allow the student to maintain her image and still be rewarded for appropriate behavior.

Treat any misbehavior that occurs after you give positive feedback as a minor interruption in the student's success. For example, if a student tears up his essay right after receiving positive feedback about it, simply tell the student, "I need you to pick up the paper and put it in the trash, please," and then go on with your classroom duties. Avoid communicating anger or sadness at the student's actions. You don't want to overreact. If you say, for example, "You were doing such a fine job, and now you do this!" you may be feeding into what the student wants you to do.

Later, at a neutral time and without an audience, talk with the student privately about his tendency to misbehave after receiving positive feedback and ask how he would like you to give feedback. Say, "I'm willing to adjust my style, but my job as a teacher is to let you know when you're doing a good job. I need to be able to do that. Can you give me some tips on how I can do that in ways that will be comfortable for you?"

If the student continues to reject your efforts to provide positive feedback, try giving only noncontingent attention, not positive feedback, when the student is behaving responsibly. Build up your ratio of positive to corrective interactions by saying hello, asking the student to help you with a task, asking if he has any questions, and saying goodbye at the end of the day or period, for example.

After 2 to 4 weeks of using only noncontingent attention, you might see the student's comfort level with your attention rising. Then try adding some praise comments. "Thanks for getting that assignment in on time." "Thanks for holding the door for that student." Avoid gushing. By interjecting some matter-of-fact positive comments into the natural flow of classroom dialogue, over time you might be able to increase the student's comfort level with positive feedback.

Analyze and adjust your correctives.

The second major topic of this task is how to be strategic in delivering correctives. First, you should understand the concept of the comparative *weight* of positives and correctives. Here's a metaphor: If someone offered you a free gift of either three $1 bills or one $10 bill, which would you take? We're betting you would take the $10 bill. You know that even though the $10 bill is only one piece of paper, it has more value—more weight—than the three $1 bills. It's possible to give a corrective that is so emotional or disrespectful that it's worth $10 compared with the $1 positives. If that happens, your 3:1 ratio of positives to correctives is skewed toward the corrective because a corrective weighs more than a positive. To keep the value of your correctives on par with your positives, keep the following points in mind.

Correctives should be unemotional. At-risk students might be so used to environments where people are often angry and abusive that they are most comfortable in those conditions. These students want to see you get emotional. If you fall into playing that game, your emotion adds weight to the corrective. "That is unacceptable! You've been repeatedly disruptive. You owe me 15 seconds after class." An unemotional corrective doesn't give the student the satisfaction of pushing your buttons: "That's disruptive—15 seconds after class. Now, class, what I was saying was . . ."

Correctives should be brief. If your corrective lasts 10 seconds and your positives last 3 seconds, the corrective has more weight. Many adults tend to talk too much when they're correcting misbehavior.

Correctives should be consistent. Inconsistency in correcting students means that sometimes students get away with misbehavior, and that can be reinforcing. Have you ever driven too fast on the highway without getting a ticket, and felt at least a little exhilarated because you didn't get caught? Getting away with it creates an intermittent reinforcement schedule. Gambling is based on intermittent rewards—the casinos allow you to win just often enough to keep you coming back and gambling some more. Getting away with it has weight.

Correctives should be respectful. Unfortunately, out of frustration, adults sometimes belittle or humiliate students when they correct. A student with a very poor self-image or an image of being tough will probably conclude that you are confirming what she thinks—that she is a loser and that adults dislike everything she does. So ensure that your corrections are respectful. Simply state the misbehavior and the consequence, with no belittlement.

Correctives should be supportive initially and neutral later. Nurturing people often correct misbehavior in ways that are very supportive. They include statements such as "I know you're capable of this" in their corrections. In the initial stages of your efforts with the student, it's OK to include some supportive statements and not be as brief as possible. But if the misbehavior continues, exclude the supportive statements and keep your tone emotionally neutral. Some students might attribute weight to supportive corrections. So be supportive initially and completely neutral thereafter.

Use the *as if* treatment. Treat all students as if they are responsible, sensible people and as if the incident or misbehavior is just a momentary interruption or mistake. The German author, scientist, and statesman Johann Wolfgang von Goethe wrote, "Treat people as if they were what they ought to be, and you help them to become what they are capable of being." That concept should always guide the way you correct.

Consider planned ignoring.

When you have made efforts to ensure that your correctives don't carry too much weight, but a student continues to misbehave frequently, consider using planned ignoring as your correction. If the student is really starved for attention, your corrections could be reinforcing the misbehavior even though the corrections are unemotional, brief, consistent, respectful, and neutral.

First, consider whether the target misbehavior is really attention seeking. Most class-clown behavior and much disruptive and disrespectful behavior is intended to elicit an adult response. If you decide that the function of the behavior is indeed

Module C: Conscious Construction of an Inviting School Climate

to gain attention, meet with the student and explain that you will no longer give attention to the misbehavior. Say, "I have so much faith in your ability to manage this behavior on your own that you don't need me to nag you about it, and I'm not going to nag you about it." Then be very consistent in ignoring the target behavior.

Planned ignoring reduces the number of times you must respond to the student's misbehavior, increasing your RPI as well as the weight of your positives.

Task 3 Action Steps (for each staff member)

1. Conduct a self-reflection exercise: Identify a student whose misbehavior is chronic. You haven't been able to improve the student's behavior even though you've increased your RPI. Ask yourself the following questions:

    - Do I provide adequate attention to the student when he is behaving appropriately?
    - Do I need to increase noncontingent attention?
    - Could my positive feedback be embarrassing to the student? What can I do to make the feedback more private?

2. Identify ways to increase the efficacy of your positive feedback with this student:

    - Is my positive feedback specific and descriptive?
    - Is my positive feedback useful and meaningful?
    - Is my positive feedback appropriate for the student's age and skill level (it doesn't insult the student)?
    - Do I avoid using attribution statements?
    - Do I avoid using "I" statements?

3. Identify ways to modify your correctives to reduce their weight:

    - Are my correctives too emotional?
    - Do I talk too much or too long?
    - Am I inconsistent—does the student sometimes get away with the misbehavior?
    - Am I respectful? Do I avoid belittling or humiliating the student?
    - Are my correctives too supportive?
    - Do I treat the student as if the misbehavior is just a momentary interruption or mistake?

4. Consider planned ignoring if you are sure that the student's behavior is attention seeking and you've fine-tuned your positive feedback and corrections.

TASK 4

Work on Ratios of Positive Interactions (RPI) continuously

In Task 4, we discuss how the Foundations Team can help keep the concept of RPI alive in your school long term. RPI is a simple concept to understand, but it's also very easy for busy staff to forget. Frequent reminders will help, but they must be done creatively because reminders about such a simple concept might be perceived as condescending or unprofessional.

A good analogy for RPI in schools is hand washing in hospitals. Hand washing is of course very simple, but it's also a life-and-death issue for the medical profession. Physicians have known about the importance of hand washing to prevent the spread of pathogens since 1847, yet these highly educated, responsible people still need constant reminders to wash their hands frequently. Steven Levitt and Stephen Dubner (2009) write in *SuperFreakonomics* about one hospital's efforts to get physicians to wash their hands.

This hospital did some research and found that about 50% of physicians were washing their hands as frequently as they should. They were able to raise that percentage a few points by building more sinks, improving access to sinks, displaying signs ("Remember to wash your hands"), and providing bottled hand sanitizer. But they didn't get close to their goal of 100% compliance until they did this: During a luncheon meeting, they had all the chief doctors of the hospital place handprints in agar plates, the medium that scientists use to culture microorganisms. More than three-fourths of the handprints (thus, three-fourths of the chief doctors) had alarming amounts of bacteria on their hands. The hospital took photos of the handprints with their growths of bacteria and created screen savers that were installed on every computer in the hospital. Every time staff logged in to a computer, they were reminded of the importance of hand washing by seeing several seconds of very dirty doctors' hands.

Although the screen savers were very effective reminders, the hospital realized that they would work for only a few weeks or months. Eventually, the staff would become inured to the bacteria-ridden handprints, and the hospital would have to come up with other creative reminders.

Like the hospital, your school might need a creative reminder system for the staff to keep the simple-but-crucial concept of RPI active. Kings Canyon Middle School in Fresno, California, developed a plan called The Power of Three: Increasing Positive Behaviors at Kings Canyon (Figure 3e on the next page shows a modified version of the plan). Kings Canyon learned about the RPI concept in October and trained its entire staff to ensure that they deliver at least three positives for every corrective. That was their goal for November—to have all staff practice and master the 3:1 ratio.

Then, as you can see in the figure, their calendar plan builds on the basic 3:1 concept. In December, they encouraged all staff to continue delivering three positives for every corrective and to spend three periods at their doors each day delivering noncontingent greetings.

In January, they added three positive parent contacts each week. In February, staff were encouraged to deliver three compliments to coworkers. Each month, a new suggestion was introduced and added to the growing repertoire of strategies for increasing positives. Although no one was required to participate, by the end of the school year almost every staff member was fluent in eight different strategies for delivering positive feedback.

The Power of Three plan is a very creative way to get staff to try something new each month and keep the concept of RPI active.

Figure 3e   *The Power of Three: Increasing Positive Behaviors at Kings Canyon (C-17); thanks to Kings Canyon Middle School and Fresno Unified School District in California*

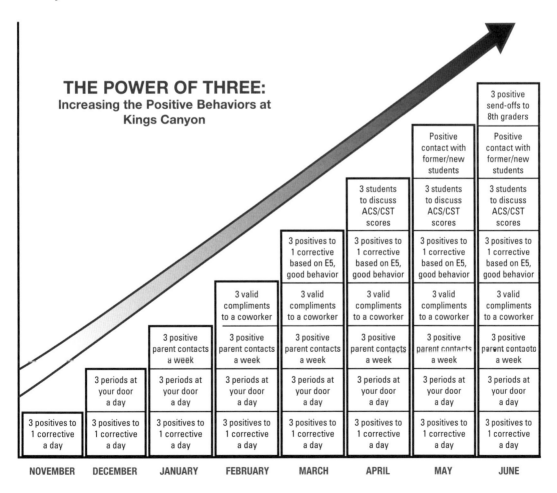

Carver Elementary School, a K–8 school in San Diego, California, developed a program to recognize staff members who provide positive reinforcement to students. It's called Caught You Caring! When staff members notice other staff members working on their RPI, overtly building positive relationships with students, or providing meaningful, positive feedback, they can nominate the staff member for the Caught You Caring! Program. The program is a twist on the Caught You Being Good! or Golden Tickets reward programs for students (we explain these types of programs in Presentation 6 of this module). Any staff member may be recognized—teachers, paraprofessionals, custodians, office staff, school nurses, and so on.

Here's how it works: Office staff prepare the blank Caught You Caring! nomination forms (see Figure 3f). The forms are kept near the staff mailboxes. To nominate a colleague, a staff member writes the colleague's name and what he or she did. Completed forms go into a Caught You Caring! container. Three forms are drawn weekly for small prizes during a recognition ceremony. Each month, all 12 winners' names are put into a bowl to draw for one winner who receives a larger prize, such as an extra hour of prep time or something equivalent arranged with the principal. Each week's Caught You Caring! forms are displayed in a window or on a board near the office.

This program demonstrates to staff that even the principal values the concept of RPI and is willing to reward staff by, for example, ensuring that classes are covered to give the winning staff member an extra hour of prep time.

Other suggestions for creative reminders about the power of RPI include encouraging staff to mark on their calendars one day each month when they will focus on one or two new strategies for increasing positive interactions. Take a couple of minutes at a staff meeting to ask staff to place reminders in their calendars or set up electronic reminders, or briefly review some of the strategies from Task 2 of this presentation.

Alternatively, have each staff member identify a negative behavior or attitude that is particularly bothersome (a pet peeve). Then ask staff to remind themselves to work on catching and giving positive feedback to students who are exhibiting the *positive opposite* of that behavior. For example, the positive opposite of flippant, disrespectful behavior is respect. If it bothers you that students don't comply easily and cooperatively with directions, make an effort to actively reinforce students who follow directions cooperatively the first time they are asked.

The principal can periodically send memos that remind staff of the importance of RPI and suggest strategies to work on. For example, think of a student who is difficult to like and make an effort to build a positive relationship with that student.

Figure 3f *Caught You Caring! instructions and nomination form (C-18)*

Caught You Caring!
Staff Incentive Program

This program is similar to our Caught You Being Good lottery ticket program for students, but it's for the amazing adults on our campus.

How It Works

- Watch for staff members you would like to recognize for their positive interactions with students.
- Pick up a nomination form near the staff mailboxes and fill it out.
- Place the form in the Caught You Caring! basket near the staff mailboxes.

Recognition Ceremony

- A drawing will be held each Monday during morning assembly.
- Three names will be drawn each week for small school-supply prizes.
- On the last Monday of each month, the 12 winners' names will be placed into a basket and one lucky grand-prize winner will be drawn.
- The winner receives an hour of prep time (with classes covered) or something equivalent to be arranged with the principal.

The Caught You Caring! Display

Each week, all the nomination forms will be displayed in the window of the Student Center. Be sure to stop by and check them out!

CAUGHT YOU CARING! NOMINATION FORM

Who did you catch? _____ Date _____
What did he or she do?
_____
_____
_____

Your name (optional) _____

 This sample can be printed from the Module C CD.

Remind staff through the all-call system or a text message to think about the students who are most likely to fade into the background. "No student should fade into the woodwork here at Franklin Middle School. Please make an effort to reach out and give lots of attention to those students."

Choose a theme for the month—a behavior, trait, or attitude the entire staff would like to encourage in students—and hold a 3-minute brainstorming session during a staff meeting on how to teach and emphasize that theme throughout the school. If the theme for the month is perseverance, for example, brainstorm activities to teach perseverance and ways to embed the concept into existing lessons and daily activities. Think of ways to reinforce and acknowledge students who display perseverance. Then during that month, staff should focus on trying to catch students exhibiting perseverance and providing positive feedback to those students.

Task 4 Action Steps & Evidence of Implementation

Action Steps	Evidence of Implementation
1. Share with staff the concept of continuous work on RPI, including the hand-washing example. Physicians are not insulted by reminders to wash their hands because they are busy, spread-too-thin professionals who sometimes forget, and they know that hand washing is very important. For teachers, RPI is the equivalent of hand washing.	Foundations Process: Presentations/ Communications With Staff, Planning Calendar
2. Find out from staff the ways they would prefer to get reminders—how can you give gentle reminders that are not insulting? Options might include email, brief agenda items during staff meetings, all-call announcements, and paper messages in mailboxes.	
3. Using the methods that staff agree on, distribute regular reminders throughout the year about the importance of RPI and strategies to try. Periodically include recommendations for monitoring RPI (see Task 1 of this presentation).	

Improving Attendance

DOCUMENTS*

- School-Based Analysis of Attendance Policies (C-06)
- How Sick Is Too Sick for School? form (C-05)
- Sample medical and dental appointment note (C-19)
- Letter to families about attendance (C-20)
- Attendance chart for families (C-21)

* All documents listed are available on the CD.

INTRODUCTION

For students to be successful in school, they need to actually be *in* school. Seems like a no-brainer, right? Educators know this intuitively, and a growing body of research points to student attendance as one of the most critical and underaddressed issues in American schools.

The extent of the attendance problem is huge. Balfanz and Byrnes (2012) estimate that as many as 7.5 million students each year are chronically absent, defined as missing 10% or more of the school year. That's 7.5 million kids in America who miss almost a month or more of school each year. This level of absenteeism has significant negative effects for the students, schools, and communities.

Task 1 presents some startling research findings on the extent and negative effects of the problem. Here's a brief preview of those findings.

Academic effects of absenteeism include:

- In the youngest school-aged children (K–1), attendance is a major predictor of whether students will read at grade level by the third grade. Third-grade reading skill is a known predictor of school success or failure (Applied Survey Research and Attendance Works, 2011).

- In secondary schools, frequent absences are one of the best predictors of whether a student will fail courses and eventually drop out (Allensworth & Easton, 2007).

- For classes with many students who are frequently absent, teachers have difficulty moving instruction forward. They have to repeat instruction and lessons. They must spend time creating and dealing with work for students who were absent, rather than designing quality, engaging initial lessons for all students. They also have more difficulty building class community and trust.

Negative social effects of absenteeism include:

- Students are deprived of social skill development and friendships.

- If students are missing school to avoid academic or social problems, they may not develop important traits like resilience and grit. The positive habits students develop in school—such as regular attendance and follow-through—will likely carry over into jobs and life.

- When students are not in school, they are more likely to be involved in illegal activities, gangs, and even kidnapping or child trafficking.

To make a difference with any school initiative—academic or behavioral—you need to ensure that students are attending so they can benefit from your efforts. So, in order to increase graduation rates, reduce achievement gaps based on income or race/ethnicity, and increase student test scores, you need to get students to attend school regularly.

Fortunately, there are many strategies that schools and districts can use to positively affect student attendance on both a schoolwide and an individual student level. You are already taking the first steps in this process. By working to establish a positive climate and reduce the use of exclusionary discipline—what you are doing through your *Foundations* implementation—you should begin to see improvements in the attendance of many students.

Students are more likely to attend when schools are safe, well managed, inclusive, and welcoming. Attendance improves when students have positive connections with staff members and with each other. All of your *Foundations* efforts should increase the likelihood that school is a place where students want to be and can be successful.

Attendance data can be a measure of your school climate initiatives—when you are doing a good job in making the school a safe, welcoming, engaging, and orderly environment, more students will come to school on a regular basis. Even a school with the best climate, however, will likely have some students who struggle with attendance. You may also find that if *many* students struggle with attendance, your other *Foundations* efforts may not be as successful as they would be if *all* students were regularly present. The four tasks in this presentation are tailored to help you improve student attendance at your school.

Task 1: Develop a Common Language and Understanding About Attendance presents some definitions you should know to be able to discuss and analyze attendance in your school. We also explain the negative outcomes associated with chronic absenteeism (these may help you get all staff, students, and families on board with your initiatives), and we discuss some of the causes of absenteeism.

Task 2: Design and Refine Attendance Policies explains why you need clear policies that emphasize the importance of attendance. You will clarify your definition of attendance and determine how you will monitor attendance. This task also covers how to address problems that might be suggested by your schoolwide data.

Task 3: Analyze Schoolwide Attendance Data and Identify Priorities for Improvement helps you examine schoolwide rates of absenteeism and common issues that can lead to high numbers of absent students. You will identify priorities for improvement from those trends. We also discuss developing systems to monitor schoolwide data and red-flag systems to connect individual students with available supports and interventions.

Task 4: Use Practical Strategies to Promote Regular Attendance discusses how to increase awareness and create a continued emphasis on the importance of regular attendance. It also looks at ways to involve families and the community in your attendance efforts.

TASK 1

Develop a common language and understanding about attendance

Most school staffs recognize that student attendance is critical for student success. Most school staffs also recognize that some—and maybe even many—students struggle with attendance and that this contributes to negative academic, social, and life outcomes. However, research suggests that schools are not doing nearly enough to address attendance or to monitor how many students are at risk because of their attendance issues.

Some of this lack of action and monitoring has to do with misunderstandings about the definitions of student attendance, so this task will help staff members develop a common language about attendance and an understanding of the metrics you should be looking at regularly. We present some of the data on the widespread nature of the problem and some of the negative outcomes associated with attendance issues. This information can build momentum among the staff to address absenteeism. You may wish to share some of these data with students and families so they can see how important regular attendance is for success in school.

This task also introduces the main causes of absenteeism so that your staff can begin thinking about how to address specific absenteeism problems in your school and prioritize your resources.

How does truancy differ from chronic absenteeism?

 Research suggests that addressing chronic absenteeism is more important than addressing truancy.”

When absenteeism is addressed in most districts, the discussion centers around student truancy, which translates to unexcused absences. Truancy is most relevant in secondary schools where students are more likely to skip school without parental permission. But research suggests that addressing chronic absenteeism is more important than addressing truancy.

Chronic absenteeism is defined as missing 10% or more of the school year for any reason, including excused absences, unexcused absences, and suspensions. Why is this metric of chronic absenteeism important? When a student is frequently absent, there will be negative effects regardless of whether those absences are excused, unexcused, or suspensions.

Recent data indicate that about 10% to 15% of students nationwide are chronically absent each year. That's as many as 7.5 million students, and this may be a conservative estimate. Chronic absenteeism is a huge problem in our schools, and it's not limited to high schools. High numbers of students are missing school at alarming rates from kindergarten all the way to 12th grade. Chronic absenteeism leads to many negative effects for students, schools, and communities, and perhaps the most obvious and most detrimental effect is on students' academic growth.

What are the detrimental effects of absenteeism on academic achievement?

A 2004–2005 survey of California students and subsequent data analyses found that of students who attended school regularly in kindergarten and first grade, 64% were proficient readers by the end of third grade (Applied Survey Research and Attendance Works, 2011). Now, 64% is not great. In fact, it's pretty bad, especially considering how critical it is that students are reading proficiently by the end of third grade. When a student is not reading proficiently by that time, it is unlikely that he or she will ever make up that lack of skills. But 64% is *significantly* better than the outcomes for students who were chronically absent. This same study found that of students who were chronically absent in kindergarten and first grade, only 17% were reading proficiently by the end of third grade. Obviously, chronic absenteeism for the youngest students can have significant negative academic effects.

Nationwide, roughly 10% of kindergarten and first-grade students are chronically absent, meaning they miss about a month or more of school each year (Chang & Romero, 2008). In some schools, as many as 50% of the students in kindergarten through third grade are chronically absent (Chang & Romero, 2008). Similarly, data show that in some secondary schools, 50% of the student body is chronically absent (Balfanz & Byrnes, 2012).

What are the effects of chronic absenteeism at the secondary level?

There are some startling statistics about how chronic absenteeism affects students at the secondary level. The main effect is the significant increased risk that these students will drop out.

Dropping out. A study in Utah found that students who were chronically absent were 7.4 times more likely to drop out than students who attended school regularly (University of Utah, Utah Education Policy Center, 2012). Researchers at Johns Hopkins University found that by sixth grade, chronic absenteeism is one of four main signs (the other three are poor behavior and course failure in math and English) that a student may drop out. If schools look at these metrics, they can get a pretty good picture of the students who are most at risk for dropping out (Balfanz & Byrnes, 2012). By ninth grade, regular attendance is a better predictor of whether students will graduate than eighth-grade test scores (Allensworth & Easton, 2007).

Life effects. There are also some significant negative life effects to consider beyond the potential lack of a high school diploma. Life effects are clearly evident in the data linking chronically absent students and the criminal justice system. In one study, researchers found that three-quarters of students who were involved in the juvenile justice system had histories of chronic absence (Balfanz & Byrnes, 2013). Numerous studies show that truant students are *far* more likely to be involved in illegal acts and arrested for offenses such as serious property crimes, assault, and drug use or sale (Baker, Sigmon, & Nugent, 2001).

Students who are chronically absent miss out on developing important life skills such as dependability. One of the main benefits of school is that students develop habits that will help them be successful in the long term. An example of an effective strategy focused on the goal of success in the long term is the Guidelines for Success that we emphasize in *Foundations*. Staff are encouraged to think about the skills, traits, and attitudes they want their students to be equipped with when they leave school and then embody those things in the Guidelines for Success.

Dependability is one of those critical life skills and habits that schools must help students develop. When employers are asked about the qualities they value the most in employees or the characteristics that differentiate a successful employee from one who may be fired, the answers all fit into the category of dependability. Employers want to hire and keep people who are on time, always show up for work, and follow through with assigned tasks. Many employers say that dependability is more important than a person's innate talent or skill in the field. Even highly talented people can risk losing their jobs if they are not dependable, especially if they often don't show up for work.

The income achievement gap. Another critical reason to address chronic absenteeism has to do with the income achievement gap. Research shows that the negative academic effects of chronic absenteeism are worse for students who live in poverty (Chang & Romero, 2008; Ready, 2010), and students who live in poverty are *far* more likely to be chronically absent (University of Utah, Utah Education Policy Center, 2012). In some states, as many as 70% of the chronically absent students are economically disadvantaged, regardless of the students' race, ethnic background, gender, or whether they live in urban, suburban, town, or rural communities (Balfanz & Byrnes, 2012). So to begin addressing the income achievement gap, which has grown more significant in our society over time, you must address chronic absenteeism.

Monitor more than average daily attendance.

With any initiative, data are important for identifying areas of concern, prioritizing resources, and monitoring efforts over time. As you know, gathering data is the starting point for any initiative. Yet despite the widespread nature of the absenteeism problem and all of the negative effects associated with chronic absenteeism, very few schools can tell you the percentage of their students who fit into the chronic absenteeism category. Most schools are not monitoring or paying enough attention to absenteeism.

Part of this problem might be because most schools look at average daily attendance (ADA). ADA is the percentage of enrolled students who are in school each day. An ADA of 93% means that on any given day, 93% of students are in school. Although ADA is a good metric to monitor, especially when it is used to motivate the whole school to improve attendance, it shouldn't be the *only* way you monitor attendance data. ADA can mask the numbers of students who are chronically absent (Bruner, Discher, & Chang, 2011).

Most schools would say that 95% ADA is pretty good—in fact, many schools use 95% ADA as their goal. But even with 95% ADA, high numbers of students can be chronically absent—as many as 30% to 40% of your student body—when it's the same students in the 5% missing on any given day. ADA doesn't take into account *which* individual students are not in school. Therefore, in addition to ADA, schools need to look at the number of students who are chronically absent.

 Although average daily attendance is a good metric to monitor, especially when it is used to motivate the whole school to improve attendance, it shouldn't be the only *way you monitor attendance data. Average daily attendance can mask the numbers of students who are chronically absent (Bruner, Discher, & Chang, 2011)."*

Establish the goal that every student attends school regularly.

Regular or satisfactory attendance can be defined as missing no more than 5% of days in an academic school year. According to research, this is the point when students are at far less risk of academic difficulties and the other associated negative outcomes of absenteeism. This figure, 5% or less, is equivalent to 9 days or fewer in a typical

180-day school year, or about one day per month on average. For example, let's say a student was sick and missed 3 days of school in one month. To have the student average one day absent per month and meet the attendance goal, she should miss no days for at least a few months.

One reason we use percentages when referring to attendance goals and rates is that you want to be able to assess students' attendance at any point during the year. You don't want to wait until the end of the year to determine if a student is at risk because of poor attendance. When you consider percentages, you can calculate that, for example, halfway through the school year your goal is that students have missed no more than 5%, or 4.5 days of a 180-day school year.

Of course, the goal of *all* students missing no more than 5% of school days is a stretch for many schools, especially when high numbers of students are chronically absent. Hence, you need to get everyone—students and families—on board with the idea that unless students are really ill or have other legitimate excuses, they need to be in school every day. This undertaking will require schoolwide approaches and targeted individual approaches that look deeper into the reasons behind absenteeism problems and attempt to address those reasons.

What's wrong with traditional approaches to addressing absenteeism?

Before we discuss the common reasons students are absent, let's look at some of the approaches that schools have traditionally taken to address absenteeism problems.

Unfortunately, some schools just ignore the issue and take the out-of-sight, out-of-mind approach. They might feel less pressure to deal with absenteeism than with disruptive and defiant behaviors because absenteeism is a less obvious problem. It's a somewhat natural reaction for them to ignore absenteeism, especially when the absent students have significant behavioral issues, because staff members get a welcome break from dealing with the students' misbehavior.

But here's the reality: Although you might breathe a bit easier on the days when Johnny is absent from class, you also know that he always comes back! And because of the compounding negative effects of absenteeism, when Johnny has been absent frequently he'll likely exhibit even worse behavior when he returns. He'll misbehave because he has fallen further behind, because he missed out on social opportunities, or because he realizes that he had more fun when he wasn't in school so he tries to get kicked out. Rather than ignoring absenteeism issues, schools should be proactive and intervene with absenteeism before it leads to other problems.

Some other methods that schools have traditionally used with absenteeism problems include parent contacts and meetings with the student. Through phone calls, letters, and in-person conferences, parents are reminded that the student needs to be in school and are possibly reprimanded or warned that the student is required to be in school.

When absenteeism, especially unexcused absences, becomes a major problem, some schools and districts send students and families to truancy court. This response is usually not initiated until the student has already missed a critical amount of school—for example, 5 days in a month or 18 days in a school year—and is a last resort in some schools and districts.

One procedure that we caution schools to move away from is the practice of suspension, especially out-of-school suspension for tardies and absences. If a student is chronically absent or chronically tardy, there is some reason or motivation behind it, and suspending the student as punishment is a little bit like punishing a drunk driver by giving her a case of beer. (In Module D, Presentation 4 we discuss alternatives to out-of-school suspension and ways to use in-school suspension productively.)

The problem with these traditional approaches is that they largely focus on punitive and reactive procedures. They shouldn't be your only approaches to addressing absenteeism. You are far more likely to effect behavioral change and improve attendance if you incorporate other kinds of solutions, especially ones that take into account the *causes* and *functions* of absenteeism.

 Punitive and reactive procedures shouldn't be your only approaches to addressing absenteeism. You are far more likely to effect behavioral change and improve attendance if you incorporate other kinds of solutions, especially ones that take into account the causes *and* functions *of absenteeism."*

Consider the possible causes and functions of absenteeism.

For any of your chronically absent students, consider these questions:

- What is preventing the student from attending regularly?
- Why does the student or parent think it is necessary to miss school?
- What is the student or parent getting from the student's absence?

Your prevention and intervention efforts at both the schoolwide and individual student levels should be designed to address these questions.

Absenteeism has four basic categories of causes and functions:

- Barriers (Barriers is a cause; e.g., the student misses school because of health, transportation, or financial issues.)
- Escape or avoidance (Absenteeism functions as escape or avoidance for the student.)
- Lack of awareness or understanding of the importance of attendance
- Access to desirables (Students obtain desirables outside of school.)

Research has shown (and your experience probably validates this finding) that chronic absenteeism is usually a complex mix of these four factors and that often more than one of them contributes to a student's absenteeism problems. Your goal should be to put measures in place that address all four of these factors.

1. Barriers cause students to be absent.

Many students face significant challenges that make regular attendance more difficult, even when they really want to attend. It can be easy to fall into a trap of thinking that students who don't attend just aren't motivated or that they or their parents just don't care about the value of education. The reality might be very different. Students and families who want to prioritize school but face significant barriers need help and support in overcoming those challenges if they are to improve their attendance.

Health. Chronic health concerns are one of the main barriers to regular attendance. The Centers for Disease Control and Prevention (CDC) reports that asthma is one of the leading causes (and the leading illness-related cause) of absenteeism in school-age children. One in ten students is likely to have asthma, and asthma is more common among minorities and students who live in low-income and poverty situations (U.S. Department of Health and Human Services, Centers for Disease Control and Prevention, 2013a). Children who live in inner cities experience more frequent emergencies, asthma-related hospitalizations, and death (American Lung Association, 2012).

What can a school do to address asthma? The student's family and health-care providers primarily need to address this problem, of course, but schools can take steps to help. Following is an example from the CDC website (U.S. Department of Health and Human Services, Centers for Disease Control and Prevention, 2013b) that describes how the Los Angeles Unified School District effectively intervened with an individual student's asthma and improved her attendance.

A young girl was frequently absent from school because of asthma-related hospitalizations. The attendance counselor noticed this pattern and referred the student's case to the school nurse. The nurse conducted a home visit and, in speaking with the mother, noted numerous environmental concerns in the home. The mother met with the landlord and asked that the environmental triggers be fixed, and they were. The home environment improved, the child was no longer being hospitalized as frequently, and her attendance improved.

That's a pretty sophisticated level of intervention and monitoring, but it's a great example of how a school district with good systems in place can really make some progress on addressing attendance problems.

If asthma and respiratory problems are identified as a significant barrier for many students, you might develop a "clean homes" initiative to teach *all* students and families how to reduce environmental triggers for respiratory infections. You can provide information to students and families about the importance of reducing smoking in the home and moving smoking outside to reduce the effects of second-hand smoke. Provide asthma and respiratory education to staff members to help students manage asthma triggers. Provide training in self-management to small groups of students who have asthma. Community organizations might be willing to partner with you to provide these kinds of services.

Other potential health barriers that might affect many of your students include dental problems and mental health issues such as depression, anxiety, and conduct disorders. Consider schoolwide and individual student efforts for these concerns.

Transportation. Transportation barriers may be prevalent, especially in neighborhoods with safety concerns such as neighborhood violence, gang violence, child trafficking, or heavy traffic. If parents in these neighborhoods can't transport students or wait with them for a bus, they might simply decide it is safer for students to remain at home.

Split-custody households might have transportation issues. If your school allows children just one legal residence but a student lives in a split-custody situation and needs to travel to school from more than one location, that student might not have school bus service several days per week. This barrier can be a major cause of absenteeism. If transportation issues affect some of your students who live in split-custody households or who have another transportation barrier, work with your transportation department, your district office, and possibly the individual families involved to find solutions that will allow students to get to school.

Financial concerns. Other barriers fall into the category of financial concerns. Students who live in unstable housing situations—they are homeless or in foster care, or their families are highly transient—are far more likely to be chronically absent (University of Utah, Utah Education Policy Center, 2012). Likewise, students who have insufficient food sources or inadequate clothing may be more likely to miss school.

*E*xample From the Field

At a school where I worked, a girl was missing school with increasing frequency. We found out that her family had lost their home and were living in their van. The girl usually missed school when her clothes were dirty and she was too embarrassed to come to school. We worked with her to develop a schedule that allowed her to come to school early, shower in the locker rooms, and launder her clothes in the consumer studies room. Her attendance improved significantly because of this relatively simple intervention.   —J.S.

Family obligations. Some students miss school because they need to work or care for older relatives or younger siblings. Some students lack effective supports—their parents are unable or unwilling to help them get up and get ready for school, for example. This situation can be a problem for elementary students, especially kindergartners through third graders, when parents are at work in the morning, asleep after working a night shift, or unavailable for some other reason.

In these cases, it is not enough for schools to just say that it's the parents' responsibility to get their kids to school. School support staff can help the student develop a checklist of things to do the night before—lay out clothes (shirt, pants, socks, shoes), pack a lunch, set the alarm, and so on—as well as a checklist for the morning. Have the student role-play the steps at school, and maybe call the student at home a few times to review the checklist. In this way, the school can help the student overcome the barrier and develop useful life skills, such as autonomy and creating a routine.

2. Absenteeism functions as escape or avoidance for the student.

Some students miss school to escape or avoid something they find aversive in the school environment. These students might have academic deficits or relationship problems with peers or adults, or they might be avoiding a negative or disengaging school climate.

Academic deficits are some of the biggest concerns and may lead to high numbers of students missing school. What child wants to be in an environment where he feels stupid, lost, frustrated, or anxious? Academic deficits can incite all those emotions. The longer absenteeism has been a problem, the more likely the student will develop an academic deficit, which further contributes to the absenteeism problem—it's a vicious cycle. Thus it's important to investigate possible academic deficits of students who are frequently absent.

Students might also miss school to avoid conflict with other students, bullying situations, or conflict with staff. Absenteeism is worse when the school climate is chaotic, negative, and punitive, and when adults (and students) do not have strong and positive relationships with students. The *Foundations* emphasis on creating a positive, inviting climate and respectful relationships will be very important in addressing absenteeism.

3. Students and families lack awareness or understanding of the importance of attendance.

Students and families may either lack awareness about the importance of attendance or simply don't see the value in education. You might think that all students and families understand that attendance is important for success in school—but the reality is that even when they do understand the relationship between attendance and success, many students and families don't fully grasp the negative effects of nonattendance.

For example, a 2005 survey showed that 80% of students who skipped school once or more per week thought this practice did not affect their grades or ability to graduate (Allensworth & Easton, 2007). This perception is very different from what the research literature shows. Schools can potentially make big gains in attendance by increasing student and family awareness about the effects attendance has on school success. Teach and disseminate concrete facts about attendance. Infuse an attendance message throughout all parts of the school throughout the entire school year. Create a campaign to tackle attendance issues and emphasize a schoolwide, let's-all-work-together approach to getting everyone to school regularly.

For some families and students, attendance is an issue of motivation, or their culture places little value or importance on education. If this is the case in your school, you might have to be creative in how your school addresses absenteeism problems. In Task 4 of this presentation, we give an example of how a rural community in Alaska effectively addressed attendance as a communitywide initiative.

Also consider the attendance practices that the adults in the school are modeling. Are many staff members absent frequently? If so, what message does this send to students? Students might have little reason to think that school is important if even the staff doesn't regularly attend. In addition, even with the greatest substitutes in the world, there is likely less learning and more climate issues when teachers are not regularly present.

4. Students obtain desirables outside of school.

The fourth category of causes and functions of absenteeism is something we call *obtain desirables*. Students are obtaining something desirable outside of school—something more rewarding to them than the rewards they get in school or the long-term goal of a diploma. They may be getting peer or adult attention, food, illegal substances, money, or access to activities such as video games, a hobby they enjoy, or unsupervised time.

Conclusion

Being aware of all of the issues we've discussed in this task will help you with your prevention and intervention efforts. As you begin looking at your schoolwide data and data about individual students who are chronically absent, consider why students are missing school. Think about possible barriers, what they might be escaping or avoiding at school, whether they and their families lack awareness or don't value school, and whether they are obtaining something desirable outside of school.

When your intervention efforts seek to address these "whys" and deal with the causes and functions of the absenteeism, you are much more likely to affect your students' behavior.

Task 1 Action Steps & Evidence of Implementation

Action Steps	Evidence of Implementation
1. Identify the information you will present to staff, students, and families to highlight the importance of attendance and to build momentum and motivation for your subsequent attendance efforts.	Foundations Process: Attendance Initiatives
2. Consider when and how you will present this information to staff, students, and families, and how frequently you will review it throughout the year. Your attendance efforts should be infused into many activities and settings throughout the school year.	
3. Identify and list the causes and functions of absenteeism that you know are affecting large numbers of your students. If you are unsure, or if your list is based on hypotheses rather than concrete data sources, plan to survey students or conduct focus groups to clarify the schoolwide causes of absenteeism.	

TASK 2

Design and refine attendance policies

Attendance policies need to be designed to emphasize the critical importance of attendance and to indicate that the school will not wait until nonattendance has reached a chronic or severely chronic level to intervene.

In this task, you will consider your current attendance policies and whether they specifically and clearly address most of the attendance issues you see in your school. You will also determine how and when attendance policies will be taught and reviewed with staff, students, and families.

This task includes a series of questions about your attendance policies. Figure 4a on the next two pages shows a document that you can use to answer these questions as you review your policy. The School-Based Analysis of Attendance Policies form is available as Form C-06 on the Module C CD. You may wish to have a copy of your current attendance policy as you read this presentation so you can make notes about potential changes. Foundations Team members should consult the current policy as they complete the Action Steps at the end of this task.

> The numbered items within this task correspond to items on the School-Based Analysis of Attendance Policies (shown in Figure 4a).

1. Does your policy refer to state laws about compulsory education and attendance?

    All states have compulsory education laws, and most states outline legal procedures for dealing with habitual truancy; that is, students and families can be referred to truancy officers and courts for excessive issues with unexcused absences. Some districts further define their truancy policies so that punitive steps or other measures are taken before court proceedings are initiated.

    The problem with these policies is that they address only unexcused absences, not excessive excused absences or suspensions, and often they are initiated only when student attendance has reached chronic or severely chronic levels. In many states, referral begins when a student has missed something like 4 or 5 unexcused days in a month (25% of days in a month) or 10 to 20 unexcused days in a year. But when a student has missed this much school, it is too late to intervene.

    In addition, these state and district laws and procedures focus on reactive rather than proactive behavior management. Although you should include them in your attendance policy, they constitute only a part of what your school should do to address the issue. In other words, they form only a portion of a comprehensive policy.

Figure 4a *School-Based Analysis of Attendance Policies (C-06)*

School-Based Analysis of Attendance Policies (p. 1 of 2)

This form is designed to help you consider your current attendance policies and whether they specifically and clearly address most of the attendance issues you see in your school. Information in the Module C, Presentation 4, Task 2 video and book complements this form.

Questions to ask yourself	Y	N	Actions
1. Does your policy refer to state laws about compulsory education and attendance?	☐	☐	
2. Does the policy clearly define what counts as an excused absence and an unexcused absence?	☐	☐	
a. Does the policy indicate legitimate reasons for absence?	☐	☐	
b. Does each legitimate reason for absence include additional information for clarification?	☐	☐	
c. Does the policy indicate reasons for absences that will *not* be considered excused, even with a parent/guardian call or note?	☐	☐	
3. Does the policy clearly define the amount of time that will qualify as an absence and indicate how this will be monitored?	☐	☐	
a. Do partial-day absences count as part of the student's absence count?	☐	☐	
b. If no, will partial-day absences accumulate toward full-day absences?	☐	☐	
c. When does a tardy become an unexcused absence? _____ _____			
d. Will the school monitor both numbers of tardies for each student as well as number of minutes missed for cumulative tardies?	☐	☐	
4. Will the school monitor school-event absences and address potential detrimental effects of these absences?	☐	☐	

 This form can be printed from the Module C CD.

School-Based Analysis of Attendance Policies (p. 2 of 2)

Questions to ask yourself	Y	N	Actions

5. Do current policies link absences with course credit or grades? (That is, students who meet an established maximum percentage of days absent are denied course credit or their grades are automatically reduced.) **Caution:** If using this procedure, ensure the following are in place:
 	
   a. How will you educate and remind students and families about the policy? _____
   _____
   _____
   _____
 	
   b. How will you warn students and families when the student is at risk of losing credit or getting a reduced grade because of high absence rates? _____
   _____
   _____
   _____
	☐	☐	

6. Does your policy include the following statements? a. The school will assist with barriers and difficulties that might be preventing regular attendance.	☐	☐	
b. The school will take measures to help the family address absenteeism before court proceedings are initiated. (Indicate specific measures; Task 4 suggests some strategies.)	☐	☐	
c. The school will override excused absences when they are found to be illegitimate.	☐	☐	
d. The school will initiate truancy court proceedings if students and families are not making serious efforts to get the student to school or work with the school to overcome barriers.	☐	☐	
7. How will the Foundations Team use the attendance policy to educate staff, students, and parents about the importance of attendance? _____ _____ _____ _____ _____			

Note: Use a separate sheet to document other policies and further actions.

The medical field provides a good analogy for attendance policies. Truancy court proceedings are like the emergency, last-chance procedure a doctor uses when a patient has reached a critical stage—emergency bypass surgery for someone who is having a heart attack, for example. To prevent others from having heart attacks and reduce the numbers of people who might need bypass surgery, doctors use many interventions.

- They identify risk factors from numerous studies.
- They advise regular medical checkups and screening for heart problems.
- They introduce healthy eating and exercise initiatives for everyone.
- They counsel about reducing risk factors—not smoking, managing stress, and limiting alcohol consumption.
- When someone is at risk, they may provide additional measures to encourage healthy eating, exercise, and reducing risk factors (they may even take behavioral therapy approaches such as referrals to specialists).
- They prescribe aspirin, beta blockers, or cholesterol-lowering medications for patients especially at risk.

Similar to the way the medical profession addresses heart health, attendance policies need to address habitual absenteeism through multiple methods. You need emergency procedures in place for students who resist other intervention plans (just as doctors are trained to perform bypass surgery when it's needed), but you also must try to drastically reduce the numbers of students who need these emergency procedures by focusing on preventive, proactive measures.

Include laws and regulations required by the state and district in your attendance policy. The rest of this task prompts you to consider other important elements that can help you be proactive and preventive. If a question is not addressed by district or state requirements, consider whether including the information would address issues that contribute to absenteeism in your school.

2. Does the policy clearly define what counts as an excused absence and an unexcused absence?

    a. Does the policy indicate legitimate reasons for absence?

    Many district policies include language similar to the following.

    A student may be excused for the following reasons:
    - Illness
    - Death of a family member or funeral
    - Medical or dental appointment

- Religious holiday
- Required court appearance
- School-sponsored curricular or extracurricular activity
- Other emergency

b. Does each legitimate reason for absence include additional information for clarification?

Detailed definitions of each of these reasons can give your students, families, and staff a clearer picture of what *excused absence* means. Illness, for example, should be clearly defined. One study in the *Journal of School Nursing* found that 76% of absences in elementary school were excused, the vast majority for illness or injury. But when the district followed up with phone calls, home visits, and so on, they found that 40% of the excused absences were actually for illegitimate reasons such as family activities, transportation problems, and family illness (Kerr et al., 2012).

Your policy can define what *illness* means with language such as, "Severe injury or illness: Too severe or contagious for the student to attend class."

Consider having families use a document similar to How Sick Is Too Sick for School? (see Figure 4b on the next page). The form outlines a series of questions that can help parents and students determine whether the illness is serious enough to miss school. If the answers to all the questions are No, the student can probably go to school.

The How Sick Is Too Sick for School? form (Form C-05) can also be used to follow up on a student who is frequently excused for illness (and you know the student does not have a chronic disease confirmed by a doctor). This student may be flagged for follow-up phone calls from the counselor, nurse, or principal, who works through the checklist with a parent before marking the student as excused or unexcused.

Medical and dental appointments should also be defined in detail. Make the following guidelines clear to parents:

- Whenever possible, schedule appointments outside school hours.

- The student must attend school before the appointment and return to school after the appointment on the same day (absent only for the time spent going to, at, and returning from the appointment)

How Sick Is Too Sick for School?

In general, children are too sick to come to school when:

- They are contagious.
- Their symptoms are serious enough to prevent them from focusing on the tasks they need to do there.

Use the checklist below to determine whether to keep your child home from school.

		YES	NO
1.	Does your child have a fever of 100° F or higher?	_____	_____
2.	Has your child vomited two or more times in a 24-hour period?	_____	_____
3.	Does your child have diarrhea?	_____	_____
4.	Are your child's eyes crusty, bright red, and/or discharging yellow or green fluid (conjunctivitis/pink eye)?	_____	_____
5.	If your child complains of a sore throat, is it accompanied by fever, headache, stomachache, or swollen glands?	_____	_____
6.	If your child complains of a stomachache, is it accompanied by fever, vomiting, diarrhea, lethargy, sharp pain, and/or hard belly?	_____	_____
7.	Does your child have a persistent, phlegmy cough?	_____	_____
8.	Does your child have lice (white, translucent eggs the size of a pinpoint on the hair or insects on the scalp)?	_____	_____

If you answered yes to any of these questions, please keep your child home from school and consider seeking medical attention. Your child could have a serious or contagious illness. Keep your child home until he or she has been symptom free for at least 24 hours or until a doctor indicates that he or she can return to school.

If children have a cold, headache, or stomachache that is not accompanied by fever, vomiting, or diarrhea, they can probably come to school.

If a child has a rash, it could be contagious. Please seek medical advice before allowing your child to come to school.

Earaches are not contagious. Children can come to school as long as they can concentrate on their work.

Once your child has been treated for lice, he or she can return to school.

 This form can be printed from the Module C CD.

- Try to vary appointment times so that the student doesn't always miss the same subject.

- A note from the doctor or dentist is required. It should include the time in and out of the appointment and the doctor or dentist's signature. (Figure 4c below shows a sample form you can provide to parents.) *Note:* Requiring signed notes from health-care providers is an optional way to increase accountability and further emphasize the importance of attendance to all families. This procedure can be mildly inconvenient for families, however, so carefully assess whether the problem of illegitimate or extended absences for medical and dental appointments is significant enough in your school to warrant requiring notes.

c. Does the policy indicate reasons for absences that will not be considered excused, even with a parent/guardian call or note?

It can be helpful to itemize reasons that should *not* be considered excused absences. For example:

- Vacation
- Minor illness (cold, stomachache, or headache without fever, vomiting, or diarrhea)
- Haircut

Figure 4c *Sample medical and dental appointment note (C-19)*

Medical professionals and parents/guardians:

Regular attendance in school is critical for students' success. In an effort to promote regular attendance, [name of school] School encourages health-care providers and parents/guardians to schedule medical and dental appointments outside of school hours when possible.

When an appointment occurs during school hours, please have the health-care provider's office list the time you entered the office in the space below and provide the time and a signature as you leave the appointment. Students will be considered excused only during the time of the appointment and reasonable transit time to and from the provider's office. Any additional time (e.g., to go out to lunch, to do errands, etc.) will be marked as unexcused on the student's attendance record. Please ensure that the student is absent only during the approved times.

Health-care Provider _____
                                              (Name and Business)

Time of Entry to Office _____   Time of Exit From Office _____

Health-care Provider _____
                                        (Signature of provider or receptionist)

A Word version of this sample is available on the Module C CD.

- Birthday
- Taking a driver's test
- Going shopping
- Car trouble
- Oversleeping (student or parent)

When you review attendance data (you'll read about this in Task 3), it may be useful to return to your policy and address common inappropriate reasons students are absent.

3. Does the policy clearly define the amount of time that will qualify as an absence and indicate how this will be monitored?

    a. Do partial-day absences count as part of the student's absence count?

    b. If no, will partial-day absences accumulate toward a full-day absence?

We recommend that you do *not* limit your count to full-day absences; include partial-day absences in your data. Partial-day absences will have an adverse effect over time, especially when they occur for the same period or class. For example, when a secondary student regularly skips one or two of the same classes but attends all other classes, your attendance data should flag that student as needing attention for attendance issues.

California's Education Code Section 48260 (a) states:

> A pupil subject to compulsory full-time education who is absent from school without a valid excuse three full days in one school year *or tardy or absent for more than a 30-minute period during the school day without a valid excuse on three occasions in one school year* [emphasis added], or any combination thereof, shall be classified as a truant and shall be reported to the attendance supervisor or to the superintendent of the school district.

You might wish to include a similar reference to partial-day absences in your policy. If you stick with counting full-day absences, ensure that you track the number by period or hour of day.

    c. When does a tardy become an unexcused absence?

When a student is 10 minutes tardy, should this count as an absence or a tardy? When a student is 30 minutes tardy, should this count as an absence or a tardy? Some schools accumulate tardies toward an absence, so three tardies, for example, count as one unexcused absence.

d. Will the school monitor both numbers of tardies for each student as well as number of minutes missed for cumulative tardies?

Some schools accumulate the tardy minutes toward unexcused absences. For example, when a student has tardies that cumulatively exceed 30 minutes, the student has earned an unexcused absence.

4. Will the school monitor school-event absences and address potential detrimental effects of these absences?

Many schools must deal with the impact of school-event absences. Most schools consider whether a student's GPA is high enough that she can participate in sports and other activities, but they don't always consider whether the absences related to school events affect the student's performance in classes. So when students are absent (excused) to travel for a football game, band tour, or debate competition, their schoolwork should be monitored and reported. If they are not successfully keeping up, take steps to ensure that academics don't take a back seat to extracurricular activities.

For example, if a student is leaving early on Fridays for sports-related events and his grade for the last class of the day is lower than expected, you might adjust the student's schedule so that PE is the last class on Friday. Or tell the student he cannot participate in the Friday events until he improves his grades or (a little more extreme) cannot participate on the team at all until he improves his grades. Many schools have eligibility requirements—students cannot participate in sports or other extracurriculars unless they meet an established minimum GPA.

5. Do current policies link absences with course credit or grades? (Are students who meet an established maximum number or percentage of absences denied course credit or are their grades automatically reduced?)

a. If so, how will you educate and remind students and families about the policy?

b. How will you warn students and families when the student is at risk of losing credit or getting a reduced grade because of high absence rates?

We are not advocating one way or the other for this policy item; it is usually mandated by the district or state. But if you do have a policy similar to this one, it is critical that you educate students and families frequently and build in warning systems so that you can tell students and families when students are at risk of losing credit or getting a reduced grade because of high absence rates. You don't want a student to lose credit, fail a class, or be at risk for not graduating because she wasn't aware that her absences were affecting her grades.

6. Does your policy include the following statements?

   a. The school will assist with reducing barriers and difficulties that might be preventing regular attendance.

   b. The school will take measures to help the family address absenteeism before court proceedings are initiated. (Indicate specific measures; Task 4 suggests some strategies.)

   c. The school will override excused absences when they are found to be illegitimate.

   d. The school will initiate truancy court proceedings if students and families are not making serious efforts to get the student to school or work with the school to overcome barriers.

   Do consider individual circumstances and situations—we caution you to avoid being too rigid with these procedures—but the school needs to be firm when students and families make no effort to improve the student's attendance.

7. How will the Foundations Team use the attendance policy to educate staff, students, and parents about the importance of attendance?

   You should do more than just tell students they need to attend school. Infuse the policy and information about the importance of attendance into the common language of the school, and teach and review the policies throughout the year. Inform students and families who are new to the school about the attendance policy. Other ideas include:

   • Review the How Sick Is Too Sick for School? form with all students and, using role-play, have students practice judging whether a student is or is not able to go to school.

   • Train family members in How Sick Is Too Sick for School? during back-to-school night.

   • During cold and flu season, conduct activities to remind students how to prevent the spread of illness, and review How Sick Is Too Sick for School? so students don't stay home unnecessarily.

   • Refer to the attendance policy when calling or meeting with families to address attendance problems.

Task 2 Action Steps & Evidence of Implementation

Action Steps	Evidence of Implementation
1. Review your current attendance policy and work through the School-Based Analysis of Attendance Policies form (Form C-06). For each question, determine whether the issue is adequately addressed or whether it needs to be refined or clarified. You might decide that some of these issues are not relevant to your school population and do not need to be included in the policy.	Foundations Process: Attendance Initiatives
2. Consider the absenteeism issues you frequently see among your students. Does the policy clearly highlight these issues?	
3. Revisit this task after you have gathered and analyzed schoolwide attendance data, as discussed in Task 3.	

TASK 3

Analyze schoolwide attendance data and identify priorities for improvement

In Task 3, we discuss who will be involved in compiling and analyzing data and identifying priorities, what attendance data should be monitored, trends to look for in your data, how to set priorities using these trends, and red-flag systems to identify individual students who need support. (More detailed information about individual behavior improvement plans appears in Module F.)

As with your other school improvement efforts, improving attendance should become a regular part of your student support process and continuous cycle of improvement. Improving attendance begins largely with data collection and analysis.

Who will be involved?

Because data collection and analysis and corresponding schoolwide initiatives are complex, time-consuming tasks, we recommend that a team lead the efforts. The team could be the Foundations Team, another leadership team, or a student-support team. If you've determined that attendance is a priority, you might create an attendance task force that is representative of all staff and departments of the school.

Even when one person is in charge of monitoring attendance, it is more effective for a team to:

- Regularly analyze attendance data.
- Red-flag students in need of intervention, link them with support systems, and provide follow-up.
- Present attendance data to staff, students, and families.
- Oversee schoolwide implementation efforts.

Collect accurate attendance data.

Ensure that all staff turn in accurate and timely attendance data. You might need to issue reminders from the office to staff members who haven't reported their attendance within the first 5 or 10 minutes of class. You might need to provide individual support to some teachers by helping them set up an attendance routine. A good strategy is to have a short assignment on the board that students can begin as soon as they enter the classroom. While they work silently at their desks, the teacher can note who is absent in the school's attendance database system (or use whatever system the school uses), then begin instruction.

Attendance records should indicate whether absences are excused, unexcused, in-school suspension, or out-of-school suspension. Also consider including a school-event category. These categories will help you break down the data into meaningful analyses.

Every 2 to 4 weeks, calculate rates for the following four categories of absenteeism. How many students fit into each category?

- **Regular attendance:** Students missed less than 5% of days year to date.
- **At risk:** Students missed 5% to 10% of days year to date.
- **Chronic absence:** Students missed 10% or more of days year to date.
- **Severe chronic absence:** Students missed 20% or more of days year to date.

For example, here's how you can calculate the number of students who are chronically absent. (Use the same procedure for the other three categories.)

1. Print a list of all students who have been absent 10% or more of the days in the current school year. For example, if school has been in session for 30 school days, list students who have been absent for 3 or more days. If school has been in session for 100 school days, list students who have been absent for 10 or more school days.

2. Calculate the schoolwide rate of chronic absence. Count the number of students on your 10% days-absent list and divide that number by the number of enrolled students. Example:

   - It is the 100th school day of the school year. 10% of 100 = 10.
   - There are 217 students on the 10% days-absent list (they have been absent 10 or more days so far this year).
   - There are 1,500 students enrolled in the school.
   - 217/1,500 = 0.145 = 14.5 %
   - 14.5% of the student body is chronically absent. (Attendance should be a high priority for improvement in this school!)

3. Include in your attendance calculations students who enroll after the school year has begun. We suggest a way to include these students in your attendance rates, but be sure to meet with your attendance and database experts to discuss whether there's an easier method within your data system. It's important to include these students not only to achieve accurate results, but also because highly mobile students often have attendance issues.

   a. Keep a list of each student who enrolls after Day 1 and write down the day of the school year they started (Day 30, Day 60).

b. For each student, calculate the number of days he or she has been enrolled. For example, Juan started school on Day 30. It is now Day 70, so Juan has been enrolled for 40 days.

c. Determine how many days each student has been absent (for students who enrolled after Day 1).

d. For each student, divide the days absent by the days enrolled. Juan has been absent 10 days, so 10/40 = 25%.

e. Figure out which attendance category the students fit into and include them when you determine schoolwide rates for each category. At 25%, Juan is in the severe chronic absence category.

Again, be sure to inquire about easier procedures for including late enrollees.

When should schoolwide procedures be emphasized?

Schoolwide procedures are probably useful in all schools, but the degree and intensity with which you implement them will vary based on your rate of chronically absent students. We recommend implementing schoolwide procedures when 10% or more of your student body is chronically absent or when the number of chronically absent students would overwhelm your staff resources for individual student support, such as individual interventions and functional behavior assessments. While you are implementing schoolwide procedures, select as many individual students as you can handle for intervention and put the remaining students who are chronically absent on a waitlist.

Use schoolwide attendance data to identify priorities for improvement.

In addition to the schoolwide rates you calculated for the four categories of absenteeism, gather data to help you understand the reasons why students miss school. Follow-up surveys can be a good source of information. For example, GradNation offers an attendance survey at guidebook.americaspromise.org/tools-directory/tool-9. An adapted version is shown in Figure 4d on the next page.

Include questions in your survey about common causes of absenteeism as well as questions that relate specifically to the reasons that students in your school are absent. You'll get a clearer picture of the issues you need to address. Also consider convening focus groups about absenteeism and having discussions with students and families to get more information.

Figure 4d   *Sample attendance survey*

Directions: Indicate how often you miss school for each of the reasons listed here.					
When I miss a day of school, it's because:	**Never**	**Once or twice a year**	**Once a month**	**A few times a month**	**Every week**
I don't feel like coming.					
I overslept.					
I had transportation problems (missed the bus, didn't have a ride, weather was too bad to walk, etc.)					
I didn't do homework or study for a test.					
I don't want to be teased or bullied by other students.					
I have to take care of siblings or a sick family member.					
I have to work.					
My classes are boring.					
I want to hang out with my friends.					
Other:					
When I miss a class but attend others, it's because:					
The class is boring.					
The teacher picks on me.					
I don't want to be teased or bullied by other students.					
I didn't do the homework or study for a test.					
Other:					
When I'm late for a class, it's because:					
I overslept.					
The class never starts on time.					
I don't walk fast enough.					
There's not enough time between classes.					
I can't find things in my locker.					
I'm talking with friends.					
Other:					

Adapted from Grad Nation Community Guidebook, guidebook.americaspromise.org.

Use of all your absenteeism data to analyze trends. Note that only the principal should look at data that are broken down by staff member; the team might analyze these data when staff names are redacted. Consider the following analyses:

- Are rates of excused absences high?
- Are suspension rates high?
- Are there patterns by week, time of day, or class period?
- Are there patterns among certain demographics, such as grade level, ethnicity, language background, or neighborhood of residence?

All of these collected data will help you and the staff identify priorities for improvement and determine how to move forward with schoolwide prevention efforts.

Develop a red-flag system.

You data will also help you develop a system to identify students with early-stage absenteeism problems. You don't want to wait to intervene until the student has missed a critical amount of school. If attendance data are available from the previous year, research which students had attendance issues then and make note of students to watch this year. After the first 30 school days of the current year, calculate absenteeism rates. Students with three or more absences and/or increasing frequency of absenteeism should be flagged for support. Several studies have shown that increasing frequency of absenteeism is a major warning sign of students at risk for dropping out.

Review all your attendance data at least once a month, and preferably more often, for students who should be flagged. Be sure to include careful review of late enrollees and highly mobile students. Refer flagged students to individual support systems as soon as possible.

Task 3 Action Steps & Evidence of Implementation

Action Steps	Evidence of Implementation
1. Identify who will print lists of students for each of the four attendance categories (regular attendance, at risk, chronic absence, and severe chronic absence) and calculate the percentage of students in each category.	Foundations Process: Attendance Initiatives, Planning Calendar
2. Identify who will be part of the task force that collects and analyzes data to identify schoolwide trends and priorities.	
3. Create a year-long task force meeting schedule.	
4. Identify who will be in charge of interventions for chronically absent students.	

TASK 4

Use practical strategies to promote regular attendance

In this task, we suggest strategies you can use to address attendance problems on a schoolwide level and with individual students who could benefit from some initial support before their absenteeism requires more intensive procedures. They fall into two categories: increase awareness of the importance of attendance, and enhance family and community involvement.

Increase awareness of the importance of attendance.

Use strategies in this category to ensure that a focus on attendance becomes a part of the everyday language and culture of the school and to campaign to get all students, families, and staff on board and excited about improving attendance.

Use available media to spread your message to staff, students, families, and the community. Examples include:

- Newsletter—maybe create a special issue that focuses on attendance to kick off your campaign, then include follow-up articles in subsequent issues
- Back-to-school night—emphasize attendance in presentations to families and in school decorations
- Staff and student slogans, videos, posters, and so on
- Press releases for local TV and radio stations and newspapers
- Enlist the help of all staff to welcome students every day and emphasize the importance of attendance during each class period.

Send an initial letter home. As you begin your campaign, one of the first strategies to consider is sending a letter to families asking for their help in monitoring students' attendance across the school year (see Figure 4e on the next page). You might include a chart similar to the example shown in Figure 4f. Whenever a student is absent, the parent (or student) logs the date and reason. Include on your chart the potential consequences of the absences; for example, after Absence 9, remind families of the negative effect so many absences can have on the student's academics, the classroom community, and the school community. Color coding (green to red) gives a visual indication of the increasing seriousness of the number of absences.

Create a focus on attendance in classrooms. Encourage all teachers to emphasize the importance of attendance in their classrooms. They should welcome students each morning and ask where they were or how they are after absences. Imagine the power of having every staff member a student encounters after an absence say, "How

Figure 4e *Sample letter to families about attendance (C-20)*

FOUNDATIONS SAMPLE

**Loganville Middle School
Home of the Trojans**

Dear families,

We are looking forward to a great year, with students in classes and ready to learn every day.

We have learned that students who miss even a few days of school each month are at far greater risk of academic failure and dropout than students who attend regularly. We have set a goal that every student in our school attends regularly (has nine or fewer absences in a year).

Because attendance is so important, please send your child to school every day unless he or she has a contagious illness or is running a fever.

We have included a chart with this letter that will help you keep track of your student's absences. If your child is at risk of missing too much school, please feel free to contact Joan Ndogo at 555-1234 for assistance. We will also monitor each student's attendance across the year so we can work with families when the number of absences puts a student at risk. We will be happy to work with you to help your student attend regularly and have greater opportunities for success.

Sincerely,

Aaron Chan, Principal

Figure 4f *Attendance chart for families (C-21)*

Date:	Date:	Date:	Date:	Date:	Date:	Date:	Date:	Date:	Absence 10+
Absence 1 Reason:	Absence 2 Reason:	Absence 3 Reason:	Absence 4 Reason:	Absence 5 Reason:	Absence 6 Reason:	Absence 7 Reason:	Absence 8 Reason:	Absence 9 Reason:	Note: Your student is at increasing risk for academic difficulties and school failure with each absence beyond this point.

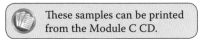
These samples can be printed from the Module C CD.

are you? We missed you. We're so glad you're back." When the student interacts with several concerned adults after each absence, that can create a strong long-term effect on the student's view of the importance of attending school.

Social stories and pledges. Primary teachers can use recited social stories or pledges to emphasize attendance. In the Los Angeles Unified School District, some teachers have their young students sing the "Morning Attendance Song" to the tune of "Frère Jacques" (see box at right). The song can become part of the classroom culture and make morning attendance fun.

See the "Social Story Example" box for a social story young students can recite at the beginning of class.

When a social story or pledge is recited regularly, it builds value for school and ingrains the idea that students should miss school only when they are truly sick.

Lessons. In secondary schools, attendance should be emphasized not only in syllabi (as it affects grades), but also in relation to life goals and future employment. This information can be presented on the school website, during student-teacher conferences, and in formal and informal lessons.

> **Morning Attendance Song**
> (Sung to the tune of "Frère Jacques")
>
> Table One, Table One,
> Who is here? Who is here?
> All of us are present. Nobody is absent.
> We are six. We are six.
>
> *When a student is absent, the lyrics are:*
> Table One, Table One,
> Who is here? Who is here?
> Some of us are present. One of us is absent.
> We are five. We are five."
>
> Developed by the Los Angeles Unified School District Attendance Improvement Program

> **Social Story Example**
>
> I'm a very important person.
> I come to school every day that I'm not sick.
> When I come to school, I see people that I know.
> I learn a lot of things.
> We have important work to do.
> I come to school every day that I'm not sick.

For example, have students brainstorm what they would do if they had a million dollars. List the items they would buy and trips they would take on the board. Then make the link: Tell them that a high school graduate makes, on average, a million dollars more than a high school dropout over a lifetime. Discuss how attendance affects the likelihood that they will graduate or drop out—if possible, work with students individually.

Another brief lesson on attendance might consist of asking students, "Why do professional football players show up regularly to practice?" Draw a T-chart on the board and have students generate ideas (see the sample T-chart below). Then connect the positives and negatives of showing up for football practice to school outcomes.

Players who show up	Players who don't show up
• Get stronger • Learn new plays and get better at old ones • Meet coaches' expectations • Get time during games	• Don't get any better or stronger • Make coaches angry • Let down the team • Don't get to play in games

Teachers can also incorporate attendance into existing lessons in their content area.

Classroom attendance graph and reward system. Another way to reinforce attendance in the classroom is to have each class develop a classroom attendance graph (see Figure 4g for a sample).

Figure 4g   *Sample classroom attendance graph*

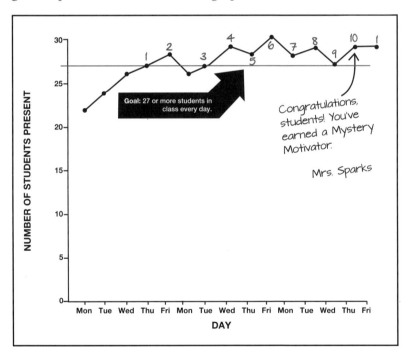

Draw a goal line for the number or percentage of students you would like to see attend each day, then graph the number (or percentage) of students who are present each day. You can use this to acknowledge and reinforce improved attendance. Pair it with a structured system for added reinforcement. For example, the class could earn 1 point each day attendance is above the goal and 2 points when attendance is 100%. When the class has accumulated x number of points, they earn a reward selected from a grab bag or with a spinner. In secondary schools, you might create a competition among class periods.

The staff at McLean Elementary School in Wichita, Kansas, developed a unique and fun attendance reward system they call No Tardy Tators. Each teacher has a plain Mr. Potato Head in his or her classroom. Each day the class has no tardies, students can select one part and add it to the potato head. After 10 days with no tardies, the class earns a certificate that they display outside the classroom. They also earn a small celebration or reward. Figure 4h shows some examples of completed Mr. Potato Heads as well as a photograph of students showing off the socks they wore for Crazy Socks Day, one of the rewards they can earn.

Figure 4h   No Tardy Tators attendance reward system; thanks to Mendie Vicin at McLean Science and Technology Magnet Elementary School and Wichita Public Schools in Kansas

Display outside classroom

No Tardy Tators certificate

Figure 4h (continued)

Samples of student-created Mr. Potato Heads

Crazy Socks Day

McLean reduced tardies in the first quarter to 118 from 224 the previous year. In the second quarter, they reduced tardies to 179 from 350 the previous year. The No Tardy Tators system didn't eliminate the tardiness problem, but it significantly reduced it. The principal, Mendie Vicin, shared this anecdote:

> *At the beginning of this year, we had a family that was tardy the first 3 days of school. On the third day, the mother called me to ask about "this potato-head thing" her daughters were telling her about. I explained our No Tardy Tators program and how we are all working together to earn Mr. Potato Head pieces. This family has not had a single tardy since that day—93 days as of this writing!*

Create a schoolwide focus on attendance. Consider using a schoolwide graph as part of an attendance routine that is conducted during each class period or over the public address system. Using a final goal of 97% or 98% (or above) average daily attendance, draw gradual increases in the goal line for improved average daily attendance. Use the graph to encourage some friendly schoolwide competition, such as most improved grade level or the grade with the best average daily attendance. You might award points to the whole school for improvements to the average daily attendance. Students earn a schoolwide celebration for a certain number of points.

Figure 4i   *Schoolwide average daily attendance graph*

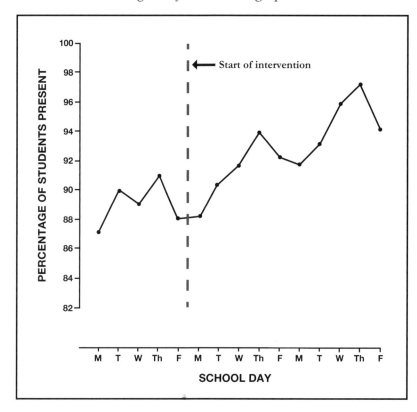

Enhance family and community involvement.

These strategies aim to increase family and community involvement by publicizing your campaign to the wider school community.

Communicate, communicate, communicate. To get families and the community to care about and get involved with school attendance issues, communication is key. You might kick off the year with a high-profile attendance campaign and then remind families and the community throughout the year with newsletters, robo-calls, website postings, and email blasts. Include information and data about the outcomes for students with poor attendance. Share data from your school and celebrate progress. Provide nonattendance guidelines and tips for getting students to school every day. Be sure that the tone of your communications emphasizes the communal "we're-all-in-this-together" aspect of your attendance initiative—when everyone cares and is involved, everyone benefits.

Reiterate your message more frequently during the holiday season, especially if families in your community tend to take long vacations during this period. Following is an example of a 30-second public service announcement (PSA) that local radio and TV stations might be willing to broadcast (perhaps local celebrities or school officials could read it), or you could include it in your newsletter or on your website. This example comes from an organization called Attendance Works.

> *This holiday season, the best gift you can give your child is a good education. And the best place to get an education is in school. It's tempting to extend your vacation by a few days, but remember, those days count as absences. Just a few missed days here and there, even if they're excused, can add up to too much lost learning time. So make sure your child is in school every day, right up until vacation starts. Our teachers will be teaching, and our students will be learning.*

Visit the Attendance Works website (www.attendanceworks.org) for more sample PSAs and additional great information about attendance issues.

In high-achievement schools, talk with families about the two weeks on both sides of school holiday periods, when students often miss class. Tell them that teachers often feel they cannot move instruction forward because if they do, so many students have to catch up on work when they finally return to school. A week's extra vacation before and after school holidays adds up to 26 weeks of lost instruction over a student's K–12 experience. When the same problem occurs around spring break, a student might miss up to 52 weeks of instruction time. By the time he or she should be graduating from high school, a student who expects to be a senior might actually be a junior because of high rates of absenteeism around vacation times.

Help students develop healthy habits. Provide tips to students and families on how to develop healthy habits that can improve attendance and success in school. For example, provide tips on improving students' sleeping habits.

> *Sleep is important. Teenagers need 8½ to 9½ hours of sleep every night. Consider the following tips to help your teenager get the sleep he or she needs to be successful:*
>
> - *Minimize activities that involve bright lights, excitement, or stress such as exercise, video games, cell phones and television in the hour before bedtime.*

- *Restrict cell phones and other electronics from the student's bedroom during sleeping hours. Parents might charge all electronics in their room at night.*

Work with families and the community to remove barriers to attendance. Conduct health and hygiene campaigns. Provide information to families about reducing asthma triggers in the home. Emphasize hand washing to reduce the spread of illness, especially during cold and flu season. You might work with community and state agencies to provide preventive health care for students and to help families navigate through the health-care system.

When many families have problems with early-morning schedules, you can provide before-school supervision and breakfast for students at school. Where neighborhood violence or heavy traffic is a problem for students who walk to school, consider creating a walking school bus. Staff members or parent volunteers walk with groups of students to school.

When certain families, cultural groups, or communities do not see the value of school, you will need to design a careful and creative approach to improving the perception of school and demonstrating the value of regular attendance. This work involves getting input from families on what they need from the school and creating meaningful partnerships with families, cultural leaders, and community members and organizations.

Example: Parent attendance initiative in Shungnak, Alaska. Shungnak School, in the Northwest Arctic Borough School District of Alaska, serves about 75 students in grades pre-K through 12. Roughly 94% of the students are Alaskan Native. The absenteeism rate was very high, in part because a cultural resistance to school had developed over time. Education was not valued, and families even viewed school as threatening because educated students were more likely to leave home after graduation and not return.

The principal of the school, Roger Franklin, recognized that although many issues needed to be addressed, community resistance to school was the first step. He started a 90% parent attendance initiative. Rather than increasing awareness of the importance of school and trying to infuse families with information about why students need to be at school, he decided to first get the parents involved with the school. The initial goal was that for every student, at least one adult family member would visit the school for 5 minutes or more each week. The adult's name was posted on a display board when he or she visited the school (see Figure 4j).

Figure 4j *The 90% Parent Attendance display at Shungnak School, Shungnak, Alaska*

Here's how Shungnak School went about engaging parents, in Roger Franklin's words:

The expectation was to get parents to fully understand the expression "we are a family"—meaning the village, school, and everyone that lives in Shungnak. All 250 people are responsible and accountable for one another. Our effort started with many home visits and listening to the parents' struggles on all levels. Many of them just wanted to know how the school was going to help.

To improve the absenteeism, we had to first look at improving the culture's perception of education and get the people to believe in a system, and we had to also understand the value of school from an Alaska Native standpoint.

The initiative was rolled out using several different media:

- *PSA announcements over the VHF (radio) several times a day*
- *Announcements at teacher-parent conferences and workshops during cultural events*
- *Through word of mouth at the post office, Native Store, airstrip, and local government organizations.*

We also spread the news while salmon fishing, ice fishing, moose and caribou hunting, and setting traps; as we enjoyed coffee with the parents and elders at the coffee house; at family homes eating moose and caribou soup; at school sporting events; and at women's sewing night.

How has Shungnak's parent attendance initiative affected attendance? The school reports the following benefits:

- Parents take pride in and responsibility for seeing their children begin to excel in school.

- Visiting the school has become a friendly competition among parents. When parents notice that other parents' names aren't posted on the 90% Parent Attendance board, they take it upon themselves to call and remind the absent parents to visit their children's classrooms for 5 minutes that week.

- Some parents stay at school longer than 5 minutes—they volunteer for lunch duty or other activities.

- The parents' presence has helped to develop a more positive school climate.

- The school reports a marked improvement in attendance for all students.

What Shungnak did so right in their initiative was get the whole community on board. Do the same with your attendance efforts; connect with local businesses, law enforcement, medical and dental offices, and so on. Enlist their help—doctors and dentists can ask families to make appointments during after-school hours; businesses can refuse service to students during hours when students should be in school. Businesses might be willing to help reinforce good attendance by offering reduced-cost insurance to school-aged drivers who have regular attendance or coupons for services and goods to students with regular attendance.

Connect early with students and families when problems are indicated. Whenever you contact families about attendance problems, ensure that school staff are welcoming and supportive. Help families identify barriers that prevent their students from getting to school, and offer support in every way possible. Provide positive feedback for improvements in student attendance, and refer the student to your individual student support and intervention process if the problem becomes chronic. It's important to be increasingly direct with the family and student as the problem persists, so include truancy officers, court, and so on in the intervention.

Task 4 Action Steps & Evidence of Implementation

Action Steps	Evidence of Implementation
1. List the schoolwide strategies that may be useful for your school, especially those that address the trends and causes of absenteeism suggested by your attendance data. 2. Decide which strategies to implement. You may decide to propose some or all of your identified strategies to staff, and then decide collectively whether to implement them. 3. For the strategies that the team, task force, or your school staff choose to implement, identify the steps needed to launch and maintain the strategy. Identify who will be responsible for each step and who will monitor the implementation.	Foundations Process: Attendance Initiatives, Planning Calendar Final procedures should be documented in Foundations Archive: Attendance Initiatives

School Connectedness: Meeting Basic Human Needs

DOCUMENTS*

- Analysis of Student Needs Worksheet (C-07)
- Summary of Student Needs (C-08)

* All documents listed are available on the CD. Other documents that are not shown in this presentation are also available on the CD (see Appendix C for a complete list).

INTRODUCTION

All people have basic human needs. Theorists and psychologists have defined the concept of basic needs in a variety of ways. We think the following eight basic needs are essential for all children and adolescents to be successful in educational settings. This particular formulation was developed by the authors of the *Administrator's Desk Reference of Behavior Management* (Sprick, Howard, Wise, Marcum, & Haykin, 1998), based on their collective experiences as counselors, teachers, and administrators.

- Acknowledgment
- Recognition
- Attention
- Belonging
- Purpose
- Competence
- Nurturing
- Stimulation/Change

Students whose basic needs are not being met are much more likely to behave inappropriately and appear unmotivated. Think about the functional behavior assessment that you might conduct for a student who misbehaves chronically. The assessment basically asks: What is the student trying to obtain (attention, for example) or avoid (schoolwork, for example) by misbehaving? In other words, what basic human need is the student not getting enough of? By meeting the needs of students proactively—providing schoolwide and Tier 2 programs and strategies that provide the eight basic human needs—you can reduce the probability that students will misbehave so chronically that you have to analyze the function of the misbehavior.

> " *Students whose basic needs are not being met are much more likely to behave inappropriately and appear unmotivated.* "

Schools play an important role in meeting the basic needs of their students. The unfortunate reality is that many students get only some of their basic needs met at home, and some students get *none* of their basic needs met at home. You can improve how well your school meets the basic needs of students by:

- Carefully analyzing the degree to which students' basic needs are being met by current school programs and practices.

- Modifying current programs and practices.

- Identifying and implementing new programs and practices to address unmet student needs.

Increasing evidence from a variety of perspectives suggests that students who are emotionally connected to school and who have meaningful relationships with staff are more likely to succeed in school and in all aspects of life. Research in the fields of mental health, school effectiveness, school connectedness, resiliency, dropout prevention, and even public health points to the importance of students' connection to their school.

As you read through the information about basic needs, we encourage you to think about the entire range of students under your care—talented, challenged, and average students. Sometimes so much attention is paid to the chronic problem students and the high-achieving students that the needs of the average students are overlooked. In Task 2, we suggest some activities that will help you determine how to help *all* students get their basic human needs met—and by so doing, you will increase the probability that students will be motivated and well-behaved.

Task 1: Understand Students' Basic Needs defines and explains the eight basic needs.

Task 2: Analyze Whether All Students' Needs Are Being Met describes the analytical process that can help you determine whether to modify current programs, develop new programs, or implement staff training on existing programs.

As your team embarks on this portion of the *Foundations* process, remind your staff that the school needs to be a great place for *all* students. The analytical processes within this and the next presentation are designed to ensure that every staff member can honestly say, "This school would be a productive, joyous, and positive place for my own children (or grandchildren, nieces, or nephews)."

TASK 1

Understand students' basic needs

Understanding these eight basic human needs will help you to determine whether staff members are doing everything possible to meet their students' needs. As you read through these descriptions, think of some particular students and how you and the school are (or are not) meeting their individual needs.

Acknowledgment

Acknowledgment is positive, noncontingent attention that staff members provide to students. The attention is not based on anything—either good or bad—that the students have done, and it demonstrates to students that the staff value them as fellow human beings, with no strings attached.

You can meet students' need for acknowledgment at school by:

- Smiling at students.
- Nodding to students.
- Greeting students by name.
- Showing interest in students by asking about their hobbies or activities they participate in.
- Offering students assistance.
- Greeting students after an absence so they know they were missed.

Every staff member should try to give noncontingent acknowledgment to students frequently. These interactions can be simple and brief. They can be made as you walk down the hallway. They can even be silent. They communicate to students that you notice them, that you are interested in who they are, and that they are important members of the student body. Everything you do in school should say to students, "We value you as a person—unconditionally." That's the concept of acknowledgment.

*E*xample From the Field

On the first day of my son's sophomore year of high school, I asked him how the day went. He said, "I think this is going to be a really good year. Every teacher made a point of saying, 'If you ever need help in this class, here's when and how you can contact me to get that help.'" From day one, the teachers in this school expressed to students that they were available and willing to help any student, no strings attached.

—R.S.

Recognition

Recognition is positive, *contingent* attention that staff members provide to students—the attention is based on something the students have done. Anytime a student has accomplished something, you can use it as an opportunity to provide recognition to the student. Keep in mind that sometimes average students don't get enough recognition because staff tend to focus on recognizing the accomplishments of low and high achievers.

 Sometimes average students don't get enough recognition because staff tend to focus on recognizing the small but important steps of low achievers and the great leaps of high achievers."

Students value recognition from school staff, but be careful not to make a big deal out of something that isn't. Students know when you're not genuine in your praise, and being praised inappropriately can be embarrassing and confusing (imagine how an average fifth grader might feel when she is praised for tying her shoes correctly). Also be cautious about publicly recognizing students because you might embarrass them in front of their peers. Older students especially will probably prefer subtle types of recognition for most accomplishments.

You can meet students' need for recognition at school by:

- Praising students.
- Putting a positive note on students' assignments or papers.
- Awarding certificates.
- Providing intermittent rewards or celebrations.
- Assigning high grades.
- Calling students' parents or family members.
- Giving points (in an established point system).
- Awarding diplomas.

Attention

By *attention*, we mean all attention (positive and corrective, contingent and noncontingent) that students receive, including acknowledgment and recognition as well as attention paid to student misbehavior.

Keep in mind the following considerations about attention:

- Different students need attention at different levels—some crave attention, others seem to avoid it.

- Students who are not getting their attention needs met through acknowledgment and recognition may misbehave to get enough attention.

- The magnitude of attention students receive rarely affects the frequency of attention that students need.

The last point might require a little more explanation. Let's say a student, Zac, had a great hour after lunch and as a reward, the teacher had the whole class applaud him and handed out snacks to everyone. But Zac needs attention every 15 minutes. If he doesn't get it, he tends to misbehave to make the teacher pay attention to him. If the teacher has to have a class party every 15 minutes to fulfill Zac's attention needs, the students are not going to learn much! Instead, the teacher should give frequent, but very brief, attention.

 No more fiendish punishment could be devised, were such a thing physically possible, than that one could be turned loose in society and remain absolutely unnoticed by all the members thereof."

WILLIAM JAMES (1842–1910), American philosopher, psychologist, and physician, from his 1890 book *The Principles of Psychology.*

Belonging

Belonging is the sense students have of being part of something bigger than themselves. A sense of belonging is fundamental to good mental and social health. Most adults meet the need to belong through family, church, clubs, social groups, and employment.

For most young people, school is a major means of fulfilling this need. Every student should feel a connection to and a sense of pride in being part of his or her school. If students feel alienated in their school setting because of peer rejection, bullying, shyness, poor social skills, changing schools frequently, or even parents who relate negatively to the school, they are likely to be less motivated to try at school. Some may become overtly antagonistic. And some, unfortunately, may even turn to gangs in a desperate attempt to belong somewhere.

You need to consider whether all of your students feel as if they are a valued part of the school. If you have high-performing students who are ostracized as geeks and nerds, lower-performing students who feel categorized as dummies, chronically misbehaving students who constantly act as if they are at war with the school, or students who seem to be outcasts, you need to do something to help all students feel they belong and are respected at school.

School spirit, average daily attendance, and numbers of students chronically absent provide rough measures of how well a school is meeting its students' need to belong.

Purpose

Purpose is the sense of intention or meaning that gives direction and coherence to students' daily actions. Every student needs to know that there is some purpose to working hard, to behaving in ways that do not interfere with the learning of others, and to contributing something of themselves to the community called school. Without a sense of purpose, students' behavior may be guided by immediate gratification (getting attention through misbehavior) rather than by goal-oriented choices and actions. While acknowledgment and nurturing needs can be met with noncontingent attention, meeting the need for purpose involves an effort to ensure that all students are goal directed and understand that the work they do is important—to themselves, to their teacher, and to the entire school community.

You can meet students' need for purpose at school by:

- Using well-designed and meaningful activities and assignments.
- Taking the time to clarify the purpose of activities and assignments so that students are less likely to consider them simply busy work.

 Striving, the usual organizer of most activity, when lost, leaves the person unorganized and unintegrated."

ABRAHAM MASLOW (1908–1970), American psychologist best known for creating Maslow's hierarchy of needs, from his 1962 book *Perceiving, Behaving, Becoming: Lessons Learned.*

Also ensure that your school's mission statement identifies the purpose of the school for students, parents, and staff members. If you assume that school is to students what jobs are to adults, then it is up to staff to help children engage in meaningful "careers"—not just endure boring menial work. This includes making sure students (justifiably) view assignments as important steps in gaining important skills rather than simply as busywork. For middle and high school students, building a sense of purpose may involve participation in community service that will help them begin to understand the purpose and benefits of altruism.

Competence

Competence is the sense students have of being able to do something well. Students, like most people, tend to engage in activities in which they are competent and avoid activities in which they are not (or are less) competent. Think of a sport or hobby that you are not good at—do you actively participate in it, or do you avoid it? You probably avoid it. Yet, every day, teachers must force some students to engage in tasks the students are not good at. The math teacher needs to teach math to every student in class, even though some students would prefer to avoid it.

You can meet students' need for competence at school primarily by ensuring that all students succeed academically. A student who is not (or does not perceive herself to be) competent at academic tasks may appear unmotivated. Here's where an important formula comes into play:

Expectancy x Value = Motivation

The Expectancy times Value theory of motivation was first used by Norman Feather in 1982 to explain a person's motivation on any given task.

> *Expectancy* = the degree to which a person expects to be successful at a task

> *Value* = the degree to which an individual values the rewards that accompany being successful at a task

The power of this theory is its recognition that a person's level of motivation on any given task is a product of both how much the person wants the rewards that accompany success and how much the person expects to be successful.

Let's say that expectancy and value are each gauged on a scale of 0 to 10, with 0 representing the lowest possible rate and 10 representing the highest possible rate. When a value rate and an expectancy rate for any given task are multiplied together, they yield a number between 0 and 100, which represents the percentage of motivation a person has for that task. A key implication of the theory is that if the rate for either expectancy or value is zero, the rate of the other factor won't matter—the resulting motivation rate will always be zero (see the table below).

Expectancy Rate	*x Value Rate*	*= Motivation*
10	× 10	= 100
10	× 0	= 0
0	× 10	= 0

Notice that the expectancy factor is just as important as the value factor in determining motivation. Many teachers, when trying to ascertain why a student appears unmotivated to behave responsibly or complete assignments, ascribe the lack of motivation to issues that involve only the value component of the formula. But if the student does not believe that he can succeed at behaving responsibly or completing assignments (he has a low expectancy rate), his motivation will also be low. Note that the rates for both expectancy and value are determined by what the student believes, not what you, the teacher, believe.

So do everything you can to structure for success, both behaviorally and academically. Jere Brophy, who was a great researcher in the education field, said, "The simplest way to ensure that students expect success is to make sure that they achieve it consistently" (Wentzel & Brophy, 2013, p. 153).

 The simplest way to ensure that students expect success is to make sure that they achieve it consistently."

Here's just one example of how to structure for competence: Let's say you are assigning an academic task, and you know that half of your students will struggle with it. Don't say, "Work on this assignment and we'll correct it in 20 minutes." Instead, say, "We'll do the first half of this assignment together." Conducting structured, guided practice with the class before you expect students to work on their own increases the success students experience. By setting students up for success, you are increasing their expectancy of success on the part of the assignment they will work on independently. All efforts to differentiate instruction are rooted in the attempt to help every student experience competence with the objectives being taught.

Guidelines for Success can also be used to increase students' expectancy of their own success. Tell students, "If you do these things (be responsible, respect others, and so on), you will be successful in this school."

Nurturing

The need for *nurturing* is the need students have for an ongoing sense of assurance that they are loved unconditionally—ideally by their family and in their home. Nurturing is not a single event, but occurs over the course of a person's life.

Unfortunately, some students are not nurtured by their families. Students who do not receive consistent nurturing may have behavior problems. Sometimes these problems appear to be random, unrelated to any discernible triggers or functions at school. Schools cannot fully compensate for a lack of family nurturing, but schools can make an effort to create nurturing relationships within the school for the students who need them. You can also work with social agencies and community groups to build and support nurturing relationships in your community's homes and neighborhoods.

You probably know or have heard of people who had horrendous childhoods marked by abuse, neglect, or parents with alcohol or drug problems, yet these people managed to grow into relatively well-adjusted, successful, happy adults. Research on people with these types of backgrounds is often referred to as the *resiliency literature*. When researchers ask these people how they were so resilient under such circumstances, the most common answer is that, as children, they relied on a family member who never gave up on them. And what is the second most common answer? "I had a *teacher* who believed in me, who stuck by me, who never gave up on me." Even though schools can't completely make up for a lack of nurturing in the home, don't underestimate the importance of the relationships you make with students. You can make a difference.

Stimulation and Change

Students need variety that fosters excitement and enthusiasm—they need *stimulation* and *change*. All of us need some variety in our school, work, and home activities to maintain interest in what we do.

For school to be a place where students are excited about what they are doing, enthusiastic about growing, and interested in learning more about life and the world they live in, their classes must be stimulating. If classes are dull and predictable, even the best system of encouragement and motivation is unlikely to foster excitement, enthusiasm, or interest.

Sometimes well-intentioned efforts fall flat due to lack of variety. For example, some schools hold monthly award assemblies to provide recognition to students. However, if this ritual becomes just a reading of names followed by applause, by the second or third repetition it will probably not serve the desired function—to motivate *all* students to strive harder. These assemblies need to be fun and entertaining so that everyone continues to pay attention and look forward to the next one.

You can meet students' need for stimulation and change at school by:

- Using effective instructional practices that include several different formats and content.

- Paying attention to and changing positive reward programs to keep them from becoming boring (and therefore less effective) over time.

- Not allowing school rituals and traditions to become dull and routine.

In Task 2, you will conduct an analysis of the degree to which your school is meeting the needs of all students. To prepare for this, discuss with the team (or the entire staff) whether the proposed list of eight basic needs or an alternative construct will work best as a vehicle to make your school a great place for all students.

In addition, make a list of all the positive programs and participation opportunities (clubs, sports, and so on) that students can access in your school.

Task 1 Action Steps & Evidence of Implementation

Action Steps	Evidence of Implementation
1. Discuss whether the proposed list of eight basic needs or an alternative construct will work best as a vehicle to make your school a great place for all students.	Foundations Process: Meeting Minutes, Students' Basic Needs
2. Create a list of all the positive programs and participation opportunities available at your school.	
3. For each program and opportunity, identify the basic needs it is designed to meet.	

TASK 2

Analyze whether all students' needs are being met

All schools should determine how well they are meeting the basic needs of *all* students, whether the students are high achievers, average, at risk, or somewhere in between. Franklin D. Roosevelt said, "I think we consider too much the good luck of the early bird and not enough the bad luck of the early worm." What that means for schools is that often programs are created to meet the needs of certain groups of students, and it's easy to think that your job is done once those programs are in place. For example, an active sports program can meet the need for belonging for some students. But if a significant number of students are not participating because they aren't interested or talented in sports, there are gaps that need to be filled. The needs of *all* students haven't been addressed.

Review the characteristics of the four categories of students.

To determine whether your school is meeting the needs of all students, you will consider the following four types of students.

Outstanding students. Most schools do a great job of meeting all the needs of outstanding students. These students are academically, socially, artistically, or athletically talented (or talented in several areas). Staff enjoy interacting with them, and students respect them. Most schools have at least a few of these shining stars. They tend to get lots of recognition for their achievements and lots of acknowledgment and attention because they are well known and well liked. Their competence is continually affirmed by their accomplishments.

Because of their success in academics, athletics, or the arts and their ease in social situations, these students usually have a good sense of purpose and belonging in the school. They might or might not receive nurturing in their homes, but it's likely they do given all the strengths they convey. The achievements of outstanding students also tend to bring variety to their daily activities—the more students are capable of doing, the more teachers and coaches allow and encourage them to do.

Students who are good athletes but average in other aspects of school deserve some extra thought. Because of the students' successes in sports, school staff tend to think that all of these students' needs are being met. But you have all heard stories of students who sailed through middle and high school because they were athletic stars only to find they weren't good enough to make college or pro teams. When sports are no longer a significant part of their lives, these students might feel adrift, with no other skills or interests to meet their needs for belonging, recognition, attention, purpose, and competence.

Average students. Average students can be easy to overlook. They have no serious behavior or academic problems, but they also do not excel in academics, the arts, athletics, or socially. Staff members often do not provide recognition and acknowledgment because these students are not very noticeable. The faculty sometimes equates average with inadequate, but it's important to remember that an academically average student might need to work hard to get a C. A grade of C can mean competence, so we should recognize that competence.

Actively at-risk students. Usually quite visible, actively at-risk students have perceptible behavior issues, ranging from the class clown who is always seeking attention to the angry, hostile student who acts out frequently. They might get a lot of attention from staff and peers for their misbehavior. In schools that have been working on positive behavior support for troubled kids, these at-risk students can also get frequent positive recognition for their small steps toward success.

As you fill out the Analysis of Student Needs Worksheet (Figure 5a on the next page) described below, ask this question: Are these students getting their needs for purpose, competence, and belonging met by being successful or by playing the role of class clown, tough guy, or bully? If they're getting those needs met in destructive ways, recognize that and place minus signs in the categories where they belong. Your goal is to help those students meet their basic needs in productive ways.

Passively at-risk students. Passively at-risk students seem to be unmotivated to even try to get their needs met. They are not as recognizably at risk as the actively at-risk students. Instead of acting out, they just *do nothing*—they don't turn in homework, don't participate in class or extracurricular activities, don't talk to teachers, and might not even attend school every day. These students require the greatest effort, creativity, and skill level from staff to try to ensure that their needs are being met.

Complete the Analysis of Student Needs Worksheet.

We suggest using a structured evaluation form to analyze how well your school is meeting the basic needs of students. Figure 5a on the next page shows the Analysis of Student Needs Worksheet (Form C-07 on the Module C CD). On this worksheet, each team member evaluates individual students who represent outstanding, average, and at-risk students.

STEP 1. Give each member of the team a copy of the worksheet. Team members should work independently on individual worksheets.

Figure 5a   *Analysis of Student Needs Worksheet (C-07)*

Foundations: A Proactive and Positive Behavior Support System

Analysis of Student Needs Worksheet

Directions:

1. Identify and write the name of one student (male or female) who is representative of each group. (Each team member completes a separate form.)
2. In the Other column, include any student who doesn't exactly fit the other defined categories, but is a student that you want to reflect on: How well does this school meet this student's basic needs?
3. Work down each column and address how well the school is meeting the student's needs. Mark a plus sign (+) for meeting, a minus sign (–) for not meeting, and a question mark (?) if you are not sure.

Basic Need	Category of Student				
	Outstanding (academically, athletically, socially) Name: _____	Average (academically, athletically, socially) Name: _____	Passively At Risk Name: _____	Actively At Risk Name: _____	Other Name: _____
Acknowledgment Positive, noncontingent attention					
Recognition Positive, contingent attention					
Attention All attention (positive and negative)					
Belonging Sense of being part of something bigger than self					
Purpose Sense of meaning that gives direction to daily actions					
Competence Sense of being able to do something well					
Nurturing Ongoing sense of assurance that student is loved and will be taken care of					
Stimulation/Change The variety in a student's activities that fosters excitement and enthusiasm					

This form can be printed from the Module C CD.

STEP 2. In the top row, have team members identify and write in the name of one student (male or female) who is representative of each group of students.

Characteristics of the students in each group are described above.

- Outstanding Student
- Average Student
- Actively At-Risk Student
- Passively At-Risk Student
- Other Student

For the Other Student column, encourage team members to include students who don't exactly fit into the other defined categories so that they can reflect on how well the school meets the basic needs of those students.

STEP 3. Have team members look at the leftmost column and review the basic needs:

- *Acknowledgment:* Positive attention that is not based on any specific thing students have done (noncontingent)

- *Recognition:* Positive attention based on something students have done (contingent)

- *Attention:* All attention that students receive, both positive and corrective

- *Belonging:* Sense students have of being part of something bigger than themselves

- *Purpose:* Sense of intention or meaning that gives coherence and direction to students' daily activities

- *Competence:* Sense of being able to do something well

- *Nurturing:* Ongoing sense of assurance that students are loved unconditionally and will be taken care of

- *Stimulation/Change:* Variety in activities that fosters excitement and enthusiasm

STEP 4. Beginning with the Outstanding Student column, team members should work down each column and identify the degree to which the school is meeting each basic need for each particular student.

Team members should mark:

- A plus sign (+) if the school is meeting the basic need of the student

- A minus sign (–) if the school is not meeting the basic need of the student

- A question mark (?) if they are unsure about whether the school is meeting the basic need of the student

STEP 5. After each team member completes a worksheet independently, have the team, as a group, compile and analyze all the worksheets.

Use the Summary of Student Needs Worksheet (Form C-08 shown in Figure 5b on the next page) for this task. Look for patterns of unmet student needs. For example, in the Average Student column, maybe only one or two basic needs consistently earn plus signs. Perhaps one need, let's say Purpose, is met across all student groups, and another, Acknowledgment, is not met for any student group.

STEP 6. Discuss how your school can address any unmet student needs.

Figure 5b *Summary of Student Needs (C-08)*

Foundations: A Proactive and Positive Behavior Support System

Summary of Student Needs Worksheet

Directions:

1. Compile the individual ratings by team members on the Analysis of Student Needs Worksheet (C-07) and look for patterns of plus (+) and (−) signs for each category of students. Consider any question mark (?) as a minus sign (−).
2. Identify any holes and gaps in your programs, services, and activities for meeting the needs of all students.

Basic Need	Category of Student				
	Outstanding (academically, athletically, socially)	Average (academically, athletically, socially)	Passively At Risk	Actively At Risk	Other
Acknowledgment Positive, noncontingent attention					
Recognition Positive, contingent attention					
Attention All attention (positive and negative)					
Belonging Sense of being part of something bigger than self					
Purpose Sense of meaning that gives direction to daily actions					
Competence Sense of being able to do something well					
Nurturing Ongoing sense of assurance that student is loved and will be taken care of					
Stimulation/Change The variety in a student's activities that fosters excitement and enthusiasm					

 This form can be printed from the Module C CD.

Review the list of current programs and participation opportunities that you compiled in Task 1, Action Step 2. Determine whether you can use any of your school's current programs and opportunities to fill in the gaps. Brainstorm ways to modify your existing programs to more effectively meet basic student needs.

Identify new programs and opportunities you might develop to help meet student needs. Suggestions are provided in Module C, Presentation 6.

Provide staff training if the unmet needs stem from the staff's lack of understanding about how to appropriately provide attention and foster the senses of competence, purpose, belonging, and so on. For example, when staff are trained in ratios of positive interactions (see Module C, Presentation 3), they can more easily provide acknowledgment, recognition, and attention. Staff who learn how to emulate an inspiring basketball coach can better help students attain purpose, competence, and belonging. To help teachers expand their repertoire of ways to provide positive recognition, have them as a group brainstorm all the different strategies they use to recognize hard work and effort. This can also help provide stimulation and change.

Assess student connectedness with adults and school activities.

Use the following strategy to assess connectedness. It is particularly useful for secondary schools.

1. Make student rosters for each grade level with a spreadsheet program such as Excel. Add two columns—Conversation and School-Based Activity—to the right of the list of names (see Figure 5c below for an example of a connectedness assessment spreadsheet created in Excel).

2. Give each staff member a copy of the rosters along with these instructions:
   a. Consider each student individually.
   b. Initial the Conversation column if you know the student well enough to have a conversation that is deeper than you would have with a complete stranger—that is, you know something about the student's interests, goals, or activities.
   c. If the student is in a school club, sport, musical group, or other activity outside the classroom that you coach or lead, write it in the School-Based Activity column.
   d. If your school is large enough that the soccer team, for example, has two coaches, only one of the adult coaches should complete the School-Based Activity column.

Figure 5c   *Example of a student connectedness assessment sheet*

	A	B	C
1	**Staff member:** Mr. Chang		
2	**Grade 8 Students**	**Conversation**	**School-Based Activity**
3	Bloom, Stuart	TC	
4	Cooper, Mary		
5	Cooper, Sheldon		Physics Club
6	Fowler, Amy Farrah		
7	Hofstadter, Beverly		
8	Hofstadter, Leonard	TC	Physics Club
9	Johnson, Penny		
10	Koothrappali, Raj		
11	Kripke, Barry		
12	Rostenkowski, Bernadette	TC	
13	Wheaton, Wil		
14	Wolowitz, Howard	TC	

Compile the data and create two separate charts for each grade level, one for Conversation and one for School-Based Activity. Sort the students from most to least conversations and activities. See Figure 5d for examples of each chart, created in an Excel worksheet. Be sure to keep this information confidential.

A horizontal bar graph illustrates the stark contrast between students who have 25 adults who know them well enough to have a conversation and students who have none. Administering one or both of these surveys is a powerful way to determine whether staff need to be more attentive to the needs of individual students, create broader ranges of extracurricular activities, or encourage even the least-connected students to find an activity of interest.

Figure 5d   *Examples of school connectedness data for (a) conversation and (b) school-based activity*

	A	B
1	**Grade 8 Students**	**Conversation***
2	Johnson, Penny	26
3	Hofstadter, Leonard	25
4	Bloom, Stuart	22
88	Fowler, Amy Farrah	13
89	Rostenkowski, Bernadette	12
90	Wolowitz, Howard	10
135	Wheaton, Wil	7
136	Hofstadter, Beverly	6
137	Cooper, Mary	5
198	Cooper, Sheldon	3
199	Kripke, Barry	2
200	Koothrappali, Raj	0
		*Number of staff members who know the student well enough to converse with him or her

(a) Conversation data and graph

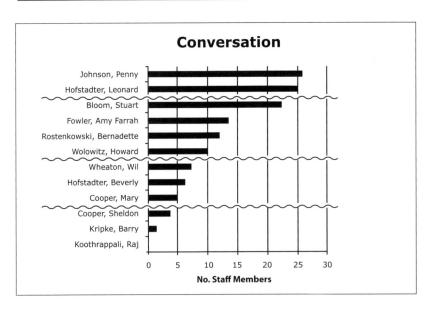

Conversation

No. Staff Members

Module C: Conscious Construction of an Inviting School Climate

Figure 5d (continued)

	A	B
1	**Grade 8 Students**	**School-Based Activity***
2	Johnson, Penny	5
3	Wolowitz, Howard	4
4	Bloom, Stuart	3
5	Wheaton, Wil	3
6	Cooper, Sheldon	3
110	Hofstadter, Leonard	2
111	Fowler, Amy Farrah	2
112	Rostenkowski, Bernadette	2
113	Kripke, Barry	2
180	Hofstadter, Beverly	1
181	Cooper, Mary	1
200	Koothrappali, Raj	0
		*Number of activities the student is involved in

(b) School-based activity data and graph

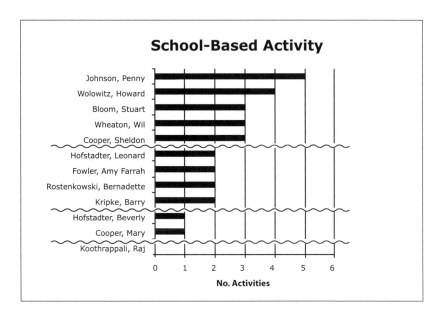

Task 2 Action Steps & Evidence of Implementation

Action Steps	Evidence of Implementation
1. Have each team member complete the Analysis of Student Needs Worksheet (Form C-07 on the CD).	Foundations Process: Meeting Minutes, Students' Basic Needs
2. Have the team compile and analyze all the worksheets together using the Summary of Student Needs (Form C-08 on the CD). Look for patterns of unmet student needs.	
3. Consider conducting the student connectedness assessment activity.	
4. Discuss how your school can address any unmet student needs. • Determine whether any of your school's current programs and procedures can be used, and brainstorm ways to modify them to be more effective. • Identify new procedures and programs you might develop to help meet student needs. Suggestions are provided in Module C, Presentation 6.	

Programs and Strategies for Meeting Needs

DOCUMENTS*

- Congratulations postcard (C-09)
- CARE Tickets and Posters (C-11a, b)
- Responsible Student Behavior (RSB) Postcard (C-10)
- Falcon Fan Club invitation and forms (C-22)
- Principal's Award nomination form (C-12)

* All documents listed are available on the CD.

INTRODUCTION

All people have basic human needs. In the previous presentation, we explained the following eight basic needs that are essential for all children and adolescents in educational settings:

- Acknowledgment
- Recognition
- Attention
- Belonging
- Purpose
- Competence
- Nurturing
- Stimulation/Change

Students whose basic needs are not being met are much more likely to behave inappropriately and lack motivation. Unfortunately, many students do not get all or even some of their basic needs met at home. It has become the school's obligation to build programs to help meet students' needs.

In Presentation 5, you learned how to analyze the degree to which students' basic needs are being met by current school programs and procedures. You also discussed, as a team, how you might address any unmet student needs by modifying current programs and procedures and by identifying and implementing new ones.

In this presentation, we suggest some programs and procedures you can implement to meet students' basic needs. Think of our suggestions as a menu from which you can pick and choose programs that might help to meet the needs of your students.

Task 1: Consider Support Programs for K–12 Students describes the following programs:

- Staff Attention
- Special Attention for Targeted Students
- Positive Reports to Parents
- Mentorship
- Lottery System (Golden Tickets)
- Connections

Task 2: Consider Support Programs for Elementary Students describes the following programs for students in grades K–6:

- Goal Achieved Book
- CARE
- Student of the Week

- Lunch With the Principal
- Responsible Student Behavior Plan
- Falcon Fan Club
- Classwide Goal of the Month
- Meaningful Work

Task 3: Consider Support Programs for Secondary Students describes programs for students in grades 6–12:

- Leadership Class
- Principal's Award
- Honor Roll
- Grades
- Attendance or Punctuality Letter
- Problem-Solving Task Force

The matrix in Table 6a lists the programs we discuss in this presentation and the basic student needs they can help meet.

Table 6a   *Programs That Meet the Basic Needs of Students*

Program	Acknowledgment	Recognition	Attention	Belonging	Purpose	Competence	Nurturing	Stimulation/Change
Grades K–12								
Staff Attention	●	●	●	●		●	●	
Special Attention for Targeted Students	●	●	●	●		●	●	
Positive Reports to Parents	●	●	●		●	●		
Mentorship	●		●	●			●	●
Lottery System (Golden Tickets)		●	●		●			
Connections		●	●	●		●		
Grades K–6								
Goal Achieved Book		●	●	●	●			●
CARE		●	●	●	●			●
Student of the Week	●		●	●				●
Lunch With the Principal	●		●	●	●			●
Responsible Student Behavior Plan		●	●		●			
Falcon Fan Club		●	●	●		●		
Classwide Goal of the Month				●	●			●
Meaningful Work	●	●	●	●	●	●	●	●
Grades 6–12								
Leadership Class	●	●	●	●	●	●	●	●
Principal's Award		●	●	●	●	●		
Honor Roll		●		●	●	●		
Grades		●				●		
Attendance or Punctuality Letter		●			●			
Problem-Solving Task Force				●	●			●

TASK 1

Consider support programs for K–12 students

In this task, we suggest six programs that can help you meet the needs of students in kindergarten through 12th grade.

- Staff Attention
- Special Attention for Targeted Students
- Positive Reports to Parents
- Mentorship
- Lottery system
- Connections

Staff Attention

This strategy is probably the most important of those in this task, and it exemplifies a theme that runs throughout all the *Foundations* modules: Students can benefit greatly from increased positive attention from adults. In the schools we've worked with, increasing positive interactions has successfully reduced misbehavior at the elementary, middle, and high school levels. We discuss this strategy in great detail in Module C, Presentation 3. The following is a relatively brief description of the basic concept.

Adults in the school simply initiate interactions by, for example, greeting students by name, conversing with them, making eye contact, smiling at them, and overtly praising them. Staff interactions with students tend to be more corrective than positive. It can be easy to fall into a pattern of negativity because students must be corrected if they are to learn, and positive interactions sometimes don't seem as necessary. However, positive interactions should be an important part of the school philosophy and staff beliefs for these reasons:

- Some students are starved for attention, and they misbehave to gain that attention. If these students are provided attention in positive ways—even brief greetings from adults can suffice—their misbehavior will decrease.

- When the adults in a school pay more attention to negative behavior than positive, they inadvertently send the message that they don't notice and don't have time for students who work hard and behave appropriately.

Your goal is to provide at least three positive interactions with each student for every one corrective interaction. But bear in mind that the 3:1 ratio may—and should—vary depending on your students' stage of learning. In the early stages of learning anything new, students can experience frustration and failure. During this time, you should strive for a much higher ratio—10 or even 15 to 1 when students are frustrated or having difficulty. When students are highly skilled, proficient, and self-motivated, 3:1 or less can be enough.

 Your goal is to provide at least three positive interactions with each student for every one corrective interaction."

You probably have some situations in your school where students don't always need a high positive to corrective ratio. Students on a high school football team, for example, usually compete for places on the team, are motivated, and voluntarily attend practice. They know that to win the next game, the coach has to tell them what they are doing wrong and how to correct it. Even these students, however, can benefit from high ratios of interactions when they are working on a new skill or a new play.

*E*xample From the Field

> When my daughter began studying flute at the university level, I noticed that her teacher gave her positive to corrective feedback at about an 8:1 ratio. As she progressed, the ratio fell to about one positive to three correctives. This ratio can work with students who are self-motivated and skilled. These students can reinforce themselves and appreciate detailed criticism because they understand that it helps them to improve. —R.S.

Teachers who structure their classrooms appropriately are constantly challenging their students, so the students are continually teetering on the edge of frustration and failure. Frequent positive feedback at much higher levels than corrective feedback can keep students from falling over that edge.

How do you do it?

Make a conscious effort to take every opportunity to interact with individual students in all school environments. Greet students in the halls. Talk to students in the cafeteria as they are standing in line. Before class begins, ask individual students about their interests. Look for opportunities to provide students with positive feedback about their academic and behavioral progress. When praising students, provide specific information about the behaviors that are contributing to their successes. "Alicia, you have been very responsible about remembering your homework on the day it is due." "Tyrone, I noticed that you picked up litter in the hall. As custodian, I really appreciate your help and your pride in how our school looks." Nonverbal communication such as a thumbs-up, a smile, and a nod of acknowledgment also count as positive interactions when they are given when the student is behaving appropriately.

Learn why and how to monitor (and adjust) your ratio of interactions with students. A great way to evaluate yourself is to audio or video record your lessons. Then, as you listen or watch yourself teach, write a + (plus sign) for every positive interaction with a student and a – (minus sign) for every corrective interaction. Then compare the numbers. If you record 30 positives and 10 correctives, your ratio is 3:1. If you record 15 positives and 20 correctives, your ratio is 3:4 and you need to work on increasing those positive interactions. Remember the definitions of *positive* and *corrective* interactions:

- An interaction is positive when the student is meeting expectations for appropriate behavior as you interact with the student.

- Contingent positive feedback occurs when you praise students who have accomplished something relatively significant, especially after making errors (but don't make a big deal out of something that isn't).

- Noncontingent acknowledgment is paying attention to students for no particular reason. Many or most of your positives can be noncontingent.

- Corrective interactions are attention to misbehavior. Remember that corrective interactions are not bad or wrong; your goal is *not* to reduce them to zero.

Administrators can help staff members remember to monitor their ratios of positive interactions by occasionally sending out meaningful reminders. For example, the memo could say something like, "This week, focus on your class clown. Try to catch that student interacting successfully and give lots of positive attention and feedback. Make a point to say, 'Good morning, Ben. It's nice to see you today.' See if you can reduce the student's negative attention-seeking behavior by launching a preemptive strike of positive interactions!"

A couple of weeks later, the administrator could send a similar memo about another group of students: "Identify a couple of average female students who tend to fade into the woodwork. Try to have at least five positive interactions every single day with those students."

A couple of weeks later, the memo might encourage staff to focus on positive interactions with angry, hostile students. Any staff member should also feel free to ask other staff members to help with providing positive interactions with specific students. The next suggested program, Special Attention for Targeted Students, describes how to involve other staff.

Basic student needs met by this procedure: Acknowledgment, Attention, Belonging, Competence, Nurturing, Recognition

Special Attention for Targeted Students

When a student exhibits chronic misbehavior, the classroom teacher can find it difficult to maintain a 3:1 ratio of positive to corrective interactions because so many of the student's behaviors need to be corrected. If other staff members make an overt effort to greet, talk to, and praise the student, collectively you can increase the number of positive interactions the student has with adults and more easily achieve the 3:1 goal. If many staff members consciously make the effort to engage the student, it is more likely that the student's needs for attention, acknowledgment, belonging, nurturing, and competence will be met. This may very well reduce the student's need to misbehave to get these needs met.

How do you do it?

When it becomes obvious that a student has a pattern of misbehavior, discuss the problem with the principal. Together you can decide whether to ask all staff to make a conscious effort to interact positively with the student.

*E*xample *From the Field*

After I conducted an inservice at a middle school, a teacher who worked with severely emotionally disturbed students wrote to tell me about a wonderful procedure he came up with for increasing positive interactions with his students. This teacher wrote:

I always thought I was very positive with my kids, but when I recorded myself teaching, as you suggested, I found that my ratio was only about 1:1. So for about a month my assistant and I worked very hard to achieve a ratio of at least 3:1 positive to negative. It made a big difference, but we realized something: With 12 kids and 2 teachers in my room, we have a teacher-student ratio of 1:6. But when my students mainstream, they go into rooms where the teacher-student ratio is something like 1:30. It's a drastic change for them. The general education teachers, no matter how skilled, cannot possibly provide the frequent positive attention to these needy students that my assistant and I can.

So with the help of the high school photography department, I enlarged each student's photograph to 8" x 10". Then I asked my principal's permission to pitch my idea at a faculty meeting. At the meeting, I explained my hypothesis: If six adults give one of my students attention as he or she walks from my room to Miss Johansson's room for math, the student's need for attention from the teacher will be reduced, and it'll be easier to have him or her in class. I held up each student's picture and said something like, "Here's Joanna. Joanna really enjoys riding horses, although she doesn't get to do it very often. Please say hello if you see her in the hallway. If you think of it, ask her about her interest in riding. It doesn't matter if you remember the name. This is Sam . . ."

The day after my plan began, the kids came into my advisory period and seemed, for lack of a better term, shell-shocked! The attention from adults outside the classroom surprised and confused them a little. But within a couple of days they were happily exchanging greetings and chatting with the other teachers.

My students are bused in from four other middle schools and did not interact with the other kids at all. Within about three weeks, the other kids—who had been afraid of my students—began to walk and talk with them in the hallway. The staff were modeling an attitude that said these students are just like everyone else. They deserve to be treated with respect, and they are part of the school. No one asked the other students to interact with the emotionally disturbed students; they simply responded to the positive model set by the adults. This simple idea to increase the positive attention to my students not only helped them behave appropriately in their general education classrooms, but it also helped them socially outside the classroom and improved the overall climate of the school. —R.S.

Basic student needs met by this procedure: Acknowledgment, Attention, Belonging, Competence, Nurturing, Recognition

Positive Reports to Parents

In addition to any regularly scheduled parent contacts such as conferences and report cards, staff members make a point of frequently reporting to parents the positive behavioral and academic accomplishments of their students. The positive report might be a simple phone call or email. Congratulatory postcards make the report special and are highly effective. A sample postcard appears in Figure 6b and can be printed from the Module C CD.

When parents receive news about their children's accomplishments, they are likely to pass along that positive feedback to the students, so the students get that much more positive attention. A simple communication via a postcard can increase parents' perceptions that staff are trying to work with them as partners in creating a positive and productive school experience for their children.

Postcards sent to families and phone calls home can celebrate successes, no matter how small, that are important to the individual student—and they don't necessarily go to just the best students. A high school principal we worked with said that initially he wondered about the value of sending postcards to parents, but then some of his toughest kids told him things like, "Don't tell any of my buddies, but my mom's got three of those postcards on the refrigerator, and she's really proud of me."

How do you do it?

1. Encourage staff to make frequent telephone contact with students' parents.

2. Give staff members preprinted Congratulations postcards that they can fill in with a specific student's name and the academic or behavioral accomplishment they wish to recognize.

3. Staff give completed cards to the office clerical staff, who address the cards to the students' homes, have the principal sign the cards, and mail them.

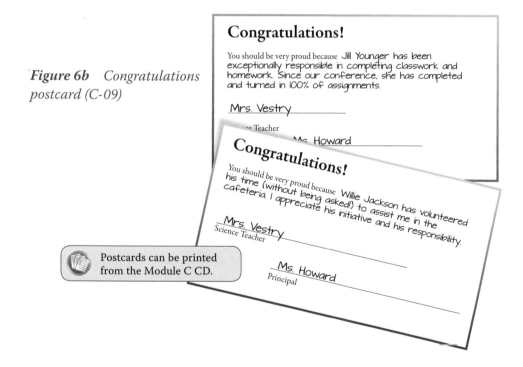

Figure 6b *Congratulations postcard (C-09)*

Postcards can be printed from the Module C CD.

Because this is an easy, quick process for the teachers, they are likely to use it.

We know of one administrator who keeps a database of the number of reports each staff member gives and which students receive them. If he sees that a teacher hasn't given any positive reports in a while, he tells the teacher, "Hey, you haven't sent any Congratulations postcards in a couple of months. Why don't you send at least 10 in the next week?" Or, "Axel Donnell hasn't received a postcard yet this year. Let's think about something we can positively reinforce him for."

Basic student needs met by this procedure: Acknowledgment, Attention, Competence, Purpose, Recognition

Mentorships

Adult volunteers are paired with individual students who would benefit from a friendly, nurturing, one-on-one relationship with an adult. Mentors meet with students on school grounds and during school hours at least once a week. Activities can include, but are not limited to, eating lunch together, playing a game, participating with the student in class activities or projects, or just taking a walk. The classroom teacher must approve any activities that will occur during class time. Mentor-student contact outside school hours and/or off school grounds must be scheduled through the office and should involve at least two mentor-student pairs together (to reduce any potential for or appearance of impropriety).

Research strongly suggests that a connection with a caring adult can reduce a student's risk of health and life failure. Students who do not have nurturing home situations (and even some students who do) often benefit from a relationship with a caring adult who consistently meets with and shows an interest in them. The one-on-one activities can be something a student eagerly anticipates and may help meet that student's need for nurturing, stimulation, change, and belonging.

How do you do it?

Each year, the counselor (or a teacher assistance team, for example) identifies students who may benefit from a mentoring relationship. These students will probably exhibit patterns of chronic misbehavior or absenteeism, appear withdrawn or shy, have failing grades, or have been recommended by their teachers. The counselor then seeks volunteers, who might be staff members, business partners, residents of a nearby retirement home, or community members. Before being accepted as mentors, volunteers should understand that the mentor relationships need to be maintained for at least one full school year. The counselor should also conduct a training session with the mentors at the beginning of the school year and then again in January (as a follow-up).

Note: Make sure your mentorship program has some form of screening to ensure that no student is paired with a mentor who might harm the student in any way.

Example From the Field

I helped a rural high school set up a mentorship program for at-risk freshmen. When I met with one of the mentors a few months later, she told me the program wasn't working with her assigned student. The student came at the appointed time every week, but would not converse with his mentor beyond one- or two-word answers to her questions:

"How are things going?"
"Fine."
"Are there any issues or problems you want to talk about?"
"No."
"Are you having a good week?"
"It's OK."
"Do you need any help with anything?"
"No."

The teacher said the meetings went like this every week. She wondered what she was accomplishing. I asked, "Does the student come every week?"

"Yes, he's here every Thursday."
"Does he *have* to come every week?"
"No."

I told the teacher, "Then don't tell me you're not helping this student." I encouraged her to keep trying to support the student. It took about a year and a half, but finally the student learned how to converse fluidly with the teacher.

All the students in the mentoring program who stayed at that high school graduated 4 years later. The local newspaper wrote an article about the students and the mentorship program. The reporter asked the student I wrote about above what he attributed his success to. His answer: "I had an adult, a mentor, who never gave up on me."

—R.S.

Basic student needs met by this procedure: Acknowledgment, Attention, Belonging, Nurturing, Stimulation/Change

Lottery System (Golden Tickets)

In a lottery system, staff members give tickets to students as recognition for good or improved behavior or grades, for working hard, for exemplifying the Guidelines for Success—any accomplishment can be rewarded. Students then enter their tickets into a drawing for a reward.

Presentation 6: Programs and Strategies for Meeting Needs

149

When a school has many at-risk students, recognizing student behavioral accomplishments with tangible rewards can help motivate students to behave responsibly. This program offers a lot of flexibility in the criteria for giving tickets, so it's easy to meet the recognition needs of all students.

How do you do it?

1. Design a ticket that includes a place for a student's name and a brief description of a specific behavioral or academic accomplishment. Think of a snappy name for the tickets that plays on the school name or mascot—Tiger Tickets, PAWS Rewards, or Pot 'o Gold Tickets, for example.

2. Distribute the tickets to all staff.

3. Staff members hand out tickets to students as a reward for appropriate behavior or other accomplishments. Staff inform the student of the specific behavior they are rewarding, write the behavior (or other accomplishment) and the student's name on the ticket, and sign the ticket. (Another option is to have the student write his or her name and accomplishment on the ticket, then have the staff member sign it.)

4. Students place their tickets in a container in the office. (Students can decide whether they want to enter or not.)

5. The principal arranges for rewards and weekly drawings. At the end of each week, a winning ticket is drawn from the container and the student wins the prize.

Weekly prizes should include a couple of small prizes and one big prize. Ask students what things or activities they might want to earn so that the rewards have more value for the students. You might display the reward in a locked case near the office.

In one inner-city middle school we worked with, we noticed that prizes for the weekly drawing were exceptional—bicycles, stereo equipment, television sets. We knew this school didn't have a big budget, so we asked how they could afford such prizes. The school social worker, who is only a half-time employee, said that one day each month she becomes a professional beggar! She calls or visits local department stores, bicycle shops, electronics stores, and the like, and asks whether they can donate a prize to the school to help motivate the students. In return, she offers publicity for the donors' businesses. With one day's work, she collects all the prizes for the month.

Basic student needs met by this procedure: Attention, Purpose, Recognition

Connections

Connections is a check-and-connect program developed by our colleague Mickey Garrison. To our knowledge, she was the first to create and use this type of program. Students check in with a program coordinator each morning and receive a daily monitoring card, which they carry with them throughout the day. Teachers rate students for specific behaviors ("Follow directions the first time," "Keep hands, feet, and objects to self," "Accept feedback without argument," for example) several times during the day. Students then take the monitoring card home for parents to sign. The coordinator meets with students the next morning, provides feedback and reinforcement, and gives them a new monitoring card for the day. Later, the coordinator compiles the data and monitors the students' progress. Students may be enrolled in the program for a few weeks, a few months, or even a few years—until their ratings are consistently high enough that they can "graduate."

Figure 6c below shows a Connections Daily Monitor. The completed monitor can be scanned to automatically add the data to the database, and reports are immediately updated. Figure 6d on the next page shows some sample reports.

Figure 6c *Connections Daily Monitor*

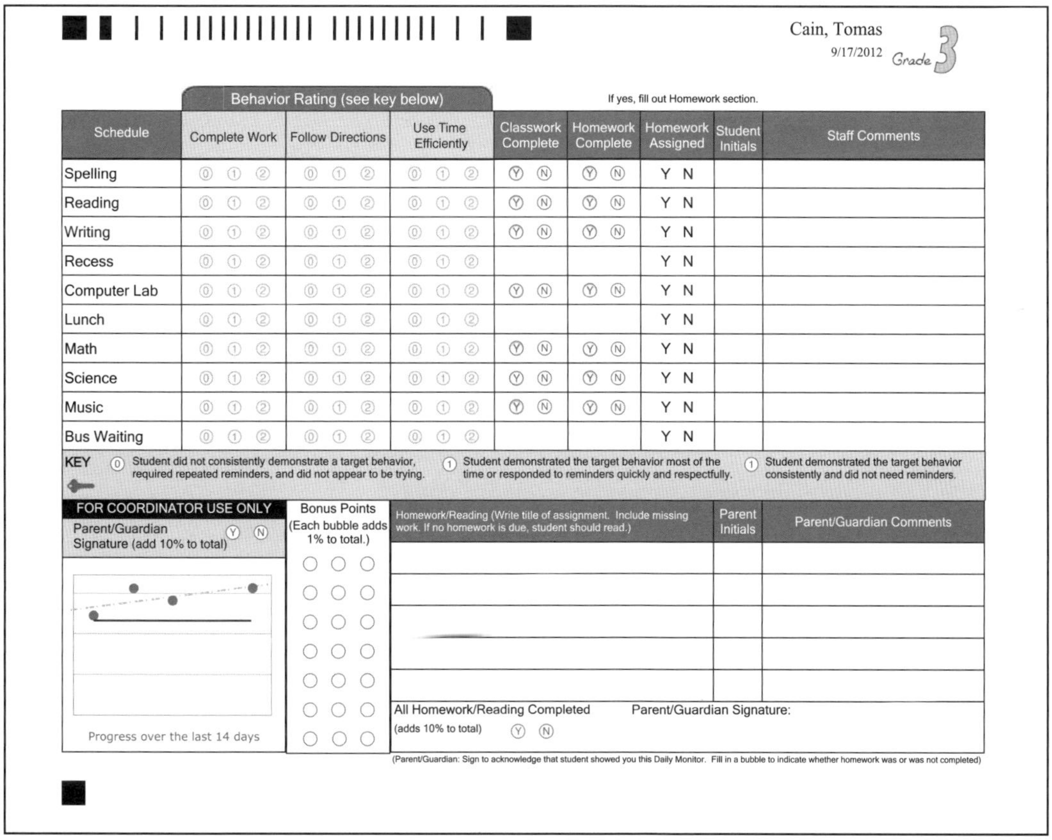
Cain, Tomas
9/17/2012 Grade 3

Behavior Rating (see key below)

If yes, fill out Homework section.

Schedule	Complete Work	Follow Directions	Use Time Efficiently	Classwork Complete	Homework Complete	Homework Assigned	Student Initials	Staff Comments
Spelling	0 1 2	0 1 2	0 1 2	Y N	Y N	Y N		
Reading	0 1 2	0 1 2	0 1 2	Y N	Y N	Y N		
Writing	0 1 2	0 1 2	0 1 2	Y N	Y N	Y N		
Recess	0 1 2	0 1 2	0 1 2			Y N		
Computer Lab	0 1 2	0 1 2	0 1 2	Y N	Y N	Y N		
Lunch	0 1 2	0 1 2	0 1 2			Y N		
Math	0 1 2	0 1 2	0 1 2	Y N	Y N	Y N		
Science	0 1 2	0 1 2	0 1 2	Y N	Y N	Y N		
Music	0 1 2	0 1 2	0 1 2	Y N	Y N	Y N		
Bus Waiting	0 1 2	0 1 2	0 1 2			Y N		

KEY (0) Student did not consistently demonstrate a target behavior, required repeated reminders, and did not appear to be trying. (1) Student demonstrated the target behavior most of the time or responded to reminders quickly and respectfully. (1) Student demonstrated the target behavior consistently and did not need reminders.

FOR COORDINATOR USE ONLY

Parent/Guardian Signature (add 10% to total) Y N

Progress over the last 14 days

Bonus Points (Each bubble adds 1% to total.)

Homework/Reading (Write title of assignment. Include missing work. If no homework is due, student should read.)	Parent Initials	Parent/Guardian Comments

All Homework/Reading Completed (adds 10% to total) Y N

Parent/Guardian Signature:

(Parent/Guardian: Sign to acknowledge that student showed you this Daily Monitor. Fill in a bubble to indicate whether homework was or was not completed)

Figure 6d *Connections Student Progress Report and Behavior Report*

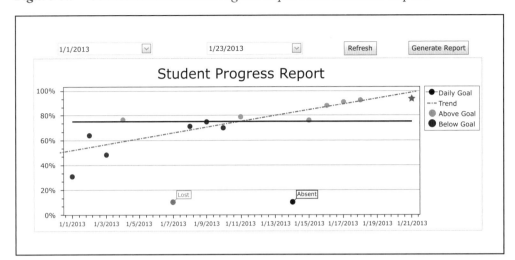

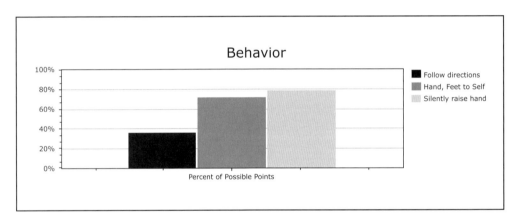

You can develop your own check-and-connect program or use a commercially available program such as Connections, an online program Mickey Garrison developed with Pacific Northwest Publishing.

Advantages of check-and connect programs include the following:

- They provide structure to the students' days.
- They establish and improve communication between home and school.
- Students get positive adult feedback and support daily.
- Students and staff can view trends across time to evaluate whether behavior is static, deteriorating, or becoming more responsible.
- Students are motivated to behave more appropriately.
- Students internalize appropriate behavior, leading to continued responsible behavior and effort.

Limitations of check-and-connect programs include the following:

- A staff member must spend time each day meeting with the students and processing monitoring cards.

- Classroom teachers must provide frequent feedback to students about performance, usually at the end of each class period. If too many students in the school are participating, general education teachers might feel undue pressure.

- If the program does not include an automated process for data entry, a staff member needs to enter data from the monitoring cards into a spreadsheet and manually record data on charts.

- The monitoring card might draw unwanted attention to the student, especially at the middle or high school level. Staff should be trained to be subtle and businesslike when they provide feedback to the student.

How do you do it?

1. Make the following initial decisions about implementing a check-and-connect program.

   What program will we use?

   The examples in *Foundations* are taken from Connections, an online program. With Connections, ratings are entered into the database through scanning and student scores are calculated and data reports are updated automatically. More information is available at pacificnwpublish.com/products/Connections. Other programs that are available commercially include:

   - *Check & Connect:* checkandconnect.umn.edu
   - *Behavior Education Program:* www.guilford.com
   - *SWIS-CICO:* www.pbisapps.org

   How will we choose students to enroll in the program?

   Universal screening is a good way to identify students who could benefit from a structured positive support system. Teachers can also nominate students, and students can be identified from a review of disciplinary referrals. Check and connect programs can often help students who:

   - Have not responded to other interventions.
   - Are completing little or no work or not turning in homework.
   - Are not participating in the learning process.

- Have emotional issues such as anxiety or are easily frustrated or angered.
- Have problems with attention or are too impulsive.
- Have poor organization.
- Are getting frequent disciplinary referrals.

When should we begin using the program?

Check-and-connect programs can probably begin anytime during the school year. Before implementing the program, ensure that the following procedures are in place.

- Tier 1 interventions should be established so that you have a chance to see how many students respond positively to them. Tier 2 check-and-connect programs are designed for students who do not respond to Tier 1 interventions.
- The principal and all staff need to be committed to participating in the program.
- A staff member or a team of staff members should be assigned to guide and coordinate the implementation of the program.

Who will administer the program?

One or more staff members can serve as check-and-connect coordinators. These staff members should have excellent communication skills with students, families, and other staff members, have time available to meet with students at the beginning and end of the school day, and know how to use data to make decisions about student progress.

2. Interpret check-and-connect data.

The Foundations Team probably won't be directly involved with a Tier 2 intervention such as Connections, although the team MTSS Coordinator should be knowledgeable about the program. If it becomes apparent that many students are having trouble with a particular behavior—following directions the first time, for example—the Foundations Team might prioritize developing a schoolwide focus on that behavior. If classroom teachers think there are too many students in the program—the teachers are struggling to give individual attention to two to seven students at the end of every class—work with the program coordinator to seek alternative interventions for some of the students, and the Foundations Team should continue to create effective Tier 1 prevention procedures.

3. Report results to staff and others.

Ask the program coordinator to share periodic reports about the overall efficacy of the program. Be sure the confidentiality of students is respected.

Ensure that the data are archived so they are available in future years.

Basic student needs met by this procedure: Attention, Belonging, Competence, Recognition

Task 1 Action Steps & Evidence of Implementation

Action Steps	Evidence of Implementation
1. Discuss whether any of the programs and procedures described in this task would help your school meet any unmet basic needs of students. • Develop an implementation proposal for any program or procedure that you determine to be useful. • Present the proposal to the entire staff for adoption or rejection. 2. If your school still has gaps in meeting the needs of its students, appoint one or more people to investigate other ways to fill those gaps. For example, other schools might be able to provide fresh ideas for programs and procedures.	Foundations Process: Students' Basic Needs

TASK 2

Consider support programs for elementary students

In this task, we present eight programs that can help you meet the needs of students in kindergarten through sixth grade. Middle schools might also benefit from some of these programs.

- Goal Achieved Book
- CARE
- Student of the Week
- Lunch With the Principal
- Responsible Student Behavior Plan
- Falcon Fan Club
- Classwide Goal of the Month
- Meaningful Work

Goal Achieved Book

Each day, each teacher recognizes a few students who have achieved a personal academic or behavioral goal by giving them "Goal Achieved!" certificates. At the end of the day, those students can go to the principal's office and sign a special book.

The goal of this procedure is to recognize the academic and behavioral progress of individual students. Staff can recognize students for any reason, so all students—troubled, average, and outstanding—can participate equally. The procedure provides students with attention from the principal, office staff, and other students who are signing the book. Going to the office for positive attention breaks up the daily routine, so the program helps meet students' needs for stimulation and change. Acknowledging the growth and success of individual students helps meet their sense of purpose.

In schools that use this program, the students also enjoy showing their parents their signatures in the Goal Achieved Book.

How do you do it?

1. Design a blank certificate that says "Goal Achieved!" or "Certificate of Merit" (or a similar phrase based on your school name or mascot). The certificate should have places for the student name, teacher signature, principal signature, and description of the goal the student achieved.

2. Distribute the certificates to all staff.

3. Create a large book with a blank, poster-size page for each school day. Display the book near or in the office where students have access to it, so they can show others where they have signed.

4. Staff can award certificates to a few students each day. They or the students can fill out the certificates.

5. During the last 15 minutes of each day, students with certificates are allowed to go to the principal's office. (Anywhere from 5 to 50 students might have certificates.)

6. The principal (or a designated person when the principal is absent) meets with the group and interacts briefly with each student individually, asks about the goal each student achieved, and has each student sign the Goal Achieved Book. The principal signs certificates for each student and gives them to the students to take home.

7. The principal might offer snacks or invent some fun rituals to make this time more celebratory.

One of the nicest Goal Achieved Books we have seen was large—it measured about 18 x 24 inches—and featured a handmade wooden cover with leather hinges. You might enlist the art teacher to create a unique, attractive cover that says "Goal Achieved!"

Basic student needs met by this procedure: Attention, Belonging, Purpose, Recognition, Stimulation/Change

CARE

This program is designed to improve student behavior in common areas by increasing the frequency of adult recognition, acknowledgment, and attention for students who behave responsibly. CARE is an acronym that stands for the following behaviors:

- **Careful Commuting** (e.g., walking or voice levels that follow hallway rules)

- **Awesome Attitude** (e.g., following school rules, being kind to others, continuing to walk and be a careful commuter)

- **Responsible Leadership** (e.g., making good decisions, following school rules, continuing to commute carefully, demonstrating an awesome attitude)

- **Exceptional Empathy** (e.g., showing concern for others, following school rules, carefully commuting, demonstrating an awesome attitude, exhibiting responsible leadership)

In the CARE program, you dedicate 4 weeks, or perhaps 4 weeks during the fall and 4 weeks during the spring, to a reinforcement system based on the CARE traits and behaviors. Staff members award tickets to students for demonstrating these qualities. (See Figure 6e below for sample tickets. These tickets are available on the Module C CD.) CARE is a little different from most schoolwide reward systems in a couple of ways. First, each behavior is rewarded for only 1 week. Students receive Careful Commuting reward tickets during the first week of the program, Awesome Attitude tickets during the second week, and so on. Second, the program runs for 4 weeks and then stops. The relatively short reward period keeps students and staff from tiring of the program, adds variety to the school year, and gives students something to antici-pate. It can reenergize both staff and students.

Note: You can use any acronym in place of CARE. Your Guidelines for Success, your school mascot (EAGLES), or a word related to the school mascot (SOAR) are good sources for meaningful acronyms. Base your decision on the behaviors you want to emphasize.

Figure 6e   *CARE Tickets (C-11a)*

How do you do it?

1. Pick one or two 4-week periods to dedicate to the program. You might pick a month in which numbers of office referrals have been high.

2. Design tickets for each letter of the acronym (see Figure 6e for examples) and distribute to the staff.

3. Explain the program to the staff and encourage them to give out lots of tick-ets. They should explain why the student earned the ticket as they reward the student.

4. Classroom teachers explain the program to students. Each classroom teacher sets a goal of 150 tickets (from any staff member) earned by the class each week. The class gets a reward such as extra recess time or game time if they reach the goal.

5. Teachers might use posters of the acronym letters like the example shown in Figure 6f below. Each letter contains 150 circles. When a student earns a ticket, he or she is allowed to color in a circle. (CARE posters are included on the Module C CD.)

6. During the first week, staff give tickets during transition times to students (who are not in their classes) for following the Careful Commuting guideline. During the second week, they award tickets (to any student) for following the Awesome Attitude guideline. Responsible Leadership is emphasized during the third week, and Exceptional Empathy is the theme for the fourth week.

7. After students show teachers their tickets, they write their names on the tickets and place them in a box in the office for a lottery drawing.

8. At the end of each week, draw 10 or 15 tickets and award small prizes such as pencils, snacks, coupons for local businesses, movies passes, and the like. At the end of the 4-week period, hold a schoolwide celebration.

Basic student needs met by this procedure: Attention, Belonging, Purpose, Recognition, Stimulation/Change

Figure 6f   *CARE Posters with 150 circles (C-11b)*

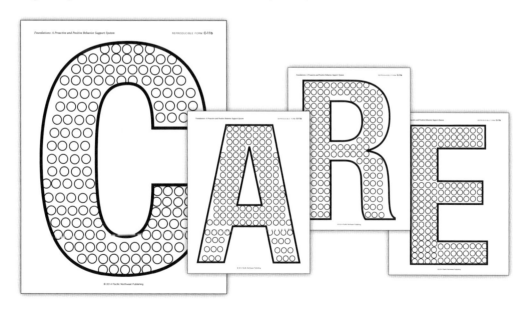

Student of the Week

In this program, a student from each classroom is spotlighted each week. Pictures of the week's chosen students are posted on a main bulletin board, and the classroom teachers celebrate the student in the classroom. Celebrating every individual student's unique contributions to the classroom and school increases students' senses of purpose and belonging, and staff are able to provide every student with acknowledgment and attention.

An important component of this program is that the sequence of student selection is entirely random and not contingent on anything. Student names should be drawn in public to make it clear to students that the order is determined by chance. Some schools use this program as contingent reinforcement, with the most responsible students selected as Students of the Week early in the year. We do not advise this procedure because it is insulting and possibly humiliating to the students chosen late in the year.

How do you do it?

1. At the beginning of the year, each classroom teacher explains the Student of the Week program. Teachers should ensure that students understand that the selection order is random—the student celebrated during the first week of the program is no more or less valuable than the student celebrated during the last week.

2. Teachers draw a student name out of a bowl (with students watching) to determine the order. The list, in order, should be posted for all students to see.

3. Every Monday, teachers provide the name of their Student of the Week to the office so the main bulletin board can be prepared. Pictures of the Students of the Week from each class should be displayed.

4. Each teacher decides how to celebrate the student within the classroom. For example:

   - Display some of the student's photographs from home. (Be prepared to take photos of students at school in case some students do not have anything to bring from home.)
   - Spend one-on-one time with the student.
   - Have the student share his or her interests or talents with the class.
   - Invite the student's parents to spend an afternoon at school.
   - Give the student a special classroom job for the week.

5. If any class has more students than there are weeks in the school year, that class will have to celebrate two students during some weeks. Those weeks should be scheduled in the middle of the school year.

Basic student needs met by this procedure: Acknowledgment, Attention, Belonging, Stimulation/Change

Lunch With the Principal

Each week, each classroom teacher chooses one student at random to have lunch with the principal. The lunch takes place in a special room or at a special table in the lunchroom that has been prepared with tablecloths, place settings, and centerpieces. During the course of the year, *every* student should get to participate one time.

This luncheon provides a wonderful opportunity for primary students to get to know the principal in a relaxed setting. With intermediate students, the luncheon can serve as an informal student council meeting. The students and principal can discuss current school issues (too much litter in the halls, for example) and brainstorm ways to solve the problem. Or students can bring prepared questions, suggestions, or concerns that their classes have generated and would like to discuss with the principal. The students can then report to their classes on the results of the discussion.

This procedure provides a break in students' weekly routines and, especially for the older students, gives a sense of belonging and purpose because they are playing a role in governing the school.

Lunch With the Principal can be easily incorporated into the Student of the Week program—the Students of the Week can be the group that gets to have lunch with the principal.

How do you do it?

1. The principal selects a day when he or she will be in school (preferably the same day every week, if possible) and arranges for a room or table to be prepared.

2. Teachers should ensure that students understand that the selection order is random—the student selected for lunch during the first week of the program is no more or less valuable than the student selected the last week. Teachers draw their students' names out of a bowl (with students watching) to determine the order. The list, in order, should be posted for all students to see.

3. If the principal plans to discuss an issue with the students, he or she tells the teachers in advance so they can discuss the issue with their classes.

4. On the appointed day, the selected students go to the front of the lunch line (if they are buying lunch) and then proceed directly to the designated room or table.

5. The principal assists the students in taking notes about their discussions so they can share key points with their teachers and classmates.

Basic student needs met by this procedure: Acknowledgment, Attention, Belonging, Purpose, Stimulation/Change

Responsible Student Behavior Plan

In this schoolwide structured program, staff members reward students who display responsible behavior with Responsible Student Behavior (RSB) forms. The students accumulate the forms until they have enough to earn a trip to the principal's office. The program offers positive recognition and attention to students.

How do you do it?

1. Design a Responsible Student Behavior (RSB) form that includes places for the student's name, teacher's signature, and a description of the behavior that earned the recognition (see Figure 6g). Distribute the forms to all staff.

Figure 6g *Responsible Student Behavior form (C-10); available on the Module C CD*

**Responsible Student Behavior!
RSB!**

_____ demonstrated especially responsible behavior by
_____
_____

Staff Member Signature: _____
When you have earned _____ RSB slips, you can go to the office to receive your special privilege.

2. Staff members award the forms to individual students to recognize responsible behavior. Staff members should compliment the students and state the specific behavior the student demonstrated. Students can fill out the form and then have the staff member sign it.

3. Students save their RSB forms until they have ten (or whatever number you choose). Primary teachers might keep the forms for students to reduce the problem of lost forms.

4. When a student has ten forms, he or she takes them to the principal.

5. The principal talks to the student about the behaviors the student demonstrated to earn the forms.

6. The student has his or her photograph taken sitting in the principal's chair at the principal's desk. The principal might also offer small rewards such as stickers or pencils.

7. The photograph is placed on a special bulletin board outside the office. The photographs can stay up indefinitely and accumulate as more and more students earn a visit to the principal.

Basic student needs met by this procedure: Attention, Purpose, Recognition

Falcon Fan Club

The Falcon Fan Club is a program created by Sarah Vaughn (behavior specialist) and Holly Hensley (counselor) at Ralph Pfluger Elementary School in Buda, Texas. (The program is the property of Hays Consolidated Independent School District.) They designed the program for a student who spent the first 7 days of the school year in the office. After they implemented it, the student did not return to the office once during the rest of the year. Figure 6h on the next two pages shows the invitation to join the club that Sarah and Holly sent to staff and some of the forms for the program. The invitation also gives instructions for setting up the program.

Basic student needs met by this procedure: Attention, Belonging, Competence, Recognition

Classwide Goal of the Month

Classroom teachers help their students choose a classwide goal for the upcoming month. For example, students may collectively decide to increase their average rate of on-time assignment completion from 85% to 95% or to collect 100 cans of food for the local food pantry. Over the course of the month, the teachers use discussions and lessons to guide their classes in achieving the collective goal. At the end of the month, each class evaluates its progress and determines whether it has met its goal. Successful classes get schoolwide recognition and a certificate from the principal.

This program gives students a clear sense of purpose and experience with goal-directed growth. It models setting a goal, striving to achieve the goal, and evaluating whether the goal has been met. The procedure can also increase students' sense of belonging because a collective goal encourages a sense of collective responsibility for working toward that goal.

How do you do it?

1. Every month, each class sets a goal—something that the students collectively wish to accomplish that month. Examples of class goals include:

    *   A school improvement project, such as picking up litter one day a week for a month
    *   A classroom improvement project, such as increasing homework completion from 81% to 90% or improving on-task behavior during work times
    *   A community service project, such as raising money for a particular charity or conducting a canned food drive

2. The students identify a way to measure whether or not they achieve the goal.

Figure 6h *Falcon Fan Club invitation and forms (C-22); thanks to Sarah Vaughn and Holly Hensley of Ralph Pfluger Elementary School and Hays Consolidated Independent School District in Buda, Texas*

Join the FALCON FAN CLUB!

The Falcon Fan Club (FFC) is the most positive, life-changing Tier 2 behavior intervention our school has seen. YOU can help change student behavior with minimal support!

Who can join? FFC is open to any support staff member who would like to participate. The support staff will pilot the program, and then we'll open the club to membership from the rest of the staff.

Who does it serve? This intervention serves a small number of highly attention-seeking students who have been identified as needing Tier 2 behavioral supports. These students crave adult interaction and will do anything to get it.

What's the rationale? Highly attention-seeking students often require additional support to respond to their high levels of misbehavior. An outside response is almost always necessary for these situations, so students learn that they will receive more attention (positive or corrective) for engaging in the inappropriate behavior than for meeting classroom expectations. With the help of adults on campus, we would like to show these students that they can receive attention (positive) for meeting the expectations! Staff who respond to these students' inappropriate behavior will strive for dullness as they respond.

How does it work?

1. If you would like to join the FFC, respond to this email and let me know. I'll add your name to an email list titled "Falcon Fan Club."

2. The classroom teachers of the target students will use a reinforcement system in their classrooms. When a student has met his or her teacher's expectations x number of times, the student is eligible for a visit from an FFC member. There are three levels of visits:

   - FFC Mini—a 2- to 3-minute visit in the hallway that could include a cheer, hug, pat on the back, or other encouragement
   - FFC Medium—a 5- to 6-minute visit during which you can take the student to a nearby staff member while bragging about the student's accomplishments
   - FFC Lunch—is just that. The student gets to eat lunch with an FFC member.

   (Please stick to the mini response if that is what is warranted. We want to fade the student off the intervention eventually.)

 These samples can be printed from the Module C CD.

SCHOOL SAMPLE

3. As soon as possible after the student has earned a visit, the classroom teacher sends an email to the list. "Falcon Fan Club" goes in the *To* line and "FFC Mini," "FFC Medium," or "FFC Lunch" goes in the *Subject* line. No message is necessary.

4. All FFC members receive the email. The first FFC member who can give a few minutes to praise the student replies to the list by adding "Got it" to the subject line. This reply lets all other members know that a response is no longer needed. (Please do not feel obligated to respond when you are in the middle of something important. Just delete the email and go on with your duties. We need only one responder per email.)

5. The person who responded goes to the classroom and delivers the type of visit specified in the email. If the student has earned a lunch, visit the student to congratulate him or her and arrange for a lunch on the earliest possible day.

Teacher Instructions: Select one or two behaviors to target, such as following directions and staying in seat. Every time you "catch" the student meeting behavioral expectations, color (or have the student color) a star. When the student has earned three stars, send an email to the Falcon Fan Club for an FFC Mini. When the student has earned 15 stars, send an email for an FFC Medium. When the student has colored in the whole page of stars, send an email for an FFC Lunch. You may adjust the criteria for earning FFC visits to fit the needs of individual students.

Congratulations!

_____
has been accepted into the
FALCON FAN CLUB!

Teacher: Reinforce your student when he/she is caught

_____
_____
_____

by coloring one star on the following page. Reinforce the student frequently. Then follow the directions at the top of the page.

Please see Holly Hensley or Sarah Vaughn for any questions!

WOW! _____ is doing AWESOME!!!

Email the Falcon Fan Club when three stars have been earned and write "FFC Mini" in the subject line. (15 stars = FFC Medium, 30 stars = FFC Lunch).

3. The teacher provides feedback and assists the students with planning and organizing the projects, identifying strategies that will help them achieve the goal, and tracking progress throughout the month. Students might take turns in leadership roles each month.

4. Teachers can conduct lessons that include role-play, positive practice, storytelling, and writing or art assignments that complement the goal.

5. Each class that meets its goal gets a visit and a certificate of congratulations from the principal. The classes can be recognized in the school newsletter and in schoolwide announcements.

6. If the goal wasn't met, the class can decide whether to renew the goal for another month, modify it, or set it aside and choose another goal.

Basic student needs met by this procedure: Belonging, Purpose, Stimulation/Change

Meaningful Work

Meaningful Work was originally developed by our colleagues B. J. Wise and Kim Marcum. It is a very powerful program based on the idea that students thrive on feeling useful, needed, and important. Staff develop school-based jobs that can be assigned to students, and individual students are offered or apply for the positions.

The program can be specifically structured to meet individual students' needs for acknowledgment, attention, belonging, competence, nurturing, purpose, recognition, and stimulation and change by engaging the students in meaningful jobs that contribute to the school. For example, a student who needs nurturing might be given a job working closely with a nurturing staff member at the library desk. A student who needs lots of attention and a sense of purpose might be given a job cleaning the disk drives of the computers in each classroom—a highly visible job that makes her feel important. And a student who just needs to *move* for a while each day could spend 15 minutes each afternoon visiting all the classrooms and collecting empty coffee cups.

The jobs are not contingent on student behavior. If a student misbehaves in the classroom, she still gets to work at her job that day as usual.

If you are interested in this program, we strongly suggest that you read *Meaningful Work: Changing Student Behavior With School Jobs* (Wise, Marcum, Haykin, Sprick, & Sprick, 2011). This excellent resource offers comprehensive instructions for developing the program in your school and describes almost 100 potential jobs for students in grades K–6.

How do you do it?

1. Identify a staff member to coordinate the program. A highly skilled paraprofessional might be a good choice. This person is responsible for tracking who has what job, the adult who supervises each job, jobs that are currently available, and so on. He or she also works with staff to identify job possibilities.

2. Identify students who might benefit from having a job. The school counselor can probably suggest some needy students. Explain the program to teachers and tell them they may nominate students for the program. Data sources such as office referrals, incident reports, anecdotal records, grades, and attendance and tardy records can help you define goals for the students.

3. Identify jobs that are truly helpful for the school and that a student is capable of doing, and identify adults who would make good job supervisors. Some examples of Meaningful Work jobs are:

   - Badge Maker
   - Bulletin Board Manager
   - Computer Technician
   - Crossing Guard
   - Gardener (water office plants)
   - Recycling Manager
   - Workroom Assistant

4. Match students with available jobs. In some schools, the program is so popular that many more students want jobs than are available. These students go through an application process that gives them an experience similar to a real-life job application process. Staff try to ensure that every student gets a chance to work, even if it means sharing a job.

5. Train supervisors to teach students how to perform the job, monitor the students' performances, provide positive and corrective feedback, and communicate with the students' classroom teachers.

Basic student needs met by this procedure: Acknowledgment, Attention, Belonging, Competence, Nurturing, Purpose, Recognition, Stimulation/Change

The following two true stories come from *Meaningful Work: Changing Student Behavior With School Jobs* (Wise et al., 2011). *Note:* The Module C DVD includes some videos of students and staff describing their experiences with Meaningful Work programs in their schools.

Devon and the Power to Change

Devon arrived like a rocket at his new school. He was impulsive, often out of his seat, and subject to frequent angry outbursts that eventually fizzled out, leaving him sobbing quietly with his head on the desk. Devon's records listed numerous office referrals in his previous schools. Disruptive behaviors included open defiance, severe classroom tantrums, and fighting during recess.

From the moment Devon arrived, staff determined that this supercharged third-grader would benefit from a high-status job with a nurturing yet professional mentor.

Devon was placed with the building technology coordinator and given the job of tech assistant. Devon showed such skill that the technology coordinator was able to assign him to sophisticated computer maintenance tasks. Devon became known as the "techno whiz kid." Not only did this delight Devon, but it also contributed to his becoming a well-behaved student—someone everyone counted on.

Unfortunately, misbehavior is generally ingrained, so from time to time even a techno whiz kid will revert to old behaviors. For Devon, this happened on the bus. He resorted to a major tantrum when provoked by another student.

Sitting across from the principal, Devon began to escalate, worried that he would get the dreaded pink slip (a behavior notice that went home to parents with a consequence). Devon warned in a high-pitched voice, "You better not give me a pink slip, or I'll . . . I'll . . ." Then in a low and determined voice he said, "Or I'll quit my job!"

Jeremy and the Power of Nurturing

Educators often feel helpless when a child experiences the loss of a parent. Jeremy, a second grader, experienced just such a loss when his mother died in the middle of the school year. To add to his grief, it was also discovered that he had been abused by a caregiver.

Jeremy began stealing from his teacher and classmates. Staff believed this misbehavior was related to the loss of his mother and the trauma of abuse. Jeremy was placed in the Meaningful Work program and assigned to a very nurturing librarian. As the weeks and months passed, Jeremy appeared happier, and the stealing stopped.

One day, a guest principal came to view Meaningful Work in action. She visited a student staff meeting in progress. Student workers were asked to share their names and their jobs. When it was time for Jeremy to share, he said in a soft voice with head lowered, "I am Jeremy. I work in the library, and they love me." Then he raised his head and repeated, "They love me."

Task 2 Action Steps & Evidence of Implementation

Action Steps	Evidence of Implementation
1. Discuss whether any of the programs and procedures described in this task would help your school meet any unmet basic needs of students. • Develop an implementation proposal for any program or procedure you determine to be useful. • Present the proposal to the entire staff for adoption or rejection. 2. If gaps remain in meeting the needs of your students, appoint one or more people to investigate ways to fill those gaps. For example, other schools might be able to provide fresh ideas for programs and procedures.	Foundations Process: Students' Basic Needs

TASK 3

Consider support programs for secondary students

In this task, we suggest six programs that work well to meet the needs of students in grades 6 through 12.

- Leadership Class
- Principal's Award
- Honor Roll
- Grades
- Attendance or Punctuality Letter
- Problem-Solving Task Force

Leadership Class

Each semester, a for-credit elective class is taught by the school counselor (or another appropriate, available staff member) to a group of approximately 20 students. The class content includes communication skills, leadership skills, confidence-building activities, and so on. The students in the class complete two major projects: They plan and implement a community service project, and they organize a school dance.

What makes this program different from most leadership classes is that staff members nominate students based on the students' lack of involvement in the school. The class is *not* for students who are already established as school leaders in some way.

In schools that have implemented this program, almost all of the nominated students have elected to participate in the class. After taking the class, these students have also become much more active in the school by joining clubs and sports teams.

How do you do it?

1. Enlist a teacher for the class and establish the class as a for-credit part of the academic schedule. Develop the class content. You might use Sean Covey's *Seven Habits of Highly Effective Teens* materials or one of the many social-emotional learning curricula available commercially. (See Covey, S. (2014) *The Seven Habits of Highly Effective Teens.* New York, NY: Touchstone.)

2. At a staff meeting near the end of the semester, have staff members nominate students they think could benefit from taking the class during the next semester. The nomination criterion is simple: noninvolvement in school activities.

3. Staff members consider each nominated student and rank them according to their involvement in school activities. Students who are in no activities rank high on the list. Those who (for example) have tried out for sports, have expressed interest in getting involved in the photography club, or have some connection with school activities will rank lower on the list. Select a final group of about 20 students.

4. To identify students with little or no involvement in school activities, you might use the strategy for assessing connectedness described in Module C, Presentation 5, Task 2.

5. The teacher approaches each student and asks whether he or she would like to participate in the class. Emphasize that the class will be fun and the students will be helping the school.

Basic student needs met by this procedure: Acknowledgment, Attention, Belonging, Competence, Nurturing, Purpose, Recognition, Stimulation/Change

Principal's Award

Each month, each teacher identifies two students from all the students enrolled in his or her classes to receive the Principal's Award. One student should be selected for being consistently responsible, and the other for making significant improvement in academics or behavior. The principal sends letters and certificates describing the students' accomplishments to the students' parents.

The goal of this program is to recognize improvements in behavioral and academic performance and motivate students to continue to strive for success. It gives students attention for behavioral and academic competence from teachers, the principal, and parents.

How do you do it?

1. At the beginning of each month, the principal distributes a form that asks teachers to nominate two students from their classes for the Principal's Award (see Figure 6i on the next page). You might establish a schedule so that in September the students are selected from first-period classes, in October from second period classes, and so on.

2. One nomination should be for a student who is consistently responsible, and one should be for a student who has made significant improvement in academics or behavior. If staff are trying to foster a particular trait in students (treating others

with respect, for example), the principal can suggest that teachers target students who have demonstrated that trait.

3. The teachers return the forms to the office. Office staff, with the help of student workers, generate parent letters and certificates for all identified students.

4. The principal sends each student's parents a letter and a certificate describing the student's accomplishments and identifies the nominating teacher.

Note: Keep track of the students who receive the awards each month. Check the current month's list against previous months. You don't want the same students to get the award every month. Also try to ensure that an approximately equal number of male and female students receive awards.

Figure 6i   *Principal's Award Nomination Form (C-12)*

Principal's Award Nomination Form

Dear Teachers:

It is once again time to identify students for the Principal's Award. This month, identify two students from your second-period class. (If you have second-period prep, disregard this notice.) Write the name of the student and a brief description (one or two sentences) of why that student deserves to be acknowledged.

The theme for this month is "Treating others with respect." If possible, identify students showing competence and improvement in this theme. However, if there is a student you wish to acknowledge for something other than this theme, do not be bound by the theme of respect.

1. Identify a student from your second-period class who consistently behaves responsibly: _____

   Describe why you are recommending this student:

2. Identify a student from your second-period class who has made significant improvement in academic progress or social behavior: _____

   Describe why you are recommending this student:

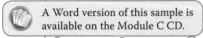

A Word version of this sample is available on the Module C CD.

Basic student needs met by this procedure: Attention, Belonging, Competence, Purpose, Recognition

Honor Roll

Many middle and high schools use an Honor Roll program to recognize students for outstanding academic performance. Students who achieve a specific grade point average for a term (3.5 or higher, for example) are automatically placed on the Honor Roll. Written notifications of their accomplishments are sent with students' report cards.

The Honor Roll provides recognition for the intelligence, competence, hard work, and discipline required by students to consistently attain high grades.

How do you do it?

1. As soon as all grades are recorded for the semester or quarter, office staff prepare the list of students who attained the grade-point average necessary for the Honor Roll.

2. Office staff also prepare letters that go home when grades are posted online or sent home.

3. The Honor Roll is usually posted in a prominent location in the school and on the school website.

Important note: This procedure is somewhat exclusionary. Because average and low-performing students have less chance of receiving this recognition, it is important for staff members to make additional efforts to acknowledge any improved performance by these students. Staff should recognize them in class, write encouraging and complimentary notes on assignments, and so on. Remember the Expectancy x Value = Motivation formula from Module C, Presentation 5? Because these students' expectancy of making Honor Roll is probably about zero, they need reminders of the value of their work and encouragement to stay motivated.

Basic student needs met by this procedure: Belonging, Competence, Purpose, Recognition

Grades

Each classroom teacher should have grading polices compatible with the schoolwide grading guidelines specified in the student handbook. Students should understand that they are in control of their grades—they should not think that grades are just something that teachers assign at the end of the semester with no discussion or preamble. The key to having students take charge of their grades is to make sure they can figure out what their current grades are at any point during the semester. Then they can work harder, arrange for extra credit and make-up assignments or tests, and get other help when necessary.

One of the major purposes of grading is to recognize successful completion of course requirements. Thus, a passing grade (or better) can be viewed as a reinforcing acknowledgment of adequate mastery of critical course content. Students can feel proud of their accomplishments and their competence.

How do you do it?

1. During the first week of a semester, teachers give students a course syllabus that explains the grading practices.

2. Teachers encourage students to keep accurate records of their own scores so that at any time during the semester each student knows his or her current grade status.

3. Teachers encourage students who are not satisfied with their current grades to meet with them to work out strategies for improving grades.

4. Staff members should be careful to avoid implying that a grade of C is a bad grade.

    *   If a student has worked hard to get a C, that C should be celebrated.
    *   However, if a student is capable of getting better than a C, that student should be counseled privately. A goal contract might help motivate the student.

5. When a student consistently gets poor grades, that student's academic or motivational needs are probably not being met. Staff members should view poor grades as a red flag that signals the student may need an individualized plan to help him or her be more successful.

Basic student needs met by this procedure: Competence, Recognition

Attendance or Punctuality Letter

Students who have exemplary attendance for one semester (zero unexcused absences and no more than three excused absences, for example) are eligible for reference letters they can use when applying for after-school and summer jobs. The letter specifies that the student had an excellent attendance record for the past semester and can be depended on to arrive at work every day.

The objective of this procedure is to motivate students to maintain good attendance and punctuality by recognizing these behaviors in a practical way that can help them get employment. The program can help all students see the connection between school behavior and workplace behavior.

How do you do it?

1. Inform students of this policy during orientation at the beginning of each year. If possible, invite a community businessperson (ideally someone who employs teenagers) to speak to the student body about how important punctuality and attendance are to employers. Encourage the person to tell students that a certificate of attendance and punctuality from the school could be of benefit when applying for after-school and summer jobs. You might even inform area businesses about the program so they know to ask for the letters when interviewing job candidates.

2. Clarify the criteria that earn a letter. A reasonable expectation might be zero unexcused absences and no more than three excused absences per semester, for example. You can include a punctuality clause—the student also has zero or no more than three excused tardies.

   A student with no unexcused absences and more than three excused absences may be eligible for a letter, but the letter should specify the number of excused absences the student had (and possibly the reason for the absences, if appropriate) and should not include an endorsement of the student's dependability.

3. Office staff can prepare the letters for qualifying students at the end of the semester for the principal to sign. The letters specify that the students have excellent attendance records and can be depended on to arrive at work.

Basic student needs met by this procedure: Recognition, Purpose

Problem-Solving Task Force

This procedure is appropriate for schoolwide problems such as tardiness, vandalism, harassment, or increased numbers of students not completing work. The principal and the counselor convene a task force of students to evaluate the problem, propose solutions, implement a plan, and evaluate the plan's effectiveness. For severe problems (illegal activity, for example), the task force should include staff and parent representatives as well.

The goal of this procedure is to actively involve students in resolving school problems. Their participation can give students a sense of belonging and purpose and increase their pride in and willingness to take care of their school. For the students on the task force, participation also provides stimulation and change.

How do you do it?

1. The principal and counselor determine which students would be best suited to serve on a task force for specific issues. The idea is to include representatives from major student factions that are part of or affected by the problem. This means that task forces will be different from student council—some of the toughest or worst-behaved students may be asked to participate on certain task forces. Once a list of recommended students has been developed, the principal or counselor can approach those students and ask if they would be willing to participate.

2. Schedule task force meetings so that the students miss relatively little class time. For example, the task force could meet on Mondays every week, but during first period the first week, during second period the second week, and so on.

3. The counselor (and/or other staff members who volunteer to guide the task force) helps students collect and review data, brainstorm solutions, develop and implement a plan, and collect data to evaluate the plan's effectiveness.

Most task forces should last no more than 2 months.

Basic student needs met by this procedure: Purpose, Belonging, Stimulation/Change

Task 3 Action Steps & Evidence of Implementation

Action Steps	Evidence of Implementation
1. Discuss whether any of the programs and procedures described in this task would help your school meet any unmet basic needs of students. • Develop an implementation proposal for any program or procedure that you determine to be useful. • Present the proposal to the entire staff for adoption or rejection. 2. If your school still has gaps in meeting the needs of its students, appoint one or more people to investigate other ways to fill those gaps. For example, other schools might be able to provide fresh ideas for programs and procedures.	Foundations Process: Students' Basic Needs

Making a Good First Impression: Welcoming New Staff, Students, and Families

INTRODUCTION

In this presentation, we discuss why and how to ensure that visitors, new students, their families, and new staff feel welcome in your school. First impressions are often lasting impressions. When a new student's first impression is negative, there is a risk that the student may have difficulty developing an affiliation with the school. So all staff members need to be aware that they set the tone of the school and they have the power to consciously create an inviting and welcoming school climate.

In unfamiliar settings, most people feel vulnerable. Imagine you are starting a new job at a new school. You don't know the names of your coworkers, the rules, or—perhaps the most difficult aspect of an unfamiliar environment—the myriad *unwritten* rules that inevitably exist. People who have been at the same school for several years might be unaware of the difficulties new staff face. People who spent their K–12 years in the same school system with the same group of peers might not realize how students feel when they move to a new city and enter a new school. And when people will be spending a lot of time in the new setting, as students will in school, they tend to feel especially vulnerable.

I (Randy) had a personal experience that illustrates the importance of welcoming newcomers. When it became clear that my elderly mother needed a little help with everyday activities, I helped her move to an independent living community. The residents of this community usually eat in a large dining room, where they serve themselves from a buffet. An employee is supposed to escort new residents to the dining room their first evenings and orient them to the buffet and the seating process. On my mother's first evening at the facility, however, the staff got busy and forgot to provide this service for her.

So my mother went to the dining room on her own. She went through the buffet line, got her food, and then began to search for a seat at a table. She walked up to a table with some empty chairs and said, "May I sit here?" The people seated there said, "No, this table is reserved." She went to another table and got the same polite response. This happened four or five times until my mother finally took her tray of food to her room.

I didn't hear about this incident until weeks later, after my mother had discovered that there are two "friendship tables" in the dining room for single people to share. Seats at those tables cannot be reserved. All of the other tables are usually occupied by longtime residents who hold seats for their friends.

Nobody explained this system to my mother. The incident was traumatic enough to color her connection to this place for months.

No one intended the dining room to be uninviting, but it was. No one intended new residents to feel alienated or bullied, but that's how my mother felt. So the lesson here is: Think about structure. Part of creating a welcoming environment for newcomers involves structural considerations. Might a new student at your school have an experience in the cafeteria similar to my mother's experience in the dining room? If so, what can you change to ensure that the cafeteria is comfortable and inviting, rather than unfriendly and unpleasant?

Another factor in creating a welcoming environment for newcomers is culture. Do you overtly and directly teach students to be welcoming and inclusive? If not, like the residents at the independent living community, students might rebuff newcomers without thinking of the new students' difficult situation and the harm their rejection might cause.

The tasks in this presentation consist mainly of questions designed to get you thinking about whether you are doing everything you can to help visitors, new students, their families, and new staff feel welcome and comfortable. As you read, try to take the perspective of a newcomer. Think deeply about how a nervous new student or staff member perceives your school. How do you bring him or her into the culture of the school? You should set a positive and welcoming tone from the minute that student or staff member becomes connected to your campus.

Task 1: Ensure That Newcomers' First Impressions of the School Are Positive prompts you to think about what it's like for students, families, staff members, and visitors when they first contact the school. What first impressions do the building and staff give?

Task 2: Welcome and Orient New Students discusses the importance of ensuring that students and their families are connected to the school right away and get all the information and support they need.

Task 3: Welcome and Orient New Staff prompts you to think about the guidance new staff members need to operate in your school.

TASK 1

Ensure that newcomers' first impressions of the school are positive

Let's begin at the beginning. Consider the impression your school makes as people first make contact. Is the building easy to navigate? Is the signage attractive and helpful? Are the physical building and foyer as inviting as possible? Do office staff welcome visitors appropriately? Is the website easily navigable and informative? Is the phone answering system efficient and professional? What kinds of first impressions do these aspects of your school create for visitors and new students, parents, and staff members?

Are directions to the office clear and inviting?

In some schools, the main entrance and main office are clearly marked and easy to find. But we have also worked in schools where it's very difficult to know where to enter. Especially when several separate buildings are scattered across the campus, a first-time visitor can't tell where to park or where to enter and find the main office.

We, as consultants, have been hired by the district to be there, so we don't hesitate to approach any staff member and ask where the office is. But what about a family who needs to enroll a student for the first time? When they must drive around the school, then search for a staff member to ask before they finally find the office, they probably do not feel particularly welcomed.

So think about the ease with which people can find the main entrance as they drive up to the school. Ensure that visitor parking is clearly marked. If visitors have to check in at the main office before going anywhere else in the school, make that process as easy as possible.

Is it easy to navigate inside the building?

If you were a new student, would you be able to find your classrooms easily, or would you have to wander the halls until you worked up the courage to ask another student for directions?

Ensure that classroom numbers can be easily seen. For example, in some schools, the numbers are above the door, but they're so small that you can't see them until you are right at the door. Other schools have big bold numbers on the doors, but when a door is open the numbers aren't visible. In large middle and high schools with multiple floors and wings and even multiple buildings, room numbers and highly visible signs giving directions to the different areas are especially important.

Think about how to make it as easy as possible for students to get from any part of the building to any other part of the building. The easier the navigation is, the more inviting the school feels to students. And with clear signage, the school may be particularly welcoming and inviting for stereotypical males who don't like to ask for directions!

Is the outside of the building as inviting as possible?

Of course, you don't have much say in the architecture of the building. Some buildings are lovely; others seem like prisons. Some campuses that were developed in the 1950s through the 1970s include an assortment of portable classrooms, pods, and buildings. Clearly you can't remodel the whole building, but think about what you can do with plantings to create an inviting feel. Ensure that signage is attractive, highly visible, and welcoming. We've worked with several schools that involved parent and community groups in fundraising efforts for improvements to plantings and other physical elements of the schools.

Is the outside signboard informative? Inspiring? Up to date?

What does it say about your school when the signboard displays September events in February? We know of many schools that organize a team of students to update the signboard every 2 weeks. The students come up with the words to display (with staff approval, of course) so the signboards are not only informative, but also sometimes a bit funny or inspiring. The students feel as though the signboard represents *them*, the students, as well as the staff, and people look forward to reading the updated signboards as they drive up to the school.

Is the foyer of the school as inviting as possible?

You probably don't have a budget for a formal remodel, but think about ways to ensure that the foyer is welcoming. Express the values the school is trying to instill in students by displaying your Guidelines for Success. Show school pride with displays of student artwork, sports trophies, photos from dramatic productions, and other student accomplishments. Enlist a community-based group to help with purchasing plants, painting walls, or small carpentry projects. You might create a student job that involves helping to keep the foyer clean and changing the displays periodically.

Do the clerical staff know how vital they are in representing the school?

The office staff play a huge role in creating the first impressions of visitors and new students, families, and staff. Ensure that they understand their importance and know how to interact appropriately with newcomers.

In many schools we visit, office staff do a great job of acknowledging adults who have entered the office while continuing to help students. "Welcome—good to see you. I need to help these students here, then I'll be right with you." Within moments, the adults know they've been noticed, but it's also clear that the students who have been waiting for help deserve respect, too. When a staff member is on the phone, just a glance and a smile, or perhaps a quick "I'll be right with you" while finishing up the phone conversation, also gives that immediate acknowledgment. These simple, brief interactions give great first impressions.

We've also visited schools where, when visitors enter the office, the office staff members immediately leave the students they've been helping (without so much as an "excuse me") and go to the adult. That behavior is disrespectful to students, and adults notice that disrespect.

*E*xample From the Field

During my first 2 years in education, I worked as a paraprofessional in an elementary school. One clerical staff member in that school was so intimidating that it was a year before I would talk to her! (I was 19 years old. Imagine the impression she made on the young students.) Once I got to know this person, I found that she was actually very nice. I think she had no idea how stern she came across and how her management style appeared so aggressive. If you have a person like this in your office, make sure you include some training in office staff demeanor as you address overall school climate. —R.S.

Is your school website informative and user friendly?

Can students and parents easily find essential information? Important announcements should be very visible, and it should be easy to find grade reports and teacher pages.

What impression does the website give to first-time visitors? Your website should give a sense of the spirit and values of your school. Imagine you are a student moving to your community and you go online to learn about your new school. Would you be disappointed or excited by what you see?

Analyze how people can make contact with the school. If you post a general email address or comment form right on the website, ensure that someone in the office is monitoring those emails daily. Clearly post at least one general phone number and the physical address of the school. We are surprised at how many school websites overlook this basic information. As consultants and trainers, we sometimes need to mail packages to schools, and it's frustrating when it takes 5 minutes or more to locate an address. Think about the contacts that community members, new students and families, and new staff might need to make with your school and ensure they can easily find the information they need.

Of course, ensure that all contact information falls within your guidelines for keeping everyone on campus safe.

Are telephone contacts appropriate?

If your school uses an automated telephone answering system, ensure that the system operates efficiently, provides essential information briefly, and allows callers to easily reach a real human being. Everyone has had frustrating experiences with answering systems that make you listen to information you don't want or need and go through multiple layers of messages. When you are finally able to leave a message, you have no confidence that anyone will actually listen to it, or, even worse, you are cut off before you can leave a message. If this description matches your answering system, imagine how uninviting it is to callers. Ensure that the system is as simple as it can possibly be.

When people answer the phone, do they understand the importance of customer service? Provide formal training in appropriate business phone etiquette so that contacts with all callers are professional and efficient.

Task 1 Action Steps & Evidence of Implementation

Action Steps	Evidence of Implementation
1. Work through the questions in this task and think about the following: • In what aspects of the school are you consciously inviting? • In what aspects of the school are you unconsciously inviting? (That is, the procedure is not formalized in any way, so it could disappear if an office staff member leaves, for example.) • In what aspects of the school are you unconsciously uninviting? (Do you push people away without realizing it?)	Foundations Process: Meeting Minutes
2. Develop and implement policies and procedures to address any issues you identify. Ensure that all parties—principal, support staff, teachers, clerical staff—know their roles in welcoming newcomers to the school. You might write a formal job description for office staff and archive it so that it is readily available for new staff members to review.	Foundations Archive: New Student Orientation, Job Descriptions

TASK 2

Welcome and orient new students

In Task 2, we discuss welcoming and orienting new students to your school. We divide these students into three basic groups.

The first group consists of grade cohorts—ninth graders who are entering a 4-year high school, sixth graders who are entering middle school, and prekindergarten students who are entering elementary school. The second group consists of students who are not part of a cohort, but are new to the school and enter either at the beginning of or sometime during the school year. The third group consists of immigrants who are not just new to the school, but also new to the country.

Welcome and orient entering grade cohorts.

What are you doing to reach out to students and families of entering grade cohorts before the first day of school? Many schools do a fabulous job of reaching out to the families of kindergartners. The schools organize times during the summer when parents and students can visit the school, meet the teachers, and learn some of the procedures they'll need to know when school starts. This orientation is also a great opportunity to emphasize the importance of attendance—it is so vital that families understand how important each school day is to their children's school career.

A process unique to prekindergarten or kindergarten is separating students from their parents on the first day. Because these grades represent the first school experience for most young children, they may experience some trauma. *Have you created smooth processes for getting the students connected with the teachers and encouraging parents to leave without a lot of drama?* You might enlist other adults in the school to help with answering parents' questions and walking parents to their cars.

What can you do to welcome entering middle school students? One middle school we work with has some of their staff members go to the feeder elementary schools during the spring. They take a basket of combination locks—the kind used on the lockers—and spend 20 minutes or so with each fifth-grade class teaching the students to open and close the locks and allowing them to practice this skill. This proactive procedure alleviates the anxiety the students might have about using lockers for the first time.

This same school has an end-of-year ritual of asking each feeder elementary school to identify three or four students who are likely to struggle the most—behaviorally, academically, or socially—as they enter the new environment of middle school. Then the principal, counselor, and classroom teachers for each child contact the parents and ask to visit the family at home before the school year begins. When they initiated this procedure, some of the families were reluctant, but in the end, all 12 families were very appreciative of the effort the school staff made to welcome them. The principal says she is able to develop positive relationships with the students before school even begins.

Do you educate students and families about how high school credits work and how they accumulate toward graduation? We see many districts where students are never taught about credits. Consider beginning this conversation with seventh graders and continuing with a deeper outreach to eighth graders. Students should know how graduation requirements work for the district and for the different high schools, the ramifications of both regular and poor attendance on credits, and how to recover credits if students fall behind. Well before the students enter high school, reach out with information about how to be successful in school and how the school can help them be successful.

Do you educate entering ninth graders about the importance of a high school diploma? You might have many students whose parents did not finish high school but are nonetheless financially secure; however, it is increasingly important in American culture to earn at least a high school diploma to be economically successful throughout a lifetime. Emphasize this point to students.

For all levels—elementary, middle, and high school—do you teach students about electives and extracurricular activities available at the school? You might reach out to students before the school year begins or when they arrive at the school. Describe the clubs, sports, service opportunities—everything that students can potentially participate in.

In general, consider how early and how often you should reach out to the new cohort that will be entering your school and what information you want to communicate to those students.

Welcome and orient students new to the school.

Also consider students who are new to your school but not part of the whole cohort of students—new 7th- and 8th-grade students entering a middle for grades 6–8, for example. This category includes students who arrive on the first day of school, but not as part of the cohort, as well as students who move in during the school year. These students are often neglected because many schools focus their time and resources on the incoming cohort, but it's important to ask: *How will new students be trained on all of your critical policies and procedures and your schoolwide expectations, and how will you make them feel welcome to the school?*

How transient is your school population? The more students who enter the school every month, the greater the probability that you can conduct group-based programs, such as the Newcomers' Club we describe below, for orienting them.

Newcomers' Club. We worked with a school in Southern California that developed a wonderful program for new students. This school has a very high level of transience, with students entering the school every week. They created a Newcomers' Club, a program run by the school counselor and a highly skilled paraprofessional supervised by the counselor. Twice each week at the end of the school day, new students are invited to meet with the counselor and paraprofessional in a dedicated area next to the counselor's office. The students attend the meetings their entire first month in the school. Students who have been in the school for a month are able to give tips to students who have been there for just a few days. The meetings are very casual, but they are a powerful way to provide support and acknowledgment to the students.

Peer-buddy program. When you don't need or want group-based orientations, consider a peer-buddy program. Train students to give school tours, teach common area and schoolwide policy expectations, and introduce key staff members to new students. The peer buddy can stay with the new student during the first few recesses, for example, to provide some support. Some schools use the terms *mentor* or *ambassador* instead of peer buddy. Encourage students to perceive being a peer buddy as a highly prized job within the school.

Videos. Another way to ensure that new students are taught expectations is to have them view orientation videos. Create orientation videos for each of the physical areas of your school: arrival, dismissal, playground, courtyards (for high school), cafeteria, and so on. You can use these videos at the start of the school year in advisory periods and during the year for review and to introduce the school to new students.

Have new students view the videos while the parents are going through the registration process. You can put those videos on a DVD or post them online so they are available to students and families at home, too. When you make the videos available online, parents of new—and not-so-new—students can get a better understanding of what the school day is like for their children. You might have the principal or counselor make a "Welcome to Our School" video—this kind of video can really show new students and families that you value them and that you want to ensure they have a great experience at your school.

If possible, have the videos available in the languages that are spoken in your students' homes. You don't have to re-create the videos in those languages—just incorporate voice-overs that explain what the people in the video are saying. This extra effort communicates respect and connects those families to the school.

New-student handbook. Another idea for providing information to new students is to create a new-student handbook or survival guide that includes all of the most important information new students need to know—how to make schedule changes, how to check items out of the library, what after-school activities are available and how to get involved, and so on.

Classroom orientation checklist. *Do all teachers have guidance for orienting students to their classrooms?* (All of your teachers should know what is included in the schoolwide orientation so they don't replicate that information in the classroom.) To develop classroom orientation guidance, we suggest that your Foundations Team—or even better, a task force of some of the more experienced teachers in your school—prepare a one-page list of suggestions for welcoming and orienting new students. A checklist format of brief bullet points is probably the easiest for busy teachers to use, but you might include a script or guided talking points, too. Before takeoff, airplane pilots, no matter how experienced they are, go through checklists to make sure they've prepared everything. Teachers with new students can also benefit from a checklist. With the hundreds of things they need to remember every day, teachers can easily forget to tell a student who joins the class in the middle of the year everything he or she needs to know.

This task force of experienced teachers should include guidance (at the secondary level) about whether all teachers for all class periods should formally introduce new students in their classes. A student who is introduced in seven different classes on the first day might be overwhelmed. The best procedure for introducing new students is probably different for every school, so teachers will likely welcome the recommendations of the experienced task force members.

Give special consideration to immigrants.

What can your school do to ease the transition for immigrant students and families—not just into the school, but also into a new culture? You might know how intimidating and confusing traveling in foreign countries can be—imagine *moving* with your family to a new country and dealing with unfamiliar transportation, housing, job, and school issues in a language you might not even understand. Be prepared with information about community agencies and services that can help support the family and connect the family with those services when necessary. Find out whether the family has connections in the community. If not, see if you can help develop a support system for them. Your district or regional service center will probably have resources for working with families of different cultural backgrounds.

Task 2 Action Steps & Evidence of Implementation

Action Steps	Evidence of Implementation
1. Work through the questions and suggestions in this task about entering grade cohorts, students who are new during the school year, and immigrant families. 2. Consider conducting a focus group or giving a brief survey to students who entered the school within the last year. Ask questions such as: • Did you feel welcome? What things did or did not make you feel welcome? • How did we do in orienting you to all of the policies, procedures, and rituals of this school?	Foundations Process: Meeting Minutes
3. Capitalize on your strengths and, where you have weaknesses, develop new policies, procedures, or rituals to help new students transition into the school.	Foundations Archive: New Student Orientation Staff Handbook: Policies and Procedures in Place

TASK 3

Welcome and orient new staff

All new staff are essentially joining a preexisting culture—your safe, orderly, and inviting school. The questions in this task will prompt you to think about the guidance new staff members need to operate within that culture. To answer the questions, consider conducting a focus group of staff members who were new within the last year or two, or perhaps have Foundations Team members working on this task reach out to new staff members individually and ask about their experiences as they transitioned into the school. What did you do well? What could you have done better?

Plan to do this with all new staff, but also think about any special considerations that you should give first-year teachers, whose first year tends to be so stressful, as well as noncertified staff.

How do you communicate all of the essential information to new staff at the beginning of the year without overwhelming them? Identify the essential information and think about how to organize it in a way that is welcoming and supportive. Essential information includes, for example, the school mission statement, the policies and procedures for student behavior and staff conduct, the weekly schedule, and requirements for committees, staff meetings, and grade-level meetings.

How well do we welcome and include the new staff member? What do we do to avoid a sense of staff cliques? When a group of staff members have been working together for some time, they tend to fall into patterns of social interaction. These networks might be formed around a grade level, by people of similar ages or with similar interests, or by the wing of the building where they work, for example. But it's important that these preexisting social networks reach out to new staff members and make it clear that anybody can join. Here are some suggestions for ensuring that new staff members feel welcome:

- Send an email to staff with a picture and a brief biography of each new staff member, including specialists, teachers, and noncertified personnel. Suggest that all staff actively welcome and include these people in staff-room conversations and staff-meeting discussions and activities.

No staff member should be intimidated about using the staff room. In fact, when a new staff member walks in for lunch on the first day, several people should say, "Hey, do you want to join us? Sit with us at this table." No one should have to stand with a tray of food, wondering whether it's OK to approach a table and say, "May I sit here?" (Remember the story about the assisted-living community dining room from the introduction of this presentation?) Similarly, people should be overtly welcoming in staff meetings. "Would you like to sit here? How's it going? We're so glad to have you in our school."

- Organize an informal eat-and-greet or reception with fun food such as cookies, pizza, donuts, or bagels.

- Display welcome banners and pictures at the school's entrance on the first day staff report to the school. Give new staff members a flower to wear so that everybody knows they are new staff.

- Create survival kits for new staff. You'll have to include instructions for these items! For example:

  ° A toothpick to remind you to pick out the good qualities in students.
  ° A rubber band to remind you to be flexible.
  ° A paper clip to remind you to try to hold it all together.
  ° An eraser to remind you to start each day with a clean slate.
  ° Life Savers to remind you that you are there when students need you and we as a staff are here when you need us.
  ° Tea to remind you to relax and take time for yourself.

  This is a fun way to communicate that you value new staff members and you want them to feel like they are an important part of the school.

Do you make a special effort to welcome and include first-year teachers? First-year teachers typically go through a period of isolation, feeling overwhelmed, and sometimes even serious depression. These feelings tend to peak in the fall and early winter and begin to abate around March. Think about what you can do to help people through that very difficult first year.

First-year teachers sometimes think that if they ask for help, it's an admission of failure. So reach out and continually offer varying levels of support. Veteran teachers might be reluctant to interfere, thinking they are just overwhelming the first-year teacher, and this reluctance can unfortunately make the experienced teachers seem unapproachable. So encourage staff to balance being approachable and inviting with not overwhelming.

Do you make a special effort to welcome and include noncertified staff? Noncertified staff might not be present for some of the initial orientation activities that you conduct with certified staff. Ensure that you have a plan for when, where, and how you communicate the essential information to them and make them feel welcome and valued by the entire staff. For example, if you provide peer mentors to first-year teachers, maybe you should provide peer mentors to first-year paraprofessionals as well.

Task 3 Action Steps & Evidence of Implementation

Action Steps	Evidence of Implementation
1. Work through the questions and suggestions in this task regarding new staff members.	Foundations Process: Meeting Minutes
2. Consider conducting a focus group of staff who began working at the school in the past year or two. Ask questions such as: • Did you feel welcome? What things did or did not make you feel welcome? • How did we do in orienting you to all of the policies, procedures, and rituals of this school?	
3. Capitalize on your strengths and, where you have weaknesses, develop new policies, procedures, or rituals to help new staff acclimate to the school. For example, document what the principal, counselor, and classroom teachers do to prepare for new staff before the school year begins.	Foundations Archive: New Staff Orientation Staff Handbook: Policies and Procedures in Place

BIBLIOGRAPHY

Adams, C. (2011). Recess makes kids smarter. *Instructor, 120*(5), 55–59. Retrieved from http://www.scholastic.com/teachers/article/recess-makes-kids-smarter

Allensworth, E. M., & Easton, J. Q. (2007). *What matters for staying on track and graduating in Chicago public schools: A close look at course grades, failures, and attendance in the freshman year.* Retrieved from http://ccsr.uchicago.edu/sites/default/files/publications/07%20What%20Matters%20Final.pdf

American Lung Association, Epidemiology and Statistics Unit, Research and Health Education Division (2012). *Trends in asthma morbidity and mortality.* Retrieved from http://www.lung.org/finding-cures/our-research/trend-reports/asthma-trend-report.pdf

Applied Survey Research and Attendance Works (2011). *Attendance in early elementary grades: Associations with student characteristics, school readiness and third grade outcomes* (mini-report). Retrieved from http://www.attendanceworks.org/wordpress/wp-content/uploads/2010/04/ASR-Mini-Report-Attendance-Readiness-and-Third-Grade-Outcomes-7-8-11.pdf

Archer, A., & Gleason, M. (1990). *Skills for school success.* North Billerica, MA: Curriculum Associates.

Baker, M. L., Sigmon, N., & Nugent, M. E. (2001). *Truancy reduction: Keeping students in school* (Juvenile Justice Bulletin). Retrieved from U.S. Department of Justice, National Criminal Justice Reference Service website: http://www.ncjrs.gov/pdffiles1/ojjdp/188947.pdf

Balfanz, R., Bridgeland, J. M., Fox, J. H., DePaoli, J. L., Ingram, E. S., Maushard, M. (2014). *Building a grad nation: Progress and challenge in ending the high school dropout epidemic.* Retrieved from http://diplomasnow.org/wp-content/uploads/2014/04/BGN-Report-2014_Full.pdf

Balfanz, R., & Byrnes, V. (2012). *Chronic absenteeism: Summarizing what we know from nationally available data.* Retrieved from Johns Hopkins University Center for Social Organization of Schools website: http://new.every1graduates.org/wp-content/uploads/2012/05/FINALChronicAbsenteeismReport_May16.pdf

Balfanz, R., & Byrnes, V. (2013). *Meeting the challenge of combating chronic absenteeism: Impact of the NYC mayor's interagency task force on chronic absenteeism and school attendance and its implications for other cities.* Retrieved from Johns Hopkins School of Education website: http://new.every1graduates.org/wp-content/uploads/2013/11/NYM-Chronic-Absenteeism-Impact-Report.pdf

Becker, W. C., & Engelmann, S. (1971). *Teaching: A course in applied psychology.* Columbus, OH: Science Research Associates.

Brophy, J. E. (1980). *Teacher praise: A functional analysis.* East Lansing, MI: Institute for Research on Teaching.

Brophy, J. E. (1986). Teacher influences on student achievement. *American Psychologist, 4*(10), 1069–1077.

Brophy, J. (1987). Synthesis of research on strategies for motivating students to learn. *Educational Leadership, 45*(2), 40–48.

Bruner, C., Discher, A., & Chang, H. (2011). *Chronic elementary absenteeism: A problem hidden in plain sight.* Retrieved from http://www.attendanceworks.org/wordpress/wp-content/uploads/2010/04/ChronicAbsence.pdf

Cameron, J., & Pierce, W. D. (1994). Reinforcement, reward, and intrinsic motivation: A meta-analysis. *Review of Educational Research, 64*(3), 363–423.

Chang, H., & Romero, M. (2008). *Present, engaged, and accounted for: The critical importance of addressing chronic absence in the early grades.* New York, NY: National Center for Children in Poverty.

Collins, J. (2001). *Good to great: Why some companies make the leap . . . and others don't.* New York, NY: HarperCollins Publishers.

Colvin, G. (Writer/Producer). (1992). *Managing acting-out behavior: A staff development program* [video]. Longmont, CO: Sopris West.

Colvin, G. (2004). *Managing the cycle of acting-out behavior in the classroom.* Eugene, OR: Behavior Associates.

Cooper, J. O., Heron, T. E., & Heward, W. L. (2007). *Applied behavior analysis* (2nd ed.). Upper Saddle River, NJ: Pearson.

Cotton, K. (1990). *Schoolwide and classroom discipline* (Close-Up #9). Portland, OR: Northwest Regional Educational Laboratory.

Donovan, M. S., & Cross, C. T. (Eds.) (2002). *Minority students in special education and gifted education.* Washington, DC: National Academy Press.

Emmer, E. T., & Evertson, C. M. (2012). *Classroom management for middle and high school teachers* (9th ed.). Upper Saddle River, NJ: Pearson.

Esler, A., Godber, Y., & Christenson, S. (2008). Best practices in supporting school-family partnerships. In A. Thomas & J. Grimes (Eds.), *Best practices in school psychology V* (pp. 917–936). Bethesda, MD: National Association of School Psychologists.

Evertson, C. M., & Emmer, E. T. (2012). *Classroom management for elementary teachers* (9th ed.). Upper Saddle River, NJ: Pearson.

Fabelo, T., Thompson, M. D., Plotkin, M., Carmichael, D., Marchbanks, M. P. III, & Booth, E. A. (2011). *Breaking schools' rules: A statewide study of how school discipline relates to students' success and juvenile justice involvement.* Retrieved from http://csgjusticecenter.org/wp-content/uploads/2012/08/Breaking_Schools_Rules_Report_Final.pdf

Feather, N. T. (1982). Expectancy-value approaches: Present status and future directions. In N. T. Feather (Ed.), *Expectations and actions: Expectancy-value models in psychology.* Hillsdale NJ: Erlbaum.

Furlong, M., Felix, E. D., Sharkey, J. D., & Larson, J. (2005). Preventing school violence: A plan for safe and engaging schools. *Principal Leadership, 6*(1), 11–15. Retrieved from http://www.nasponline.org/resources/principals/Student%20Counseling%20Violence%20Prevention.pdf

Get Schooled and Hart Research (2012). *Skipping to nowhere: Students share their views about missing school.* Retrieved from https://getschooled.com/system/assets/assets/203/original/Hart_Research_report_final.pdf

Glossary of Education Reform for Journalists, Parents, and Community Members. Retrieved from http://edglossary.org/school-culture/

Gottfredson, D. C., Gottfredson, G. D., & Hybl, L. G. (1993). Managing adolescent behavior: A multiyear, multischool study. *American Educational Research Journal, 30*(1), 179–215.

Jensen, E. (2009). *Teaching with poverty in mind: What being poor does to kids' brains and what schools can do about it.* Alexandria, VA: Association for Supervision and Curriculum Development.

Jenson, W., Rhode, G., & Reavis, H. K. (2009). *The Tough Kid tool box.* Eugene, OR: Pacific Northwest Publishing.

Kerr, J., & Nelson, C. (2002). *Strategies for addressing behavior problems in the classroom* (4th ed.). Englewood Cliffs, NJ: Merrill/Prentice Hall.

Kerr, J., Price, M., Kotch, J., Willis, S., Fisher, M., & Silva, S. (2012). Does contact by a family nurse practitioner decrease early school absence? *Journal of School Nursing, 28*, 38–46.

Kim, C. Y., Losen, D. J., and Hewitt, D. T. (2010). *The school-to-prison pipeline: Structuring legal reform.* New York, NY: New York University Press.

Klem, A. M., & Connell, J. P. (2004). Relationships matter: Linking teacher support to student engagement and achievement. *Journal of School Health, 74*(7), 262–273.

Kounin, J. S. (1977). *Discipline and group management in classrooms.* Huntington, NY: Krieger Publishing.

Losen, D. J. (2011). *Discipline policies, successful schools, and racial justice.* Boulder, CO: National Education Policy Center. Retrieved from http://nepc.colorado.edu/publication/discipline-policies

Losen, D. J., & Martinez, T. E. (2013). *Out of school & off track: The overuse of suspension in American middle and high schools.* Retrieved from http://civilrightsproject.ucla.edu/resources/projects/center-for-civil-rights-remedies/school-to-prison-folder/federal-reports/out-of-school-and-off-track-the-overuse-of-suspensions-in-american-middle-and-high-schools/OutofSchool-OffTrack_UCLA_4-8.pdf

Maag, J. (2001). *Powerful struggles: Managing resistance, building rapport.* Longmont, CO: Sopris West.

Marzano, R. J. (2003). *Classroom management that works: Research-based strategies for every teacher.* Alexandria, VA: Association for Supervision and Curriculum Development.

Maslow, A. H. (1962). Some basic propositions of a growth and self-actualization psychology. In A. W. Combs (Ed.), *Perceiving, behaving, becoming: A new focus for education* (pp. 34–49). Washington, D.C: Association for Supervision and Curriculum Development.

McNeely, C. A., Nonnemaker, J. A., & Blum, R. W. (2002). Promoting school connectedness: Evidence from the National Longitudinal Study of Adolescent Health. *Journal of School Health, 72*(4), 138–146.

National Association for Sport and Physical Education (2006). *Recess for elementary school children* (Position Statement). Retrieved from http://www.eric.ed.gov/PDFS/ED541609.pdf

National Center for Education Statistics (2012). *Digest of Education Statistics* (NCES 2014-015). Retrieved from http://nces.ed.gov/programs/digest/d12/ and http://nces.ed.gov/programs/digest/d12/tables/dt12_122.asp

O'Leary, K. D., & O'Leary, S. G. (1977). *Classroom management: The successful use of behavior modification* (2nd ed.). New York, NY: Pergamon Press.

O'Neill, R. E., Horner, R. H., Albin, R. W., Storey, K., & Sprague, J. R. (1996). *Functional assessment and program development for problem behavior: A practical handbook* (2nd ed.). Belmont, CA: Cengage.

Payne, C. (2008). *So much reform, so little change: The persistence of failure in urban schools.* Boston, MA: Harvard Education Press.

Purkey, W. W., & Novak, J. M. (2005). *Inviting school success: A self-concept approach to teaching, learning, and democratic practice in a connected world* (4th ed.). New York, NY: Wadsworth Publishing.

Ready, D. (2010). Socioeconomic disadvantage, school attendance, and early cognitive development: The differential effects of school exposure. *Sociology of Education, 83*(4), 271–289.

Rhode, G. R., Jenson, W. R., & Reavis, H. K. (2010). *The Tough Kid book: Practical classroom management strategies* (2nd ed.). Eugene, OR: Pacific Northwest Publishing.

Sheets, R. H., & Gay, G. (1996). Student perceptions of disciplinary conflicts in ethnically diverse classrooms. *NASSP Bulletin, 80*(580), 84–94.

Skiba, R. J., Horner, R. H., Chung, C.-G., Rausch, M. K., May, S. L., & Tobin, T. (2011). Race is not neutral: A national investigation of African American and Latino disproportionality in school discipline. *School Psychology Review, 40*(1), pp. 85–107.

Skiba, R. J., Michael, R. S., Nardo, A. C., & Peterson, R. L. (2002). The color of discipline: Sources of racial and gender disproportionality in school punishment. *Urban Review, 34*(4), 317–342.

Skiba, R., & Peterson, R. (2003). Teaching the social curriculum: School discipline as instruction. *Preventing School Failure, 47,* 66–73.

Sparks, S. D. (2010). Districts begin looking harder at absenteeism. *Education Week, 30*(6), 1, 12–13.

Spinks, S. (n.d.). Adolescent brains are works in progress. *Frontline.* Retrieved from http://www.pbs.org/wgbh/pages/frontline/shows/teenbrain/work/adolescent.html

Sprague, J. R., & Walker, H. M. (2005). *Safe and healthy schools: Practical prevention strategies.* New York, NY: Guilford Press.

Sprague, J. R., & Walker, H. M. (2010). Building safe and healthy schools to promote school success: Critical issues, current challenges, and promising approaches. In M. R. Shinn, H. M. Walker, & G. Stoner (Eds.), *Interventions for achievement and behavior problems in a three-tier model including RTI* (pp. 225–258). Bethesda, MD: National Association of School Psychologists.

Sprick, R. S. (1995). School-wide discipline and policies: An instructional classroom management approach. In E. Kame'enui & C. B. Darch (Eds.), *Instructional classroom management: A proactive approach to managing behavior* (pp. 234–267). White Plains, NY: Longman Press.

Sprick, R. S. (2009a). *CHAMPS: A proactive and positive approach to classroom management* (2nd ed.). Eugene, OR: Pacific Northwest Publishing.

Sprick, R. S. (2009b). *Stepping in: A substitute's guide to managing classroom behavior.* Eugene, OR: Pacific Northwest Publishing.

Sprick, R. S. (2009c). *Structuring success for substitutes.* Eugene, OR: Pacific Northwest Publishing.

Sprick, R. S. (2012). *Teacher's encyclopedia of behavior management: 100+ problems/500+ plans* (2nd ed.). Eugene, OR: Pacific Northwest Publishing.

Sprick, R. S. (2014). *Discipline in the secondary classroom: A positive approach to behavior management* (3rd ed.). San Francisco: Jossey-Bass.

Sprick, R. S., & Garrison, M. (2000). *ParaPro: Supporting the instructional process.* Eugene, OR: Pacific Northwest Publishing.

Sprick, R. S., & Garrison, M. (2008). *Interventions: Evidence-based behavior strategies for individual students* (2nd ed.). Eugene, OR: Pacific Northwest Publishing.

Sprick, R. S., Howard, L., Wise, B. J., Marcum, K., & Haykin, M. (1998). *Administrator's desk reference of behavior management.* Longmont, CO: Sopris West.

Sprick, R. S., Swartz, L., & Glang, A. (2005). *On the playground: A guide to playground management* [CD program]. Eugene, OR: Pacific Northwest Publishing and Oregon Center for Applied Sciences.

Sprick, R. S., Swartz, L., & Schroeder, S. (2006). *In the driver's seat: A roadmap to managing student behavior on the bus* [CD and DVD program]. Eugene, OR: Pacific Northwest Publishing and Oregon Center for Applied Sciences.

Sugai, G., Horner, R. H., Dunlap, G., Hieneman, M., Lewis, T., Nelson, C. M., & Wilcox, B. (2000). Applying positive behavior support and functional behavioral assessment in schools. *Journal of Positive Behavioral Interventions, 2,* 131–143.

U.S. Department of Education. (2000). *Safeguarding our children: An action guide.* Retrieved from http://www2.ed.gov/admins/lead/safety/actguide/action_guide.pdf

U.S. Department of Health and Human Services, Centers for Disease Control and Prevention (2009). *Fostering school connectedness: Improving student health and academic achievement.* Retrieved from http://www.cdc.gov/healthyyouth/protective/pdf/connectedness_administrators.pdf

U.S. Department of Health and Human Services, Centers for Disease Control and Prevention. (2012). *Youth violence: Facts at a glance.* Retrieved from http://www.cdc.gov/violenceprevention/pdf/yv_datasheet_2012-a.pdf

U.S. Department of Health and Human Services, Centers for Disease Control and Prevention. (2013a). *Asthma and schools.* Retrieved from http://www.cdc.gov/healthyyouth/asthma/index.htm

U.S. Department of Health and Human Services, Centers for Disease Control and Prevention. (2013b). *State and program examples: Healthy youth.* Retrieved from http://www.cdc.gov/chronicdisease/states/examples/pdfs/healthy-youth.pdf

U.S. Department of Justice, Office of Justice Programs, Office of Juvenile Justice and Delinquency Prevention. (2006). *Statistical briefing book.* Retrieved from http://www.ojjdp.gov/ojstatbb/offenders/qa03301.asp

University of Utah, Utah Education Policy Center. (2012). *Research brief: Chronic absenteeism.* Retrieved from Utah Data Alliance website: http://www.utahdataalliance.org/downloads/ChronicAbsenteeismResearchBrief.pdf

Wald, J., & Losen, D. J. (2003). Defining and redirecting a school-to-prison pipeline. *New Directions for Youth Development, 99,* 9–15. doi:10.1002/yd.51

Walker, H. (1995). *The acting-out child: Coping with classroom disruption.* Longmont, CO: Sopris West.

Walker, H. M., Colvin, G., & Ramsey, E. (1995). *Antisocial behavior in school: Strategies and best practices.* Pacific Grove, CA: Brooks/Cole.

Walker, H., Ramsey, E., & Gresham, F. M. (2003–2004a). Heading off disruptive behavior: How early intervention can reduce defiant behavior—and win back teaching time. *American Educator, Winter,* 6–21, 45–46.

Walker, H., Ramsey, E., & Gresham, F. M. (2003–2004b). How disruptive students escalate hostility and disorder—and how teachers can avoid it. *American Educator, Winter,* 22–27, 47–48.

Walker, H. M., Ramsey, E., & Gresham, F. M. (2004). *Antisocial behavior in school: Evidence-based practices* (2nd ed.). Belmont, CA: Cengage Learning.

Walker, H. M., Severson, H. H., & Feil, E. F. (2014). *Systematic screening for behavior disorders* (2nd ed.). Eugene, OR: Pacific Northwest Publishing.

Walker, H., & Walker, J. (1991). *Coping with noncompliance in the classroom: A positive approach for teachers.* Austin, TX: Pro-Ed.

Wentzel, K. R., & Brophy, J. E. (2013). *Motivating Students to Learn* (4th ed.). New York, NY: Taylor & Francis.

Wise, B. J., Marcum, K., Haykin, M., Sprick, R. S., & Sprick, M. (2011). *Meaningful work: Changing student behavior with school jobs.* Eugene, OR: Pacific Northwest Publishing.

Wright, A. (n.d.). Limbic system: Amgdala. In J. H. Byrne (Ed.). *Neuroscience online.* Retrieved from http://neuroscience.uth.tmc.edu/s4/chapter06.html

APPENDIX A
Foundations Implementation Rubric and Summary

The rubric is a relatively quick way for the Foundations Team to self-reflect on the implementation status of each of the modules. If you are just beginning *Foundations*, you might use this rubric toward the end of your first year of implementation. Thereafter, work through the rubric each year in the spring and consider using it in mid- to late fall to guide your work during the winter.

Each column—Preparing, Getting Started, Moving Along, and In Place—represents a different implementation status. The text in each row describes what that status looks like for each *Foundations* presentation. For each presentation, read the four descriptions from left to right. If the statements in the description are true, check the box. Each description assumes that the activities preceding it in the row have been attained. Stop working through the row when you reach a description that you cannot check off because you haven't implemented those tasks.

Notice that the descriptions for the In Place status include a section about evidence, which suggests where to find objective evidence that the described work is truly in place. If no documentation exists, think about whether the work has really been thoroughly completed. Throughout *Foundations*, we recommend archiving all your work so that policies and procedures are not forgotten or lost when staff changes occur.

When you've worked through every row, summarize your assessment on the Rubric Summary. If any items are rated as less than In Place, or if it has been more than 3 years since you have done so, work through the Implementation Checklist for that module. Of course, if you know that you need to begin work on a module or presentation, you can go directly to the corresponding content.

For Module B, evaluate (separately) the common areas and schoolwide policies that you have implemented—that is, you've structured them for success and taught students the behavioral expectations. Use the rows labeled Other for your school's common areas and schoolwide policies that do not appear on the rubric by default.

Figure A-1 shows a summary form completed by an imaginary school in the spring of their second year of *Foundations* implementation. They have highlighted the checkboxes to create a horizontal bar graph, giving the evaluation an effective visual component. They've done a great job on most of Module A, the common areas they've prioritized so far (hallways and cafeteria), and Welcoming New Staff, Students, and Families (C7). They need to work a bit more on staff engagement and unity (A5)

> Print the summary and rubric (Form C-01) from the Module C CD.

and most of Module C, which they began in Year 2. Modules D, E, and F are blank because they plan to work on them in future years.

Figure A-1 *Sample Foundations Rubric Summary*

Date _____

Foundations Implementation Rubric and Summary (p. 8 of 8)

	Preparing (1)	Getting Started (2)	Moving Along (3)	In Place (4)
Module A Presentations				
A1. Foundations: A Multi-Tiered System of Behavior Support	X	X	X	X
A2. Team Processes	X	X	X	X
A3. The Improvement Cycle	X	X	X	X
A4. Data-Driven Processes	X	X	X	X
A5. Developing Staff Engagement and Unity	X	X		
Module B Presentations				
Hallways	X	X	X	X
Restrooms				
Cafeteria	X	X	X	X
Playground, Courtyard, or Commons				
Arrival				
Dismissal				
Dress Code				
Other:				
Other:				
Other:				
Other:				
Module C Presentations				
C2. Guidelines for Success	X	X	X	
C3. Ratios of Positive Interactions	X	X		
C4. Improving Attendance	X	X	X	
C5 & C6. School Connectedness and Programs and Strategies for Meeting Needs	X	X		
C7. Welcoming New Staff, Students, and Families	X	X	X	X
Module D Presentations				
D1. Proactive Procedures, Corrective Procedures, and Individual Interventions				
D2. Developing Three Levels of Misbehavior				
D3. Staff Responsibilities for Responding to Misbehavior				
D4. Administrator Responsibilities for Responding to Misbehavior				
D5. Preventing the Misbehavior That Leads to Referrals and Suspensions				
Module E Presentations				
E1. Ensuring a Safe Environment for Students				
E2. Attributes of Safe and Unsafe Schools				
E3. Teaching Conflict Resolution				
E4. Analyzing Bullying Behaviors, Policies, and School Needs				
E5. Schoolwide Bullying Prevention and Intervention				
Module F Presentations				
F2. Supporting Classroom Behavior: The Three-Legged Stool				
F3. Articulating Staff Beliefs and Solidifying Universal Procedures				
F4. Early-Stage Interventions for General Education Classrooms				
F5. Matching the Intensity of Your Resources to the Intensity of Your Needs				
F6. Problem-Solving Processes and Intervention Design				
F7. Sustainability and District Support				

Additional information about the rubric appears in Module F, Presentation 7, Task 1.

Thanks to Carolyn Novelly and Kathleen Bowles of Duval County Public Schools in Florida. We modeled the Foundations Implementation Rubric on a wonderful document they developed called the School Climate/Conditions for Learning Checklist. Thanks also to Pete Davis of Long Beach, California, for sharing samples of rubrics and innovation configuration scales.

Foundations Implementation Rubric and Summary (p. 1 of 8)

Directions: In each row, check off each description that is true for your *Foundations* implementation. Then summarize your assessment on the Rubric Summary form. For Module B, evaluate each common area and schoolwide policy separately; and use the rows labeled Other for common areas and schoolwide policies that do not appear on the rubric by default. *Note:* Each block assumes that the activities in previous blocks in the row have been attained.

Presentation	Preparing (1)	Getting Started (2)	Moving Along (3)	In Place (4)
A1 Foundations: A Multi-Tiered System of Behavior Support	☐ Staff are aware of the *Foundations* approach and basic beliefs, including that *Foundations* is a process for guiding the entire staff in the construction and implementation of a comprehensive approach to behavior support.	☐ *Foundations* multi-tiered system of support (MTSS) processes are coordinated with academic MTSS (RTI) processes, and team organization has been determined (e.g., one MTSS Team with a behavior task force and an academic task force).	☐ Staff have been introduced to the STOIC acronym and understand that student behavior and motivation can be continuously improved by manipulating the STOIC variables: Structure, Teach, Observe, Interact positively, and Correct fluently.	☐ A preliminary plan has been developed for using the *Foundations* modules. For a school just beginning the process, the plan includes working through all the modules sequentially. For a school that has implemented aspects of positive behavior support, the team has self-assessed strengths, weaknesses, and needs using this rubric. **Evidence:** Foundations Implementation Rubric
A2 Team Processes	☐ Foundations Team members have been identified. They directly represent specific faculty and staff groups, and they have assigned roles and responsibilities.	☐ Foundations Team attends trainings, meets at school, and has established and maintains a Foundations Process Notebook and Foundations Archive.	☐ Foundations Team members present regularly to faculty and communicate with the entire staff. They draft proposals and engage staff in the decision-making process regarding school climate, behavior, and discipline.	☐ Foundations Team is known by all staff and is highly involved in all aspects of climate, safety, behavior, motivation, and student connectedness. **Evidence:** Staff members represented by Foundations Team members and presentations to staff are documented in the Foundations Process Notebook.
A3 The Improvement Cycle	☐ Foundations Team is aware of the Improvement Cycle and keeps staff informed of team activities.	☐ Foundations Team involves staff in setting priorities and in implementing improvements.	☐ Foundations Team involves staff in using multiple data sources to establish a hierarchical list of priorities and adopt new policies. Team members seek input from staff regarding their satisfaction with the efficacy of recently adopted policies and procedures.	☐ All staff actively participate in all aspects of the Improvement Cycle, such as setting priorities, developing revisions, adopting new policies and procedures, and implementation. Foundation Team presents to staff at least monthly. **Evidence:** Memos to staff and PowerPoint presentation files are documented in the Foundations Process Notebook.
A4 Data-Driven Processes	☐ Administrators and Foundations Team review discipline data and establish baselines.	☐ Common area observations and student, staff, and parent climate surveys are conducted yearly.	☐ Discipline, climate survey, and common area observation data are reviewed and analyzed regularly.	☐ Based on the data, school policies, procedures, and guidelines are reviewed and modified as needed (maintaining the Improvement Cycle).
A5 Developing Staff Engagement and Unity	☐ Foundations Team regularly communicates with staff through staff meetings, scheduled professional development, memos, and so on.	☐ Foundations Team members understand that they play a key role in staff unity. They periodically assess whether any factions of staff are disengaged and how they can develop greater staff engagement in the *Foundations* process.	☐ A building-based administrator attends most *Foundations* trainings and plays an active role in team meetings and in assisting the team in unifying staff.	☐ For districts with more than five or six schools, a district-based team meets at least once per quarter to keep the *Foundations* continuous improvement processes active in all schools. **Evidence:** Meeting minutes and staff presentations are documented in the Foundations Process Notebook.

If any items are rated as less than In Place or if it has been more than 3 years since you have done so, work through the Module A Implementation Checklist.

Foundations Implementation Rubric and Summary (p. 2 of 8)

Common Area	Preparing (1)	Getting Started (2)	Moving Along (3)	In Place (4)
Hallways	☐ Common area observations are conducted and data from multiple sources are collected and analyzed.	☐ Current structures and procedures have been evaluated and protected, modified, or eliminated.	☐ Lesson plans have been developed, taught, practiced, and re-taught, when necessary.	☐ Common area supervisory procedures are communicated to staff and monitored for implementation. **Evidence:** Policies, procedures, and lessons are documented in the Foundations Archive and, as appropriate, in the Staff Handbook.
Restrooms	☐ Common area observations are conducted and data from multiple sources are collected and analyzed.	☐ Current structures and procedures have been evaluated and protected, modified, or eliminated.	☐ Lesson plans have been developed, taught, practiced, and re-taught, when necessary.	☐ Common area supervisory procedures are communicated to staff and monitored for implementation. **Evidence:** Policies, procedures, and lessons are documented in the Foundations Archive and, as appropriate, in the Staff Handbook.
Cafeteria	☐ Common area observations are conducted and data from multiple sources are collected and analyzed.	☐ Current structures and procedures have been evaluated and protected, modified, or eliminated.	☐ Lesson plans have been developed, taught, practiced, and re-taught, when necessary.	☐ Common area supervisory procedures are communicated to staff and monitored for implementation. **Evidence:** Policies, procedures, and lessons are documented in the Foundations Archive and, as appropriate, in the Staff Handbook.
Playground, Courtyard, or Commons	☐ Common area observations are conducted and data from multiple sources are collected and analyzed.	☐ Current structures and procedures have been evaluated and protected, modified, or eliminated.	☐ Lesson plans have been developed, taught, practiced, and re-taught, when necessary.	☐ Common area supervisory procedures are communicated to staff and monitored for implementation. **Evidence:** Policies, procedures, and lessons are documented in the Foundations Archive and, as appropriate, in the Staff Handbook.
Arrival	☐ Common area observations are conducted and data from multiple sources are collected and analyzed.	☐ Current structures and procedures have been evaluated and protected, modified, or eliminated.	☐ Lesson plans have been developed, taught, practiced, and re-taught, when necessary.	☐ Common area supervisory procedures are communicated to staff and monitored for implementation. **Evidence:** Policies, procedures, and lessons are documented in the Foundations Archive and, as appropriate, in the Staff Handbook.
Dismissal	☐ Common area observations are conducted and data from multiple sources are collected and analyzed.	☐ Current structures and procedures have been evaluated and protected, modified, or eliminated.	☐ Lesson plans have been developed, taught, practiced, and re-taught, when necessary.	☐ Common area supervisory procedures are communicated to staff and monitored for implementation. **Evidence:** Policies, procedures, and lessons are documented in the Foundations Archive and, as appropriate, in the Staff Handbook.
Other: _____	☐ Common area observations are conducted and data from multiple sources are collected and analyzed.	☐ Current structures and procedures have been evaluated and protected, modified, or eliminated.	☐ Lesson plans have been developed, taught, practiced, and re-taught, when necessary.	☐ Common area supervisory procedures are communicated to staff and monitored for implementation. **Evidence:** Policies, procedures, and lessons are documented in the Foundations Archive and, as appropriate, in the Staff Handbook.
Other: _____	☐ Common area observations are conducted and data from multiple sources are collected and analyzed.	☐ Current structures and procedures have been evaluated and protected, modified, or eliminated.	☐ Lesson plans have been developed, taught, practiced, and re-taught, when necessary.	☐ Common area supervisory procedures are communicated to staff and monitored for implementation. **Evidence:** Policies, procedures, and lessons are documented in the Foundations Archive and, as appropriate, in the Staff Handbook.

If any items are rated as less than In Place or if it has been more than 3 years since you have done so, work through the Module B Implementation Checklist.

Foundations Implementation Rubric and Summary (p. 3 of 8)

Schoolwide Policy	Preparing (1)	Getting Started (2)	Moving Along (3)	In Place (4)
Dress Code	☐ Foundations Team has discussed the clarity and consistency of the current schoolwide policy.	☐ Data from multiple sources about the efficacy of the policy have been gathered and analyzed.	☐ The policy has been analyzed for clarity, efficacy, and consistency of enforcement.	☐ Schoolwide policies, lessons, and procedures have been written and are reviewed as needed with staff, students, and parents. **Evidence:** Policies, lessons, and procedures are documented in the Foundations Archive and, as appropriate, in the Staff Handbook.
Other: _____	☐ Foundations Team has discussed the clarity and consistency of the current schoolwide policy.	☐ Data from multiple sources about the efficacy of the policy have been gathered and analyzed.	☐ The policy has been analyzed for clarity, efficacy, and consistency of enforcement.	☐ Schoolwide policies, lessons, and procedures have been written and are reviewed as needed with staff, students, and parents. **Evidence:** Policies, lessons, and procedures are documented in the Foundations Archive and, as appropriate, in the Staff Handbook.
Other: _____	☐ Foundations Team has discussed the clarity and consistency of the current schoolwide policy.	☐ Data from multiple sources about the efficacy of the policy have been gathered and analyzed.	☐ The policy has been analyzed for clarity, efficacy, and consistency of enforcement.	☐ Schoolwide policies, lessons, and procedures have been written and are reviewed as needed with staff, students, and parents. **Evidence:** Policies, lessons, and procedures are documented in the Foundations Archive and, as appropriate, in the Staff Handbook.
Other: _____	☐ Foundations Team has discussed the clarity and consistency of the current schoolwide policy.	☐ Data from multiple sources about the efficacy of the policy have been gathered and analyzed.	☐ The policy has been analyzed for clarity, efficacy, and consistency of enforcement.	☐ Schoolwide policies, lessons, and procedures have been written and are reviewed as needed with staff, students, and parents. **Evidence:** Policies, lessons, and procedures are documented in the Foundations Archive and, as appropriate, in the Staff Handbook.
Other: _____	☐ Foundations Team has discussed the clarity and consistency of the current schoolwide policy.	☐ Data from multiple sources about the efficacy of the policy have been gathered and analyzed.	☐ The policy has been analyzed for clarity, efficacy, and consistency of enforcement.	☐ Schoolwide policies, lessons, and procedures have been written and are reviewed as needed with staff, students, and parents. **Evidence:** Policies, lessons, and procedures are documented in the Foundations Archive and, as appropriate, in the Staff Handbook.
Other: _____	☐ Foundations Team has discussed the clarity and consistency of the current schoolwide policy.	☐ Data from multiple sources about the efficacy of the policy have been gathered and analyzed.	☐ The policy has been analyzed for clarity, efficacy, and consistency of enforcement.	☐ Schoolwide policies, lessons, and procedures have been written and are reviewed as needed with staff, students, and parents. **Evidence:** Policies, lessons, and procedures are documented in the Foundations Archive and, as appropriate, in the Staff Handbook.
Other: _____	☐ Foundations Team has discussed the clarity and consistency of the current schoolwide policy.	☐ Data from multiple sources about the efficacy of the policy have been gathered and analyzed.	☐ The policy has been analyzed for clarity, efficacy, and consistency of enforcement.	☐ Schoolwide policies, lessons, and procedures have been written and are reviewed as needed with staff, students, and parents. **Evidence:** Policies, lessons, and procedures are documented in the Foundations Archive and, as appropriate, in the Staff Handbook.
Other: _____	☐ Foundations Team has discussed the clarity and consistency of the current schoolwide policy.	☐ Data from multiple sources about the efficacy of the policy have been gathered and analyzed.	☐ The policy has been analyzed for clarity, efficacy, and consistency of enforcement.	☐ Schoolwide policies, lessons, and procedures have been written and are reviewed as needed with staff, students, and parents. **Evidence:** Policies, lessons, and procedures are documented in the Foundations Archive and, as appropriate, in the Staff Handbook.

If any items are rated as less than In Place or if it has been more than 3 years since you have done so, work through the Module B Implementation Checklist.

School Name _____ Date _____

Foundations Implementation Rubric and Summary (p. 4 of 8)

Presentation	Preparing (1)	Getting Started (2)	Moving Along (3)	In Place (4)
C2 Guidelines for Success (GFS)	☐ All staff understand what Guidelines for Success (GFS) are and why they are important.	☐ Foundations Team has drafted proposals and engaged all stakeholders in the decision-making process of developing GFS.	☐ GFS have been finalized and posted and are reviewed regularly.	☐ GFS are embedded into the culture and are part of the common language of the school. **Evidence:** Procedures for teaching and motivating students about GFS are documented in the Foundations Archive, Staff Handbook, and Student and Parent Handbook.
C3 Ratios of Positive Interactions	☐ Staff have been taught the concept of 3:1 ratios of positive interactions and the importance of creating a positive climate and improving student behavior.	☐ Staff have been taught how to monitor ratios of positive interactions and are encouraged to evaluate their interactions with students.	☐ Administrator plans for teachers to observe and calculate other teachers' classroom ratios of interactions; the teachers involved meet to discuss outcomes.	☐ Observation data show that most staff at most times strive to interact with students at least three times more often when students are behaving responsibly than when they are misbehaving. **Evidence:** Procedures for teaching and motivating staff are documented in the Foundations Archive and Staff Handbook.
C4 Improving Attendance	☐ Average daily attendance is monitored to view long-term trends and patterns. Faculty and staff have been made aware of the importance of encouraging regular attendance by all students.	☐ All students with chronic absenteeism (absent 10% or more of school days) are identified at least quarterly; Foundations Team determines whether universal intervention is warranted.	☐ Each student with chronic absenteeism is identified and assigned one school-based support person who monitors whether additional support is needed. Foundations Team has analyzed attendance data and analyzed policies for clarity and efficacy.	☐ Every student with chronic absenteeism that has been resistant to universal and Tier 2 supports becomes the focus of a multidisciplinary team effort. **Evidence:** Data on average daily attendance and chronic absenteeism as well as efforts to improve attendance (e.g., parent newsletters) are documented in the Foundations Process Notebook.
C5 & C6 School Connectedness and Programs and Strategies for Meeting Needs	☐ Foundations Team has analyzed the degree to which current programs and practices meet the needs of all students (outstanding, average, and at risk).	☐ Foundations Team has developed proposals for programs and practices that might help meet unmet needs of students (e.g., the average student's need for purpose and belonging).	☐ Faculty and staff have implemented programs and practices designed to meet basic needs of all students (e.g., Mentorship, Student of the Week, Meaningful Work).	☐ Programs to meet students' basic needs are in place and analyzed at least once per year to determine their effectiveness and assess whether the needs of any student groups are not being met. **Evidence:** Analysis is documented in the Foundations Process Notebook, and programs and practices for meeting needs are documented in the Foundations Archive.
C7 Welcoming New Staff, Students, and Families	☐ Foundations Team has reviewed the welcoming aspects of the school, such as signage, website, and phone and front office procedures, and has suggested improvements.	☐ Foundations Team has analyzed and suggested improvements for welcoming and orienting new students and families at the beginning of the school year. (New students include those in a new grade-level cohort [e.g., ninth graders in high school] and students who are not part of that cohort.)	☐ Foundations Team has analyzed procedures and suggested improvements for welcoming new students and families who arrive during the school year. Improvements might include written information about rules, procedures, GFS, and so on.	☐ Foundations Team has analyzed procedures and suggested improvements for welcoming new staff members, both professional and nonprofessional, at the beginning of the year. New staff members are oriented to essential procedures and the culture and climate defined by the school's behavior support procedures. **Evidence:** All policies and procedures for welcoming and orienting staff, students, and families are documented in the Foundations Archive.

If any items are rated as less than In Place or if it has been more than 3 years since you have done so, work through the Module C Implementation Checklist.

Foundations Implementation Rubric and Summary (p. 5 of 8)

Presentation	Preparing (1)	Getting Started (2)	Moving Along (3)	In Place (4)
D1 Proactive Procedures, Corrective Procedures, and Individual Interventions	☐ Foundations Team is aware of data and staff opinions about consistency in correcting misbehavior, including clarity of staff roles in discipline compared with administrative roles.	☐ Staff understand the potential limitations of office referral as a corrective procedure and avoid using it whenever possible.	☐ Staff have been made aware of the limited benefits and potential drawbacks (including disparate impact) of out-of-school suspension (OSS) as a corrective consequence.	☐ Staff avoid pressuring administrators to use OSS. Staff perceptions of consistency and administrative support for disciplinary actions are documented in staff survey results. **Evidence:** Discussions on these topics are documented in the Foundations Process Notebook.
D2 Developing Three Levels of Misbehavior	☐ Staff are aware of the concept of three levels of misbehavior: Level 1 (mild), Level 2 (moderate), and Level 3 (severe) misbehavior.	☐ Annually, staff discuss and agree on what behavior *must* be sent to the administrator, what can be sent to the administrator, and what should be handled in the setting in which the infraction occurred (3-level system for responding to misbehavior).	☐ A referral form that reflects the agreed-upon definition of Level 3 misbehavior has been developed. A notification form that reflects the agreed-upon definition of Level 2 misbehavior has been developed. (Alternatively, both Level 2 and Level 3 may be on one form.) Accurate data are kept and analyzed quarterly for all Level 2 and Level 3 misbehaviors and consequences.	☐ Data are collected on the implementation of the 3-level system for responding to misbehavior and on staff and administrator satisfaction with the system. **Evidence:** All aspects of the policy are documented in the Foundations Archive and Staff Handbook.
D3 Staff Responsibilities for Responding to Misbehavior	☐ Staff have generated and administrators have approved a menu of corrective consequences for use in common areas.	☐ Staff have generated and administrators have approved a menu of corrective consequences for use in classrooms.	☐ Staff have been trained in how to use Level 2 notifications as a process for moving toward collaborative planning for severe or chronic behavior problems.	☐ Staff have been trained in writing objective and appropriate office referrals for Level 3 misbehavior. **Evidence:** Menus and procedures are documented in the Foundations Archive and Staff Handbook.
D4 Administrator Responsibilities for Responding to Misbehavior	☐ Procedures have been developed for responding to Level 2 notifications to ensure that the reporting staff member receives timely feedback and that administrators and support staff take appropriate actions.	☐ Office procedures for dealing with students sent to the office have been analyzed and streamlined. Students do not get too much attention from office staff or staff members who visit the office	☐ Administrators are familiar with the game plan for dealing with Level 3 incidents. The game plan includes a menu of alternative consequences to out-of-school suspension.	☐ If the school has an ISS program, that program has been analyzed and revised as needed to ensure that it is highly structured and includes an instructional component. **Evidence:** All procedures for Level 2 and Level 3 infractions are documented in the Foundations Archive.
D5 Preventing the Misbehavior That Leads to Referrals and Suspensions	☐ Foundations Team has examined data on Level 2 and Level 3 infractions to determine what misbehaviors get students into trouble.	☐ Foundations Team has reviewed the lessons in Module D (how to interact appropriately with adults) and discussed whether they might reduce misbehaviors that get students into trouble.	☐ To avoid duplication, the Foundations Team has compared the Module D lessons with other social skills or social-emotional curricula currently in use. Staff have agreed on a plan for when and how to teach expected behaviors to all students.	☐ Foundations Team has discussed whether re-teaching the Module D lessons (or similar) in ISS or detention settings would be beneficial; if so, the team has planned when and how to re-teach. **Evidence:** Lesson plans and teaching logistics and schedule are documented in the Foundations Archive.

If any items are rated as less than In Place or if it has been more than 3 years since you have done so, work through the Module D Implementation Checklist.

School Name _____ Date _____

Foundations Implementation Rubric and Summary (p. 6 of 8)

Presentation	Preparing (1)	Getting Started (2)	Moving Along (3)	In Place (4)
E1 Ensuring a Safe Environment for Students	☐ Team members are aware of their responsibilities for overseeing school safety efforts. The team coordinates with other teams or task forces that may be doing similar work and avoids duplicating other efforts.	☐ Foundations Team has viewed or read Module E and has compared that content with the school's current efforts toward safety, managing conflict, and bullying prevention. The team has developed a proposal for closing any gaps in the current efforts.	☐ Foundations Team has made staff aware of the importance of a comprehensive view of safety that includes preparing for outside attackers as well as the more common occurrences of playground injuries, student fights, bullying, and so on.	☐ Foundations Team has assessed problems with safety, conflict, and bullying within the last 3 years. If problems exist, a plan for using or adapting information from this module and integrating them with current curriculum or procedures has been completed. **Evidence:** Data analyses are documented in the Foundations Process Notebook, and final policies and procedures are documented in the Foundations Archive.
E2 Attributes of Safe and Unsafe Schools	☐ Team members and other staff directly involved with safety concerns have viewed or read Presentation 2 and have completed (individually) the form Understanding the Attributes of Safe and Unsafe Schools.	☐ Foundations Team has compiled individual responses to Understanding Attributes of Safe and Unsafe Schools and correlated those data with safety assessments completed in the last 3 years. Information about strengths and concerns has been shared with staff, and priorities have been set.	☐ Foundations Team and other staff involved with safety concerns have completed the form Assessing Emergency Preparedness, evaluated current plans for natural disasters and man-made emergencies, revised any weak procedures, including training on policies regarding seclusion and restraint.	☐ Foundations Team has completed the form Lessons to Increase Safety and Belonging, reviewed the Module E sample lessons, and evaluated whether current problems and policies address all features of the sample lessons. If there are gaps, a plan to teach some or all of the *Foundations* lessons is established. **Evidence:** Lesson plans and procedures are documented in the Foundations Archive.
E3 Teaching Conflict Resolution	☐ Foundations Team has assessed whether the school has a conflict resolution strategy that students and staff use when necessary. If so, document the effective procedures in the Foundations Archive (and skip the rest of this row).	☐ Foundations Team has reviewed the concepts and lessons in the Stop-Think-Plan (STP) approach and has prepared an implementation plan for staff.	☐ With staff input, lessons have been revised, an implementation plan has been established, and a process is in place for training all staff in how to encourage students to use the conflict-resolution strategy.	☐ Foundations Team has established a process for evaluating the effectiveness of STP by analyzing multiple data sources. The policy and lessons are revised and staff are retrained when necessary, and successes are celebrated. **Evidence:** Data analyses are documented in the Foundations Process Notebook, and lessons and teaching procedures are documented in the Foundations Archive.
E4 Analyzing Bullying Behavior, Policies, and School Needs	☐ Foundations Team is aware of the content of this presentation and can compare it with current policies and procedures related to bullying.	☐ Foundations Team has completed the form School-Based Analysis of Bullying Data and has identified whether new or revised procedures need to be implemented to enhance the current use of data related to bullying.	☐ Foundations Team has completed the form School-Based Analysis of Bullying Policies and has identified whether new or revised policies need to be implemented to enhance current policies related to bullying.	☐ Quarterly, the Foundations Team reviews data related to bullying. Annually, the team uses those data to answer each of the questions in the form STOIC Analysis for Universal Prevention of Bullying (or an equivalent process), and improvement priorities are established. **Evidence:** Data analyses are documented in the Foundations Process Notebook.
E5 Schoolwide Bullying Prevention and Intervention	☐ Foundations Team has completed the form Staff Training in Preventing and Responding to Bullying and has developed and implemented a plan to fill in any identified gaps in current practices.	☐ Foundations Team has completed the form Student Training in Preventing and Responding to Bullying. As part of a previously adopted bullying curriculum or through the *Foundations* lessons, students are taught about bullying prevention.	☐ Foundations Team has completed the form Family Training in Preventing and Responding to Bullying and developed an implementation plan to fill in any identified gaps in current practices.	☐ Foundations Team has completed the form Active Engagement for the Prevention of Bullying and has developed an implementation plan to fill in any gaps in current practices. Bullying issues are a regular part of the team's work and are integrated into staff development efforts. **Evidence:** Ongoing discussions are documented in the Foundations Process Notebook. Established programs to enhance student engagement are documented in the Foundations Archive.

If any items are rated as less than In Place or if it has been more than 3 years since you have done so, work through the Module E Implementation Checklist.

Foundations Implementation Rubric and Summary (p. 7 of 8)

Presentation	Preparing (1)	Getting Started (2)	Moving Along (3)	In Place (4)
F2 Supporting Classroom Behavior: The Three-Legged Stool	☐ A research-based model for classroom management has been adopted at the building or district level. All teachers have access to training, and teachers new to the building or district receive the same training.	☐ School and district personnel are identified as resources for teachers who would like observations, feedback, and coaching. An effort is made to actively market the benefits of coaching support.	☐ The administrator has communicated clear outcomes and goals of effective classroom management: • 90% engagement • 95% respectful interactions • 95% of behavior matches posted expectations	☐ The model creates a common language among teachers, support staff, coaches, and administrators for problem solving and intervention. Data are collected and analyzed to evaluate classroom management efforts. **Evidence:** Information on the model, administrative walk-through visits, and coaching supports is included in the Foundations Archive and Staff Handbook.
F3 Articulating Staff Beliefs and Solidifying Universal Procedures	☐ Foundations Team has reviewed sample staff beliefs about behavior management.	☐ In faculty and staff meetings, faculty and staff have examined and discussed sample staff beliefs about behavior management.	☐ All staff have developed and adopted a set of written staff beliefs regarding discipline and behavior, and ensured that it aligned with the school's mission statement.	☐ To solidify the culture of the school and to guide the ongoing development of school policies and procedures, staff beliefs are reviewed, discussed, and revised as needed at least annually. **Evidence:** Staff beliefs and the review process are documented in the Foundations Archive and Staff Handbook.
F4 Early-Stage Interventions for General Education Classrooms	☐ Foundations Team and support staff (counselor, school psychologist, and so on) understand the concept of early-stage intervention.	☐ Foundations Team, support staff, and principal (or district administrators) agree on the interventions that should be included in the early-stage protocol.	☐ All teachers and support staff have been trained on the interventions in the school or district early-stage protocol, including how and why to keep records of each intervention.	☐ Data Collection and Debriefing (or an equivalent) is adopted as a required intervention for most chronic behavioral problems. Data must be charted before assistance is requested from support staff or problem-solving teams. **Evidence:** Expectations about when and how to get assistance are included in the Foundations Archive and Staff Handbook.
F5 Matching the Intensity of Your Resources to the Intensity of Your Needs	☐ Foundations Team and support staff (counselor, psychologist, and so or) have identified a set of red-flag criteria and (if possible) have conducted universal screening to identify students who may need individual behavior support.	☐ Foundations Team, support staff, and principal (or district administrators) agree on who can serve as advocates for students who need additional support.	☐ The advocates meet regularly to discuss progress and case studies to ensure that each student's needs are being met. Patterns of need are communicated to the Foundations Team so prevention efforts can be implemented.	☐ All support staff and problem-solving teams have written brief job descriptions that outline the services they can provide. The documents are shared with staff to inform them about available resources. **Evidence:** Suggestions for accessing these services are in the Foundations Archive and Staff Handbook.
F6 Problem-Solving Processes and Intervention Design	☐ Foundations Team understands that it will not conduct staffings (team-based problem solving) on individual students, but the team should examine current processes for supporting students and staff.	☐ Foundations Team and support staff (counselor, school psychologist, and so on) have discussed the range of problem-solving support (individuals and teams) currently available to students and staff.	☐ Foundations Team and support staff have discussed the problem-solving processes suggested in *Foundations* (e.g., the 25-Minute Planning Process), and have determined whether the processes would strengthen current practices.	☐ A flowchart or description of how the school meets the needs of students and staff has been created. It clarifies how the intensity of student needs matches the intensity of both problem-solving processes and intervention design and implementation. **Evidence:** This information is documented in the Foundations Archive and summarized in the Staff Handbook.
F7 Sustainability and District Support	☐ Foundations Team archives data, in-process work, and all completed policies and procedures, and builds on this work each year.	☐ Foundations Team orients new staff and re-energizes returning staff about all policies and procedures, and emphasizes unity and consistency.	☐ Foundations Team uses the rubric annually and the Implementation Checklists as individual modules near completion and every 3 years thereafter. The team uses this information to guide staff in setting improvement priorities.	☐ In larger districts (more than four schools), a district-based team works on sustainability. The team reminds schools about important milestones (e.g., surveys, year-end tasks, etc.) and ongoing staff development opportunities on behavior support. **Evidence:** This information can be found in district communications (e.g., emails) to schools and agenda items for principals' meetings.

If any items are rated as less than In Place or if it has been more more than 3 years since you have done so, work through the Module F Implementation Checklist.

Foundations Implementation Rubric and Summary (p. 8 of 8)

	Preparing (1)	Getting Started (2)	Moving Along (3)	In Place (4)
Module A Presentations				
A1. Foundations: A Multi-Tiered System of Behavior Support				
A2. Team Processes				
A3. The Improvement Cycle				
A4. Data-Driven Processes				
A5. Developing Staff Engagement and Unity				
Module B Presentations				
Hallways				
Restrooms				
Cafeteria				
Playground, Courtyard, or Commons				
Arrival				
Dismissal				
Dress Code				
Other:				
Other:				
Other:				
Other:				
Module C Presentations				
C2. Guidelines for Success				
C3. Ratios of Positive Interactions				
C4. Improving Attendance				
C5 & C6. School Connectedness and Programs and Strategies for Meeting Needs				
C7. Welcoming New Staff, Students, and Families				
Module D Presentations				
D1. Proactive Procedures, Corrective Procedures, and Individual Interventions				
D2. Developing Three Levels of Misbehavior				
D3. Staff Responsibilities for Responding to Misbehavior				
D4. Administrator Responsibilities for Responding to Misbehavior				
D5. Preventing the Misbehavior That Leads to Referrals and Suspensions				
Module E Presentations				
E1. Ensuring a Safe Environment for Students				
E2. Attributes of Safe and Unsafe Schools				
E3. Teaching Conflict Resolution				
E4. Analyzing Bullying Behaviors, Policies, and School Needs				
E5. Schoolwide Bullying Prevention and Intervention				
Module F Presentations				
F2. Supporting Classroom Behavior: The Three-Legged Stool				
F3. Articulating Staff Beliefs and Solidifying Universal Procedures				
F4. Early-Stage Interventions for General Education Classrooms				
F5. Matching the Intensity of Your Resources to the Intensity of Your Needs				
F6. Problem-Solving Processes and Intervention Design				
F7. Sustainability and District Support				

APPENDIX B
Module C Implementation Checklist

The Implementation Checklist is a detailed checklist of the processes and objectives in each *Foundations* module. The Module C checklist (Form C-02) appears in this appendix and can be printed from the Module C CD.

As you near completion on the module, use the Implementation Checklist to ensure that you have fully implemented all recommendations. If you've decided not to follow some recommendations—you've adapted the procedures for your school—indicate the reason on the checklist. If data show problems later, this record of what you implemented and what you chose not to implement could be helpful in deciding what to do to address the problem.

In addition to using the checklists as needed, plan to work through all *Foundations* checklists every 3 years or so. See the sample schedule below. Additional information about Implementation Checklists appears in Module F, Presentation 7, Task 1.

Sample Long-Term Schedule: Improvement Priorities, Data Review & Monitoring

Year 1	Work on: • Modules A and B (continuous improvement process, common areas and schoolwide policies) • Cafeteria • Guidelines for Success In late spring, work through the Foundations Implementation Rubric for Modules A, B (cafeteria), and C2 (Guidelines for Success). Use the Modules A and B Implementation Checklists to assess status as you near completion of those modules.
Year 2	Work on: • Module C (inviting climate) • Hallways In the fall, evaluate cafeteria data. In late spring, work through the Foundations Implementation Rubric for Modules A, B (cafeteria and hallways), and C. Use the Module C Implementation Checklist to assess status as you near completion of Module C.

Year 3	Work on:
	• Module D (responding to misbehavior) • Playground
	In the fall, evaluate hallway data.
	In late spring, work through the Foundations Implementation Rubric for Modules A, B (cafeteria, hallways, and playground), C, and D.
	Use the Module D Implementation Checklist to assess status as you near completion of Module D.
Year 4	Work on:
	• Module E (safety, conflict, bullying prevention) • Arrival and dismissal
	In the fall, evaluate playground data.
	In late spring, work through the Foundations Implementation Rubric for Modules A, B (cafeteria, hallways, arrival and dismissal), C, D, and E.
	Use the Module E Implementation Checklist to assess status as you near completion of Module E.
	Monitor Year 1 priorities:
	• Module A Implementation Checklist • Module B Implementation Checklist for cafeteria • Module C Implementation Checklist for Guidelines for Success (C2 only)
Year 5	Work on:
	• Module F (classroom management and sustaining *Foundations*) • Assemblies • Guest teachers
	In the fall, evaluate arrival and dismissal data.
	In late spring, work through the Foundations Implementation Rubric for Modules A, B (playground, arrival and dismissal, assemblies, guest teachers), C, D, E, and F.
	Use the Module F Implementation Checklist to assess status as you near completion of Module F.
	Monitor Year 2 priorities:
	• Module B Implementation Checklist for hallways • Module C Implementation Checklist

Year 6	In the fall, evaluate assemblies and guest teacher data.
	Work through the Foundations Implementation Rubric for all modules.
	Monitor Year 3 priorities:
	• Module B Implementation Checklist for playground • Module D Implementation Checklist
Year 7	In the fall, work through the Foundations Implementation Rubric for all modules and all common areas and schoolwide policies.
	Monitor Year 4 priorities:
	• Module A Implementation Checklist • Module B Implementation Checklist for arrival, dismissal, and cafeteria • Module C Implementation Checklist for Guidelines for Success (C2 only) • Module E Implementation Checklist
Year 8	In the fall, work through the Foundations Implementation Rubric for all modules and all common areas and schoolwide policies.
	Monitor Year 5 priorities:
	• Module B Implementation Checklist for assemblies, guest teachers, and hallways • Module B Implementation Checklist for hallways • Module C Implementation Checklist • Module F Implementation Checklist
Year 9	In the fall, work through the Foundations Implementation Rubric for all modules and all common areas and schoolwide policies.
	Monitor Year 6 priorities:
	• Module B Implementation Checklist for playground • Module D Implementation Checklist

Module C Implementation Checklist (1 of 5)

Implementation Actions	Completed Y/N	Evidence of Implementation	Evidence Y/N
Presentation 1: Constructing and Maintaining a Positive Climate	✓		✓
1. The team has presented to or reviewed with all staff the concept of and the role staff members play in consciously constructing a positive, inviting school climate.	☐	Foundations Process: Presentations/ Communications With Staff	☐
2. The team has presented to or reviewed with all staff how an inviting climate affects school connectedness, which in turn affects academic achievement, dropout rates, the health choices students make, and more.	☐	Foundations Process: Presentations/ Communications With Staff	☐
Presentation 2: Guidelines for Success			
1. During initial development, the team has determined whether the school already has something comparable to Guidelines for Success (GFS), such as schoolwide goals or a pledge, and whether it is used by staff throughout the school, taught to students, and communicated to families. If yes, skip development tasks 2 and 3 below.	☐	Foundations Process: Guidelines for Success	☐
2. When developing the school's GFS, the team or task force presented the concept and usefulness of GFS to the entire staff.	☐	Foundations Process: Presentations/ Communications With Staff	☐
3. When developing the school's GFS, the team or task force gathered suggestions from staff, students, and families on both the content of and the name for the GFS, and the team or task force designed a development process that actively involved the staff and created a sense of value and ownership among staff.	☐	Foundations Process: Guidelines for Success	☐
4. GFS (or equivalent) are highly visible throughout the school, in all classrooms, in communications with parents, and in staff and student handbooks.	☐	Observable; Staff Handbook; Student and Parent Handbook; Foundations Process: Communications With Parents	☐
5. GFS are relaunched and directly taught to students at the beginning of each new school year.	☐	Foundations Archive: Lesson Plans for Teaching GFS	☐
6. A GFS implementation calendar is developed to ensure that GFS are woven into the fabric of school life and used as the hub of all behavior management and motivation practices.	☐	Foundations Process: Planning Calendar	☐

Implementation Actions	Completed Y/N	Evidence of Implementation	Evidence Y/N
Presentation 3: Ratios of Positive Interactions	✓		✓
1. The team has presented to or reviewed with all staff the concept of ratios of positive interactions (RPI) and the differences between and definitions of attention to positive behavior (positives) and attention to corrective behavior (correctives).	☐	FoundationsProcess: Presentations/ Communications With Staff	☐
2. Staff have received training and understand the potential negative impact of ratios skewed to correctives—specifically, that some students learn that it is easier to get adult attention by breaking rules than by following rules. Conversely, staff understand that a ratio skewed at least 3 to 1 toward the positive can be a powerful tool in setting a positive climate and encouraging responsible behavior.	☐	Foundations Process: Presentations/ Communications With Staff	☐
3. Staff have received training in how to identify and count both positives and correctives.	☐	Foundations Process: Presentations/ Communications With Staff	☐
4. At least once per year, staff use the Ratios of Positive Interactions Monitoring Form (Reproducible Form C-03a, b, and c) to monitor and analyze their RPI with students during the most challenging 30 minutes of the school day.	☐	Interviews With Staff	☐
5. Annually, staff use the document Strategies for Increasing Positive Interactions (Reproducible Form C-04) and place reminders in their planning calendars to consciously work on keeping the positives at a very high level.	☐	Interviews With Staff	☐
6. Staff are encouraged (perhaps even required) to observe a colleague and count RPI.	☐	Interviews With Staff	☐
7. Whenever a student exhibits chronic motivation or behavior problems, staff consider the RPI concepts and establish a plan to modify some aspect of their current interactions with that student.	☐	Interviews With Staff	☐
8. The team involves staff in developing a plan for giving respectful, attention-grabbing reminders about RPI to staff.	☐	Foundations Process: Meeting Minutes, Planning Calendar	☐

Implementation Actions	Completed Y/N	Evidence of Implementation	Evidence Y/N
Presentation 4: Improving Attendance	✓		✓
1. The Foundations Team has developed information about the importance of attendance and presents it to staff, students, and families regularly throughout the school year.	☐	Foundations Process: Presentations/ Communications With Staff, Communications With Parents	☐
2. The team has reviewed the current attendance policy and revised it as needed to increase clarity and to address any absenteeism concerns.	☐	Foundations Process: Attendance Initiatives	☐
3. The team (or attendance task force) meets regularly (at least once a month) to review attendance data, identify schoolwide trends and priorities, and link individual students who meet red flag criteria with individual support systems.	☐	Foundations Process: Meeting Minutes	☐
4. The team (or attendance task force) has identified and implemented schoolwide strategies (as described in Module C, Presentation 4) to address the trends and causes of absenteeism suggested by attendance data.	☐	Foundations Archive: Attendance Initiatives	☐
5. Each student with chronic absenteeism has been assigned one school-based support person who monitors whether additional support is needed. When a student has been resistant to universal and Tier 2 supports, the student becomes the focus of a multidisciplinary team effort.	☐	Foundations Process: Attendance Initiatives	☐
6. The team has a plan to provide a comprehensive review of the importance of attendance with staff, students, and parents every 3 years (or more frequently).	☐	Foundations Archive: Long-Term Planning Calendar	☐

Module C Implementation Checklist (4 of 5)

Implementation Actions	Completed Y/N	Evidence of Implementation	Evidence Y/N
Presentation 5: School Connectedness—Meeting Basic Human Needs and Presentation 6: Programs and Strategies for Meeting Needs	✓		✓
1. The Foundations Team has discussed whether the proposed list of eight basic needs or an alternative construct will work best as a vehicle to make the school a great place for all students.	☐	Foundations Process: Meeting Minutes, Students' Basic Needs	☐
2. The team has generated a list of the school's current positive programs and practices, and that list has been analyzed for the basic needs the various programs might address.	☐	Foundations Process: Students' Basic Needs	☐
3. Each team member has completed the Analysis of Student Needs Worksheet (Reproducible Form C-07), and the team has compiled the data and analyzed them for patterns of unmet needs. The team plans to conduct this analysis every 3 years (or more frequently).	☐	Foundations Process: Students' Basic Needs	☐
4. The team (particularly at the secondary level) has considered asking the staff to identify students who have no involvement in school activities and no or few staff members they can converse with.	☐	Foundations Process: Students' Basic Needs	☐
5. The team has discussed ways to modify existing programs and practices to get nonconnected students involved in school activities.	☐	Foundations Process: Meeting Minutes, Student's Basic Needs	☐
6. The team has reviewed the programs and practices described in Module C, Presentation 6 to determine whether new programs or practices might be developed to meet the needs of students whose needs are not currently being met.	☐	Foundations Process: Meeting Minutes, Student's Basic Needs	☐

Module C Implementation Checklist

Implementation Actions	Completed Y/N	Evidence of Implementation	Evidence Y/N
Presentation 7: Making a Good First Impression— Welcoming New Staff, Students, and Families	✓		✓
1. The team has analyzed the physical building (especially signage), website, and office staff skills (both in person and on the phone) to assess how welcoming and helpful the school is to visitors and new arrivals. Problems and gaps have been addressed. The team plans to conduct this analysis every 3 years (or more frequently).	☐	Foundations Process: Meeting Minutes	☐
2. *Elementary level:* The team has collected data from focus groups or surveys of a new cohort of parents (e.g., entering kindergarten students) to learn what the school can do to improve the orientation and acculturation of entering students and families.	☐	Foundations Process: Data Summaries	☐
3. *Secondary level:* The team has collected data from focus groups or surveys of a new cohort of students (e.g., entering sixth graders or ninth graders) to learn about what the school can do to improve the orientation and acculturation of entering students.	☐	Foundations Process: Data Summaries	☐
4. The team analyzes how well the school welcomes new cohorts, students entering at the beginning of the year who are not part of the cohort, and students entering midyear. Extra thought is given to recent immigrants. Adjustments are made so that the school is as supportive and welcoming as possible to these students.	☐	Foundations Archive: New Student Orientation	☐
5. The team analyzes how well the school welcomes and acculturates new staff members. Additional thought goes into the needs of first-year teachers and new noncertified staff. Adjustments are made so that the school is as supportive and welcoming as possible for these staff members.	☐	Foundations Archive: New Staff Orientation	☐

APPENDIX C
Guide to Module C
Reproducible Forms and Samples

The CD provided with this book contains many materials to help you implement *Foundations*. A thumbnail of the first page of each form, figure, or sample on the CD appears in this appendix. Most forms can be completed electronically. See the Using the CD file for more information about using fillable forms. Unless otherwise noted, all files are in PDF format.

Folders included on the CD are:

- Forms (C-01 through C-12)
  - Fillable Forms
  - Print Forms
- Samples (C-13 through C-22)
- Guidelines for Success Examples (C-23 through C-34)
- Lessons for Guidelines for Success
  - Lesson 1
  - Lesson 2
- PowerPoint Presentations (C1 through C7)
  - C1 Introduction.pptx
  - C2 Guidelines for Success.pptx
  - C3 RPI.pptx
  - C4 Attendance.pptx
  - C5 Basic Needs.pptx
  - C6 Meeting Needs.pptx
  - C7 Newcomers.pptx

Forms
(C-01 to C-12)

C-01 *Foundations Implementation Rubric and Summary (8 pages)*

C-02 *Module C Implementation Checklist (4 pages)*

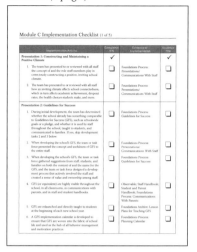

Form C-03a, b, c *Ratios of Positive Interactions Monitoring Forms (3 versions)*

Form C-04 *Strategies for Increasing Positive Interactions*

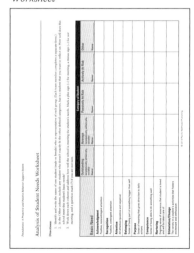

C-05 *How Sick Is Too Sick for School?*

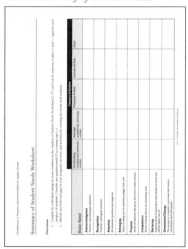

C-06 *School-Based Analysis of Attendance Policies (2 pages)*

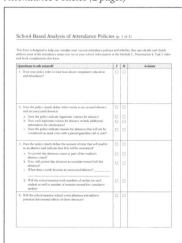

C-07 *Analysis of Student Needs Worksheet*

C-08 *Summary of Student Needs*

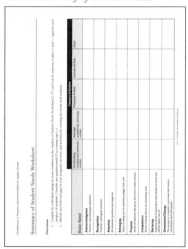

C-09 *Congratulations postcards*

C-10 *Responsible Student Behavior postcards*

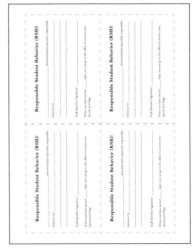

C-11a, b *CARE tickets and posters (8 pages)*

C-12 *Principal's Award nomination form (Word format)*

Samples
(C-13 to C-22)

C-13 *Grateful Dads program flyer*

C-14 *Behavior Rubric (Elementary)*

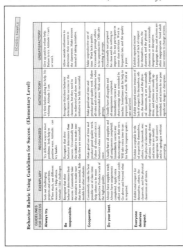

C-15 *Behavior Rubric (Secondary)*

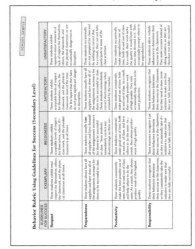

C-16 *Sample Staff Handbook Entry for Guidelines for Success*

C-17 *Power of Three: Increasing Positive Behaviors at Kings Canyon*

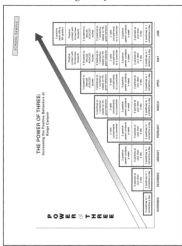

C-18 *Caught You Caring! instructions and nomination form*

C-19 *Medical and dental appointment note*

C-20 *Attendance letter for families*

C-21 *Attendance chart for families*

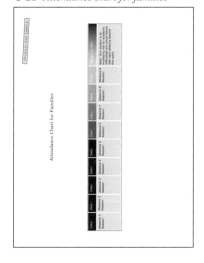

C-22 *Falcon Fan Club invitation and forms (4 pages)*

Guidelines for Success Examples
(C-23 to C-34)

C-23 *Bee Attitudes*

C-24 *Humanity, Integrity, Scholarship*

C-25 *KNIGHTS*

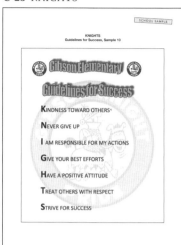

C-26 *Maturity, Humanity, Scholarship*

C-27 *PAWSitive Attitude*

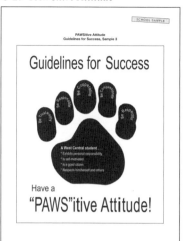

C-28 *PRIDE*

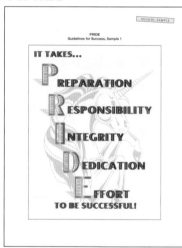

C-29 *Puesta del Sol*

C-30 *REACH District Cultural Mission Statement and Contract*

C-31 *ROAR*

C-32 *Spearman Elementary's Guidelines for Success*

C-33 *Steps to Success*

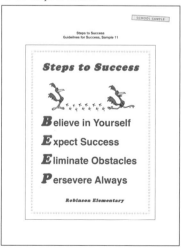

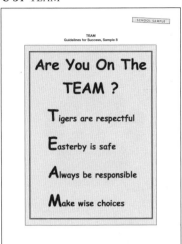

Lessons

Guidelines for Success

Guidelines for Success
Lessons 1

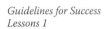

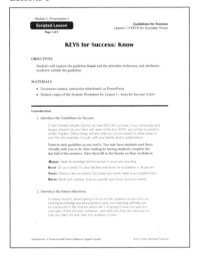

Guidelines for Success
Lesson 2

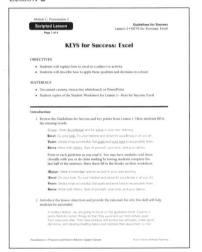

PowerPoint Presentations

(C1 to C7)